ATTITUDE PROBLEMS

ATTITUDE PROBLEMS

An Essay on Linguistic Intensionality

GRAEME FORBES

CLARENDON PRESS · OXFORD

OXFORD
UNIVERSITY PRESS

Great Clarendon Street, Oxford OX2 6DP

Oxford University Press is a department of the University of Oxford.
It furthers the University's objective of excellence in research, scholarship,
and education by publishing worldwide in

Oxford New York

Auckland Cape Town Dar es Salaam Hong Kong Karachi
Kuala Lumpur Madrid Melbourne Mexico City Nairobi
New Delhi Shanghai Taipei Toronto

With offices in

Argentina Austria Brazil Chile Czech Republic France Greece
Guatemala Hungary Italy Japan Poland Portugal Singapore
South Korea Switzerland Thailand Turkey Ukraine Vietnam

Oxford is a registered trademark of Oxford University Press
in the UK and in certain other countries

Published in the United States
by Oxford University Press Inc., New York

© Graeme Forbes 2006

The moral rights of the authors have been asserted
Database right Oxford University Press (maker)

First published 2006

All rights reserved. No part of this publication may be reproduced,
stored in a retrieval system, or transmitted, in any form or by any means,
without the prior permission in writing of Oxford University Press,
or as expressly permitted by law, or under terms agreed with the appropriate
reprographics rights organization. Enquiries concerning reproduction
outside the scope of the above should be sent to the Rights Department,
Oxford University Press, at the address above

You must not circulate this book in any other binding or cover
and you must impose this same condition on any acquirer

British Library Cataloguing in Publication Data

Data available

Library of Congress Cataloging in Publication Data

Data available

Typeset by the Author
Printed in Great Britain
on acid-free paper by
Biddles Ltd., King's Lynn, Norfolk

ISBN 0–19–927494–0   978–0–19–927494–9

1 3 5 7 9 10 8 6 4 2

Preface

This preface contains two confessions. First, I confess to a disreputable desire that, because it is so-called, *Attitude Problems* should be purchased in bulk, sight unseen, by large corporations seeking to improve the attitudes of their most difficult employees. Universities and other organizations that have a tenure system might also be tempted by the title. Such potential misunderstanding does not keep me awake at night, for like many of my colleagues,[1] I have pursued the semantics of natural language in order to become rich and famous (perhaps I am less fussy than others about the means).

And so I let the cat out of the bag: *Attitude Problems* is yet another essay on the logico-semantic problems to which attitude ascriptions and their near-neighbours give rise. More exactly, it is about *objectual* attitude ascriptions, ascriptions of attitudes towards objects that we make with psychological intensional transitive verbs such as 'want', 'seek' and 'fear'.[2] I also discuss other intensional transitive verbs, such as transaction verbs and depiction verbs, which behave in similar ways.

Those familiar with the literature on intensional verbs would expect the topic of substitution failure to loom large in this book. It does not. Instead, I have focused on another peculiarity of many

---

[1] See, for instance, (Chierchia and McConnell-Ginet 2000:xi, xv).
[2] Throughout, I use single quotes to mention expressions of natural language, except expressions which contain an apostrophe, for which I use double quotes. Double quotes are also used as scare quotes. Expressions of formal languages double as names of themselves.

intensional transitives, that with almost any kind of complement, they give rise to an ambiguity that has been called 'specific/unspecific', 'particular/no particular', and 'relational/notional'. In Quine's famous illustration (1956:185), if we paraphrase 'I want a sloop' as 'there exists a sloop such that I want it', this gives the wrong idea if all I really want is 'mere relief from slooplessness'. The 'mere relief' reading is the notional or unspecific one, and the details of how it gets expressed are by no means evident.

One thing is clear, that in advance of a theory of substitution-resistance and a theory of the relational/notional distinction, there is no reason to be confident that the same mechanism underlies the two phenomena. It is not even the same verbs that give rise to them. Which brings me to my second confession, that in the mid-nineties I nevertheless published an article on substitution-resistance in a prominent journal, in which I suggested that my account of it automatically explained the relational/notional ambiguity as well. Naturally, I blame the editors and referees for letting this pass.

In more recent years, I have published papers on the topic, some of the content of which I have incorporated into this essay in what I think is improved form. I thank the editors and publishers of *The Philosophical Review, The Proceedings of the Aristotelian Society, Linguistics and Philosophy*, and *Facta Philosophica*, for their permission to use the original material. All those papers contained extensive thanks to various colleagues, which I repeat here without spelling out the lengthy list of names, though Jennifer Saul deserves another mention for her response at the Aristotelian Society meeting in Glasgow, Scotland (where I was either local-boy-makes-good or prophet-without-honour, I am still unsure which).

There are others to whom I am grateful for assistance directly related to writing *Attitude Problems:* Johan van Benthem, Bob Carpenter, David Dowty, Geoffrey Pullum, François Recanati, Tom Sattig, Roger Schwarzchild, Mandy Simons, Jason Stanley, Zoltan Szabó, Achille Varzi, and especially Richmond Thomason and Ede Zimmerman. Obviously, I need to hear from more people in the middle of the alphabet, unless the Press's anonymous readers, from whom I received very helpful comments, were such.

Discussions with Kit Fine, Christopher Peacocke, and Mark Richard were as invaluable to me again as they have been throughout my career. Kathrin Koslicki and Teresa Robertson read drafts of chapters and suggested a number of improvements. I am also grateful to audiences at the Society for Exact Philosophy, especially Diana Raffman; at the first Bellingham Summer Philosophy Conference, especially Ted Sider; at Logica 2003, especially Philip Kremer; at the University of Notre Dame's Ernan McMullin Perspective Series in Philosophy meeting on the work of Terence Parsons, especially Peter van Inwagen, Barbara Partee, and, of course, Terence Parsons, to whom I have accumulated a large debt in drinks promised but not yet bought; and at a workshop at the Institut d'Histoire et de Philosophie des Sciences et des Techniques, especially Friederike Moltmann, Thomas Hofweber, Ede Zimmerman, and my commentator, Isidora Stojanovic.

The last stages of preparation of the proofs of *Attitude Problems* were carried out in less than ideal circumstances, for I was completing the project while I was a Hurricane Katrina evacuee.[3] I thank the University of Alabama in Huntsville for extending facilities to me that proved very useful, and Andrew Cling for arranging it.

Finally, I thank the National Endowment of the Humanities for the Summer Grant that facilitated the writing and revising of later chapters. To be sure, any views, findings, conclusions, or recommendations expressed in this publication do not necessarily reflect those of the NEH.

But I'm not done yet. Though what follows may be out of date by the time it reaches its audience, I would like to end by saying something about the impact of Hurricane Katrina on Tulane University, where I have taught for twenty-three of the last twenty-four years, and the city of New Orleans, where I have lived for the same period.

I am confident that Tulane's current leaders have formulated a sound plan to bring the university back. But their task has been made very much harder by the fact that Tulane has no financial cushion that would allow it room for manoeuvre in weathering this crisis. Significant responsibility for this rests with successive Boards

---

[3] For those interested in such matters, proofs were prepared in Adobe *FrameMaker* running on Macintosh computers. The text font is Robert Slimbach's *Kepler*, the display font for formulae is *AG Rounded*, both from Adobe, and the logic symbols are from *Lucida NewMath* by Y&Y.

of Administrators and the four decades of deficit spending on ball games that they have insisted on to gratify their obsession with remaining in Division 1A of the American intercollegiate athletics system. The total cost in subsidies and lost opportunities relating to these deficits, for the period 1964 to 1995, was calculated by a Tulane economist as reaching nine figures,[4] an amount of money that would be, to put it mildly, rather welcome right now.

But Tulane does not exist in a vacuum, and whether or not it can function again depends on its environment as well as its finances: New Orleans also needs to be functioning. Bringing New Orleans back will require political will, and a certain competence, at city, state, and federal levels. So far, there have been few hopeful signs in these areas. On the other hand, there is a small army of ordinary people working hard at rebuilding. They range from emergency-services personnel from around the country who volunteered and drove hundreds of miles to the city in their official vehicles to help restore order,[5] to the clean-up crews who have the arduous, unpleasant, and monumental task of disposing of all the trash and rubble, to the tradesmen who will do most of the reconstruction work on the ground. Some members of this army might be rather nonplussed to be presented with copies of *Attitude Problems*, but the author nevertheless records his admiration for all of their efforts.

New Orleans
May 2006

---

[4] See (Tanner 1995). His final estimate of the cost for this period was $115 million, assuming a 12% return on money that might have been invested instead of being used to cover athletics deficits (12% was the average return on US stocks in the period 1945–94). [Tanner's budget number for 1992–3 is inaccurate, but the effect of this on his overall calculation is negligible. In 1994, the value of Tulane's endowment was $280 million.]

[5] In a report about a visit to New Orleans not long after the hurricane, Michael Lewis writes: 'I walked down St. Charles Avenue and watched the most eclectic convoy of official vehicles ever assembled. It included...the New York City Police Department, the Alameda County Fire Department, the Aspen Fire Department, the S.P.C.A. from somewhere in Kentucky, emergency-rescue trucks from Illinois and Arizona, the Austin Fire Department, the U.S. Coast Guard, the Consulate of Iceland, and several pickup trucks marked, mysteriously, FPS: Federal Protection Services' (*The New York Times Magazine*, 9th October 2005, p. 51).

Table of Contents

Preface v

Chapter 1: Compositionality 1

1. The age of the universe 1
2. Extensionalism 5
3. Problems for extensionalism............................ 7
4. Intensionalism... 9
5. Beyond intensionality 12
6. Hyperintensional logic 13

Chapter 2: A Brief Guide to Type Theory 16

1. Extensional type-theory............................... 16
   - 1.1 Intransitive verbs... 16
   - 1.2 Transitive verbs 18
   - 1.3 Binary truth-functions 19
   - 1.4 Common nouns and adjectives............................20
   - 1.5 Quantified noun phrases................................. 22
   - 1.6 The lambda operator 23
   - 1.7 Type shifting and systematic ambiguity 26
   - 1.8 Interpretations of $\mathcal{L}_x$.................................29
2. Hyperintensional semantics 30

Chapter 3: Intensional Transitives 36

1. A taxonomy of intensional "transitives" 36
2. Relational versus notional readings 40
3. Existence-independence................................ 46
4. Non-relational, anti-relational, notional 47

Chapter 4: Propositionalism — 52

1. The Quinean strategy 52
2. Verbs of requirement and desire......................... 55
3. Search verbs 58
4. Depiction verbs 61
5. Verbs of evaluation..................................... 64
6. Conclusion 68

Chapter 5: Quantifiers and Characterization — 69

1. Quantifiers as arguments................................ 69
2. Event semantics for action verbs 73
3. ITV's as predicates of events or states................. 75
4. The notional as non-thematic............................ 77
5. Deriving interpretations 85

Chapter 6: Unspecificity and Inference — 91

1. Simplification... 92
2. Weakening... 94
3. The disjunction problem 96
4. Outcome postulates...................................... 98
5. Possibility as conceivability 102
6. A theory of conjunctive force 107
7. Characterization by compound QNP's......................112
8. Compound complements with singular terms 117
9. Applying the postulates 118
10. The serendipity problem................................121
11. Negative quantifiers 124

Chapter 7: Verbs of Creation and Depiction — 130

1. Parsons' theory..131
2. Characterizing processes of creation 133
3. Verbs of depiction..................................... 138
4. Depiction verbs and the definiteness effect 142
5. The pure inventory account............................. 147

Chapter 8: Substitutivity 151

1. Substitution and side-effects 151
2. 'so-called'...154
3. 'as such' 157
4. Opacity and unspecificity together 164
5. Simple sentences.. 166

Bibliography 175

Index 189

1

Compositionality

1 THE AGE OF THE UNIVERSE

Natural languages are *compositional*, or *have compositional semantics:* the meaning of a meaningful complex expression is "composed" from the meanings of its immediate constituents, in a way that reflects the syntactic configuration of those constituents. For example, if we suppose that 'Mary loves John' consists syntactically in the combination of the proper name 'Mary' and the verb phrase (VP) 'loves John', then the meaning of 'Mary loves John' will be the result of composing the meaning of 'Mary' with the meaning of 'loves John'. In turn, the meaning of 'loves John' will be the result of composing the meaning of 'loves' and the meaning of 'John'. 'Mary', 'loves' and 'John' are not themselves complex (grant this for 'loves'), so their meanings are not composed from simpler ones. Instead, their meanings have to be learned individually.

A little more formally, compositionality can be understood to say that the meaning of a complex expression is a *function* of its syntax and the meanings of its immediate constituents. A function is a black box which operates on inputs to produce an output. The workings of the box are such that different inputs may produce the same output, but the same inputs never produce different outputs (thus functions are said to be *deterministic*). For instance, the function of exponentiation produces the same output, 64, for the two different inputs (i) 2 and 6 in that order, and (ii) 8 and 2 in that order. The inputs 8 and 2 always produce 64, as do the inputs 2^3 and 2. Thus the output of a correct application of exponentiation depends only on the input numbers, and is not sensitive to the way the inputs are expressed or described ('8' versus '2^3').

We will use the brackets ⟦ and ⟧ to abbreviate 'the meaning of _', so that we can write, say, '⟦loves John⟧', instead of "the meaning of 'loves John'". And let us think of a meaning-generator for a natural language as a deterministic black box. Then giving it the three inputs ⟦Mary⟧, ⟦loves John⟧, and the syntactic configuration '[Mary [loves John]]', it will produce ⟦Mary loves John⟧ (i.e., the meaning of 'Mary loves John') as output. Repeating this procedure over and over never changes the output, and if the meaning of 'MaryBeth' is the same as that of 'Mary', then the inputs ⟦MaryBeth⟧, ⟦loves John⟧, and the syntactic configuration '[MaryBeth [loves John]]', will produce the same meaning as that of 'Mary loves John' as output. In other words, granted ⟦Mary⟧ = ⟦MaryBeth⟧, compositionality guarantees that ⟦Mary loves John⟧ = ⟦MaryBeth loves John⟧.

A good illustration of the rationale for the thesis that natural languages are compositional is provided by examples such as

(1) The universe is about fourteen thousand million years old.

There will be some readers for whom (1) is a novel sentence, one they have not encountered before, either in speech or writing. But in terms of grasping what (1) says, these readers are in no worse a position than those to whom the thought occurs every day. Typical English-speakers understand (1), even if it is novel to them, because they understand its constituent words, they perceive its syntax, and they can compose its meaning from these resources.[1] If there is a significantly different and equally plausible explanation of the ability to understand novel sentences, it has yet to be discovered.

As this example suggests, compositionality can constrain what kinds of thing the meanings of expressions can be. This constraint

---

[1] This example suggests, correctly, I think, that if compositionality is to be explained in terms of functional dependence, not just any old function will do: the function must be tailored to supporting these capacities. Such restrictions may make available a response to the objections in (Szabó 2000:499–500) to the functional dependence account of meaning-composition.

Compositionality 3

on the nature of meanings[2] may be broken into two parts:

(i) if the phrase $e_1\widehat{\ }e_2$ with constituent expressions e_1 and e_2 is meaningful, the meanings of e_1 and e_2 must be of such a nature as to permit some way of being composed with one another;

(ii) composition of meanings in whatever way that (i) provides must produce the right results – if $e_1\widehat{\ }e_2$ is meaningful, its meaning should be the item that is produced when the meaning of e_1 is composed with the meaning of e_2.

Following word order and writing $x(y)$ for the composition of x with y, (ii) above can be stated briefly as the constraint that $[\![e_1\widehat{\ }e_2]\!] = [\![e_1]\!]([\![e_2]\!])$, for all expressions e_1 and e_2 such that $e_1\widehat{\ }e_2$ is meaningful.

As an example of what the combination of (i) and (ii) exclude, consider the phrase 'pet fish' (Osherson and Smith 1981) and the view that the meanings of (simple *and* complex) expressions which apply to individual objects are *lists of features weighted by typicality* ('t-weighted lists of features'). If this is so, then according to (i) we should be able to *compose* lists of t-weighted features into lists of t-weighted features. And according to (ii), the list of t-weighted features that is in fact the one for 'pet fish' should be the one we get by composing the list of t-weighted features for 'pet' with the one for 'fish', by whatever method of composition we have in hand from (i). In our meaning-bracket notation, this is to say that the list $[\![\text{pet fish}]\!]$ must be equal to the result of composing the list $[\![\text{pet}]\!]$ with the list $[\![\text{fish}]\!]$: we need $[\![\text{pet fish}]\!] = [\![\text{pet}]\!]([\![\text{fish}]\!])$.

It is a non-trivial problem for the proponent of meanings as lists of t-weighted features to explain composition so that (i) and (ii) are satisfied simultaneously. Suppose that in the list for 'pet fish', the heavily weighted features are those of a typical goldfish and a typical small multi-colored tropical fish. For $[\![\text{pet}]\!]$ the heavily weighted features are 'four legs', 'furry/hairy', 'playful', and so on, while for $[\![\text{fish}]\!]$, think of the features of something like a cross between a trout and a salmon, with a bit of shark thrown in. The problem is to describe a methodical operation on the lists $[\![\text{pet}]\!]$ and $[\![\text{fish}]\!]$ that gets us a list

---

[2] It is extensively argued for in (Fodor and Lepore 1996; 2002b, Chs. 1–3). But in my choice of example to follow, I am respecting some replies in (Horwich 2006: Ch. 8).

⟦pet fish⟧ that has heavy weights on goldfish-features and small multi-colored tropical fish features, and handles all similar cases.

A unification operation may suggest itself, but it is far from obvious how to unify lists when they differ over the same feature. Legs seem nearly as important to the typical pet as leglessness is to the typical fish. Does this mean that it is *open* whether or not pet fish have legs, or that leggedness is *moderately* t-weighted in ⟦pet fish⟧?

An alternative is to suppose that ⟦fish⟧ already has 'pet' as a feature with moderate to low weight, and ⟦pet fish⟧ is obtained simply by increasing the weight of 'pet' in ⟦fish⟧ to the maximum (this is the core of the 'selective modification model' of Smith *et al.* 1988). But it is a standard objection to this that the weights on fish-features are not independent. If we increase the weight of 'pet' to the maximum, then in order to get ⟦pet fish⟧, the weights in ⟦fish⟧ of (for example) habitat features like 'river', 'loch' and 'ocean' must plunge, while that of 'glass bowl' should soar. So composition of t-weighted features will *follow* the (purported) facts about what the things to which 'pet fish' applies are like. And presumably one must first understand the complex phrase to identify the things whose prominent features should be the heavily weighted ones (someone who, amazed to learn that people keep fish as pets, asks 'what are pet fish like?', understands her own question). So it is viciously circular to claim that such weighted features constitute the meaning of the complex phrase.

It is not hard to see that the underlying problem is the attempt to absorb contingent *a posteriori* matters into meanings.[3] Even if we

---

[3] This point seems insufficiently appreciated in (Robbins 2002), which proposes to assimilate such items as lists of weighted features to Fregean senses or narrow contents (328–9). But however these latter are explained, they must not embody what is just widely-shared collateral information. Someone who thinks that pet fish are only kept in rectangular plastic acquaria thinks exactly *that* without qualification, so his failure to accord high weight to 'glass bowl' as a habitat-feature does not impugn his grasp of ⟦pet fish⟧. Instead, it merely indicates a false belief about pet fish. Quite extraordinary false beliefs are consistent with firm grasp of meaning. Certainly, as the number of apparently sincere avowals of extraordinary falsehoods about pet fish mounts in a single speaker, the hypothesis that his understanding of 'pet fish' is deviant grows in plausibility. But that this might be the best explanation of the avowals, does not justify *identifying* ⟦pet fish⟧ with the list of t-weighted features given by normal belief-avowals using 'pet fish'. It is simply that, among those who understand 'pet fish', much the same collateral information is in the air and easily acquired.

can predict from ⟦pet⟧ that rivers, lochs and oceans are unlikely habitats for pet fish, there is no particular reason to expect *bowls*. And it is entirely contingent and *a posteriori* that those who seek the companionship of fish are not predominantly piranha enthusiasts (I believe tarantulas are the most popular pet spider). So we cannot predict just from ⟦pet⟧ and ⟦fish⟧ that the weight of 'carnivorous' in ⟦pet fish⟧ is lower, or even *thought* to be lower, than in ⟦fish⟧. The weights of features in ⟦pet fish⟧ result from empirical and contingent facts about what kinds of *fish* people are generally inclined to favour as pets, and these are not necessarily predictable from, or a function of, the empirical and contingent facts about what fish are like and about what kinds of *creatures* (let's forget about rocks) people are generally inclined to favour as pets. But the meaning of 'pet fish' *is* graspable just from grasp of the meaning of 'pet', the meaning of 'fish', and the manner of their combination in 'pet fish'. So the meaning of 'pet fish' cannot be a list of t-weighted features.[4]

2 EXTENSIONALISM

What accounts of meaning *are* compatible with compositionality? The set of things to which a predicate of objects applies is called its *extension*. For example, the common noun 'cordate' has as its extension the set of creatures with a heart; the common noun 'renate' has as its extension the set of creatures with a kidney. We will use $^\vee$ for 'the extension of', so '$^\vee$cordate' means "the extension of 'cordate'", and $^\vee$cordate = $\{x: x$ is a cordate$\}$. Similarly, $^\vee$renate = $\{x: x$ is a renate$\}$. A traditional candidate for the meaning of an atomic predicate is its extension: ⟦cordate⟧ = $^\vee$cordate, ⟦renate⟧ = $^\vee$renate, ⟦fish⟧ = $^\vee$fish, and so on. The equation of the meaning of a predicate with its extension we refer to as *extensionalism* about predicates.

Extensionalism about predicates solves the pet-fish problem:

(2) a. ⟦pet⟧ = $^\vee$pet = $\{x: x$ is someone's pet$\}$.
 b. ⟦fish⟧ = $^\vee$fish = $\{x: x$ is a fish$\}$.

---

[4] This section has merely dipped a toe into very deep water. There is a vast literature, including (Davies 1987; Evans 1981; Fodor and Lepore 2001; Higginbotham 1986; Horwich 1998, 2006; Partee 1984; Pelletier 1994; Recanati 2003; Szabó 2000).

To satisfy principle (i) on page 3, we may explain modifier-noun composition as set-intersection. So ⟦pet⟧(⟦fish⟧) will be the set that results from taking the intersection of {x: x is someone's pet} and {x: x is a fish}, which we write $^\vee$pet ∩ $^\vee$fish. $^\vee$pct ∩ $^\vee$fish is the set of things which are both someone's pet and a fish. This set is exactly the extension of 'pet fish', hence according to extensionalism about predicates, it is ⟦pet fish⟧. Therefore principle (ii) on page 3 is also satisfied: ⟦pet⟧(⟦fish⟧) = $^\vee$pet ∩ $^\vee$fish = $^\vee$(pet fish) = ⟦pet fish⟧. Thus extensionalism can accommodate this type of complex predicate.

The concept of extension is applicable to other categories of expression. We can identify the extensions of proper names with their referents and the extensions of sentences with their truth-values. For *quantified noun phrases* (QNP's), expressions such as 'every dog', 'no black cat', 'three blind mice', and so on, the extension is the set of all sets that contain the relevant quantity of items from the extension of the predicate in the QNP.[5] Thus the extension of 'every dog' is the set of all sets that include every dog; the extension of 'no black cat' is the set of all sets that include no black cats; and the extension of 'three blind mice' is the set of all sets that include three blind mice. This is the correct choice of extension for compositional calculation of the truth-values of sentences (s) that consist in a QNP followed by a verb phrase (VP), for example,

(3) [$_S$[$_{QNP}$three blind mice] [$_{VP}$ran from a farmer's wife]].

(3) is true iff the set x of things that ran from a farmer's wife is one of the sets in the extension of 'three blind mice', which is to say, iff x is a set that includes three blind mice. The general rule is:

(4) $^\vee$[$_S$ QNP VP] = ⊤ iff $^\vee$VP ∈ $^\vee$QNP.

Extensionalism about sentences, about proper names, and about quantified noun phrases, are three different claims. Each is a thesis that identifies the meanings of expressions of certain classes with their extensions. Extensionalism about an entire language $\mathcal{L}$ is the thesis that identifies the meaning of *any* meaningful expression of $\mathcal{L}$ with its extension: ⟦e⟧ = $^\vee e$ for every meaningful e of $\mathcal{L}$.

---

[5] See (Barwise and Cooper 1982); for exposition, (Larson and Segal 1995, Ch. 8).

3 PROBLEMS FOR EXTENSIONALISM

Extensionalism is more plausible for some classes of expression than others. Extensionalism about proper names is not easily refuted. But extensionalism is rather implausible for whole sentences: classically, there are only two truth-values, TRUE (for short, ⊤) and FALSE (⊥), so there would only be two meanings, all true sentences would be synonymous, and all false sentences would be synonymous. Except for expressively impoverished languages, this is almost impossible to square with compositionality (see the argument below about predicates).

Extensionalism for predicates may solve the pet-fish problem, but it is doubtful that it is the *right* way of solving it. Suppose what is anyway close to being the case, that $^\vee$cordate = $^\vee$renate. In other words, suppose $\{x: x$ is a cordate$\} = \{x: x$ is a renate$\}$, that is, that these two sets have the same members. Then if extension is meaning, we have to say that 'cordate' and 'renate' mean the same. But this sounds wrong: saying that you have a heart isn't *synonymous* with saying that you have a kidney. And if ⟦cordate⟧ ≠ ⟦renate⟧ even though $^\vee$cordate = $^\vee$renate, extensionalism about predicates is refuted.

This is just an appeal to intuitions about synonymy. It would be better if we could produce a pair of examples which differ in construction only by one's having 'cordate' where the other has 'renate', yet the two examples have different truth-values. If the only difference between the examples is that one has 'cordate' where the other has 'renate', and ⟦cordate⟧ = ⟦renate⟧, then by compositionality, the two sentences must be synonymous. But it is impossible for synonymous sentences to have different truth-values – whether or not we think of the meaning of a sentence *as* its truth-value, meaning certainly *determines* truth-value (given the facts), hence same meaning guarantees same truth-value. So consider the examples in (5):

(5) a. Cordates could have evolved without kidneys.
 b. Renates could have evolved without kidneys.

'Could have' expresses broadly logical possibility, so (5a) seems uncontroversial: presumably no *logical* necessity drove evolutionary forces to select kidneys as the engineering solution to performing the functions that kidneys in fact perform. (5b), on the other hand, makes little sense, since 'renate' just means 'creature with a kidney'. Apparently, then, (5a) is true, (5b) false. But since the only difference between the meanings of (5a) and (5b) is that one has ⟦cordate⟧ where the other has ⟦renate⟧, compositionality requires that ⟦(5a)⟧ = ⟦(5b)⟧ if ⟦cordate⟧ = ⟦renate⟧. By the difference in truth-value, ⟦(5a)⟧ ≠ ⟦(5b)⟧, so ⟦cordate⟧ ≠ ⟦renate⟧.

More carefully, we should only say that (5b) has a *reading* on which it differs in truth-value from (5a). By (5b) we might mean something like 'the creatures which in fact are renates could have evolved without kidneys', which might be true: the very same creatures, or ones of the very same type, which *actually* have kidneys, could have evolved a somewhat different array of organs. But this is not the reading intended here for (5b); its existence illustrates a *scope ambiguity* in the sentences in (5), roughly concerning which of the bare plural noun *versus* the 'could have' is processed first in interpreting the sentence. For (5b) we can bring out the alternatives with the following paraphrases:

(6) a. In some possible world w, the renates of w evolve in w without kidneys.
 b. The renates of the actual world evolve in some possible world w without kidneys.

The term 'possible world' corresponds to the intuitive idea of a way things could have gone, so (6a) claims that there is a way things could have gone in which, contradictorily, renates evolve without kidneys. (6b) says that for the actual renates there is a way things could have gone in which *they* evolve without kidneys (and hence are not renates in *that* course of events). If (5b) is taken in the sense (6a), we are giving 'could have' wide scope, or scope over 'renates', but if it is taken in the sense (6b), we are giving 'could have' narrow scope and 'renates' wide scope. It is only in sense (6a) that (5b) is contradictory. So suppose we are careful to read both (5a) and (5b) so that 'could have' has wide scope. This gives us sense (6a) for (5b) and its counterpart for (5a). (5a) and (5b) have different truth-values on this pair of parallel readings. But if ⟦cordate⟧ = ⟦renate⟧ they should have the *same* truth-values on any parallel readings we care to consider. So our demonstration that ⟦cordate⟧ ≠ ⟦renate⟧ still stands.

4 INTENSIONALISM

The argument of Section 1.3 indicates that we should not identify the meanings of predicates with their extensions. However, example (5) suggests that meanings could be identified with *intensions*, which are generalizations of extensions designed to cater for precisely the distinction that (5) brings out. We write $^\wedge e$ for the intension of an expression e. (5) shows that 'cordate' and 'renate' are only *contingently* coextensive: their extensions coincide in the actual world, but at other possible worlds, for instance ones where some cordates lack kidneys, their extensions diverge. The intension of a predicate, on the usual account, is its *possible-worlds profile*. This is not the set of things it applies to in the actual world, but rather a collection of pairs, each pair consisting in a possible world w and the set of things the predicate applies to in w (these are the things the predicate would have applied to if things had gone as they do in w).

Writing '@' for the actual world, the intension of a predicate F has the shape

(7) $\{\langle @, \{a_1, a_2, a_3,...\}\rangle, \langle u, \{b_1, b_2, b_3,...\}\rangle, \langle v, \{c_1, c_2, c_3,...\}\rangle,...\}$.

$\{a_1, a_2, a_3,...\}$ is the (actual) extension of F. $\{b_1, b_2, b_3,...\}$ is the set of things which would have been F if things had gone as they do in u, $\{c_1, c_2, c_3,...\}$ is the set of the things which would have been F if things had gone as they do in v, and so on. In terms of our running example, we then have $^\wedge$cordate $\neq$ $^\wedge$renate, because for at least one w, there will be sets X and Y such that $X \neq Y$, $\langle w, X\rangle$ is in $^\wedge$cordate, and $\langle w, Y\rangle$ is in $^\wedge$renate. Since $^\wedge$cordate $\neq$ $^\wedge$renate and we wanted ⟦cordate⟧ $\neq$ ⟦renate⟧, we are encouraged to identify meaning with intension, at least for predicates.

Intensionalism about predicates solves the pet-fish problem as well as extensionalism does. To satisfy principle (i) on page 3, we can explain composition of predicates in terms of second-co-ordinate intersection for corresponding pairs. In other words, if $\langle w, X\rangle$ is in ⟦pet⟧, and $\langle w, Y\rangle$ is in ⟦fish⟧, we will have $\langle w, X \cap Y\rangle$ in ⟦pet⟧(⟦fish⟧). But $X \cap Y$ is exactly the extension of 'pet fish' at w. Therefore, we also have $\langle w, X \cap Y\rangle$ in ⟦pet fish⟧, and conversely. So principle (ii) on page 3 is also satisfied.

The predicate's intension is said to be *flexible* if its extension at some world is a different set from its extension at some other; all the predicates we have used so far, 'cordate', 'pet', 'fish' and 'renate', have flexible intensions. Kripke (1972, 1980) has convincingly argued that by contrast, the intensions of proper names are inflexible or *constant* (names are, in his terminology, *rigid designators*). So the intension of a name will have the form $\{\langle @, x\rangle, \langle u, x\rangle, \langle v, x\rangle,...\}$, where x is a fixed object. This captures the fact that if we say

(8) Socrates could have been a cordate without being a renate

we are making a claim about Socrates, not someone else, so we are keeping the extension of 'Socrates' fixed.[6] But we must allow the extensions of 'cordate' and 'renate' to come apart at some world, otherwise (8) would be refuted. Granted that 'cordate' and 'renate' are actually co-extensive, at least one must be flexible if (8) is to be true.

The constancy or otherwise of the intensions of other types of expression will depend on the constituents of the expression. For sentences, necessary truths and necessary falsehoods have constant intensions, while contingencies have flexible ones. The intension of a sentence is a collection of pairs, each pair consisting in a possible world and the truth-value of the sentence at that world. So the intension of a necessary truth has the form $\{\langle @, \top\rangle, \langle u, \top\rangle, \langle v, \top\rangle,...\}$. The intension of a sentence is sometimes called the *proposition* it expresses. The proposition, in this technical sense, can also be identified with a set of possible worlds, on the understanding that to say that a world w is in a proposition p is to say that $\langle w, \top\rangle$ is in p, and to say that w is not in p is to say that $\langle w, \bot\rangle$ is in p.

---

[6] To forestall any confusion: Kripke is of course happy to agree that there are ways things could have gone in which someone other than Socrates is *called* 'Socrates' (Kripke 1980:77–8). We can say, if we like, that there are worlds *in* which 'Socrates' does not denote Socrates: Socrates' parents choose a different name for him, and maybe his brother gets the name 'Socrates'. But (8) is true iff the indicative sentence 'Socrates is a cordate but not a renate' is made true by some possible world. In evaluating this sentence at a given possible world, we interpret 'Socrates' as standing for Socrates (who else?). But we need not interpret 'cordate' and 'renate' by their actual extensions. Since 'Socrates' is always interpreted by Socrates, we can say that it stands for Socrates *at*, or *with respect to*, every possible world. (For 'Socrates might not have existed' to be true, we need a world at which 'Socrates does not exist' is true. For uniform treatment with 'Socrates is a cordate but not a renate', we should still take 'Socrates' to denote Socrates with respect to such worlds.)

More generally, the intension $^\wedge e$ of any expression e is the set of pairs $\langle u, {}^\vee u e\rangle$, where ${}^\vee u e$ is the extension of e at the world u. For example, the intension of 'three blind mice' is the set of pairs $\langle u, X\rangle$, where X is the set of all sets in u that include three blind mice of u. Since 'blind mouse' has a flexible intension, so does 'three blind mice'. There are intensionalist theses for specific classes of expression in a language $\mathcal{L}$, and also global intensionalism, which says that for any meaningful expression e of $\mathcal{L}$, $[\![e]\!] = {}^\wedge e$.

Call an expression e_1 *extensional* iff for any expression e_2 such that $e_1\widehat{\ }e_2$ is meaningful, the extension of $e_1\widehat{\ }e_2$ depends on the *extension* of e_2, as opposed to its intension: ${}^\vee(e_1\widehat{\ }e_2) = {}^\vee e_1({}^\vee e_2)$. Call e_1 *intensional* iff the extension of $e_1\widehat{\ }e_2$ depends on the *intension* of e_2, that is, iff ${}^\vee(e_1\widehat{\ }e_2) = {}^\vee e_1({}^\wedge e_2)$. This is a distinction that is orthogonal to extensionalism/intensionalism: the meaning of every expression may be its extension, its intension, or something else, but expressions still *have* extensions, and the extension of a compound expression $e_1\widehat{\ }e_2$ may or may not be a function of the extensions of both e_1 and e_2.

'Pet' is extensional, since the extension of, say, 'pet fish', is obtained by intersecting the extensions of 'pet' and 'fish' – the *intension* of 'fish' does not get involved. But 'it is necessary that', as in

(9) It is necessary that all cordates are renates,

is intensional. To calculate the extension of (9), that is, its truth-value, we need the *extension* of 'it is necessary that' and the *intension* of 'all cordates are renates'. The extension of 'it is necessary that' is such that when 'it is necessary that' is combined with a sentence, the resulting expression (e.g., (9)) has a truth-value as its extension. But the relevant feature of the embedded sentence is its *in*tension. For example, the extension of 'all cordates are renates' does not suffice to fix the extension of (9), given the extension of 'it is necessary that': the extension of (9) depends on what type of intension 'all cordates are renates' has. If its intension is flexible, as we proposed in connection with (5a), then (9) is false, but if it is constantly true, making 'all cordates are renates' a necessary truth, then (9) is true. More explicitly, the extension of 'it is necessary that _' is such that when 'it is necessary that _' composes with a complete sentence S, the resulting complex sentence is true iff the intension of S is the set of pairs $\langle w, \top\rangle$ for every possible world w.

5 BEYOND INTENSIONALITY

Examples like (5) appear to show that extensions are inadequate candidates for meanings. Are there examples of a similar nature, which show that intensions are inadequate candidates? Apparently so, as the following pairs attest.

(10) a. Lex Luthor fears Superman.
b. Lex Luthor fears Clark Kent.

(11) a. No-one doubts that water is water.
b. No-one doubts that water is H_2O.

(12) a. Obviously, there are infinitely many numbers.
b. Obviously, there are infinitely many prime numbers.

'Superman' and 'Clark Kent' have the same intension (assume the fiction to be factual), as do 'water' and 'H_2O',[7] and as do 'there are infinitely many numbers' and 'there are infinitely many prime numbers'. So if meaning is intension, we have ⟦Superman⟧ = ⟦Clark Kent⟧, ⟦water⟧ = ⟦H_2O⟧, and ⟦there are infinitely many numbers⟧ = ⟦there are infinitely many prime numbers⟧. Hence by compositionality, the meaning of each (a)-sentence above is the same as its companion (b)-sentence. So the members of each pair must have the same truth-values. But in each pair, the (a)-sentence appears to be true and the (b)-sentence false. Granted appearances, it follows that identifying meaning with intension is a mistake.

---

[7] 'H_2O' is a rigid designator because of how it is related to the rigidly designating description, 'the substance whose chemical composition is two parts of hydrogen to one of oxygen'. This description rigidly designates because (i) 'hydrogen' and 'oxygen' rigidly designate and (ii) when two parts of hydrogen combine with one part of oxygen in one possible world, the result is the same substance as in any other world where the same combination occurs. Since this substance is water in the actual world, it is water in every world where the combination occurs. However, to get the same intension for 'H_2O' as for 'water', granted the rigidity of the latter, we also require that water could not have had a different chemical composition, or more broadly, that the fundamental physical properties of substances (let's take chemical composition to be fundamental) are essential to them, and we need to be willing to treat the description 'H_2O' and the unstructured term 'water' the same way *vis à vis* worlds where there is no water, hydrogen, or oxygen.

However, the three examples are rather disparate. In (11) and (12), the differences in meaning are based on differences in complexity. The term 'water' is unstructured, and the term 'H₂O' is structured. The former can be mastered without any grasp of 'hydrogen', but not the latter (assuming it is not learned as an unstructured term). Similarly, the difference in meaning of the sentences in (12) traces to the presence of *prime* number' in (12b). But for (10) there are no structural differences to cite in explaining why ⟦Superman⟧ ≠ ⟦Clark Kent⟧: each name is a semantic primitive. So it is natural to posit *hidden* differences. However, this leads to a dilemma. The more recondite we make the hidden difference, the more doubtful it is that it is grasped, even implicitly, by ordinary speakers. But a less recondite difference runs the risk of resembling the 'famous-deeds descriptions' theory discredited in (Kripke 1972, 1980).

In fact, the only candidate we have so far come up with for the meaning of a name is the object the name stands for.[8] But since Superman is Clark Kent, this would give those two names the same meaning, and promote the counterintuitive conclusion that the sentences in (10) cannot differ in truth-value. This is a problem to which we will return in Chapter 8.

6 HYPERINTENSIONAL LOGIC

An expression e is said to be *hyperintensional* iff there are expressions e_1 and e_2 of the same syntactic category such that $e\hat{\ }e_1$ and $e\hat{\ }e_2$ are meaningful, e_1 and e_2 have the same intension, but the intensions of $e\hat{\ }e_1$ and $e\hat{\ }e_2$ are different ($^\wedge e_1 = {^\wedge}e_2$ but $^\wedge(e\hat{\ }e_1) \neq {^\wedge}(e\hat{\ }e_2)$). We can use examples (10), (11), and (12) to show that their psychological vocabulary is hyperintensional, for instance, by putting 'fears' for e, 'Superman' for e_1, 'fears Superman' for $e\hat{\ }e_1$, 'Clark Kent' for e_2, and 'fears Clark Kent' for $e\hat{\ }e_2$. By compositionality for intensions,

---

[8] The intension of a name is not its referent α but rather, the set of pairs $\langle w, \alpha \rangle$ for each world w. However, this is simply a technical convenience, and should not distract attention from the fact that it is the referent that does the work in distinguishing one intension from another. It is trivial to convert an intensional theory in which names have intensions which are sets of pairs into one in which the intension of a name is identified with its extension.

^(fears Superman) ≠ ^(fears Clark Kent), otherwise composing each with ^(Lex Luthor) would produce the same intension. But granted that (10a) and (10b) have different truth-values at the actual world, they have different intensions. Thus 'fears' is a hyperintensional transitive verb by the criterion.

If we were to proceed as before, we would now discuss the hypothesis that the meaning of an expression is to be identified with its *hyper*intension. But there is no commonly accepted characterization of hyperintensions that leaves it open whether or not meaning is hyperintension. Nevertheless, we can use (11) and (12) to draw a conclusion about what hyperintensions must be like: they must not collapse evident differences in structure and constituents. In particular, the hyperintensions of 'water' and 'H_2O' must in some way reflect the fact that only the second of these involves ⟦hydrogen⟧, and the hyperintensions of 'there are infinitely many numbers' and 'there are infinitely many prime numbers' must differ in a way that traces to the presence of ⟦prime⟧ in the second but not the first. What to say about the cases in (10) is not settled at this point.

There are, broadly, two ways in which these distinctions might be realized. On one approach, the hyperintension of an expression is a structured entity that reflects the structure of the expression itself: the meanings of the primitive expressions are the basic constituents of the hyperintension of the complex expression, and they are configured in some set-theoretic arrangement that mirrors the syntax of the complex expression. A version of this says that the hyperintensions of names are their referents, and the hyperintensions of predicates are the properties they express. The hyperintension of a sentence is said to be a *state of affairs* or a *Russellian proposition*.[9] But on this account, (10a) and (10b) have the same hyperintension, which, some would say, defeats the hypothesis that hyperintension is meaning (we will see, in Chapter 8, why this is wrong).

A distinct, non-structuralist, approach, takes sentence-meanings

---

[9] See (Forbes 1989:137–149) on states of affairs, and (Soames 1987) on Russellian propositions. There is a hybrid account in (Lewis 1972:182–6) on which a sentence-meaning is a tree at each node of which we find the intension of the corresponding phrasal constituent of the sentence. So presumably there is also a hybrid account of meaning-composition, as tree-composition and intension-composition.

to be primitive (though there is no harm in thinking of them, extra-theoretically, as structured). In part, the motivation is that taking the notion of truth-value as primitive does not lead to an adequate conception of sentence-meaning, and taking the notion of possible world as primitive effects insufficient improvement. So it may be a mistake to try to identify sentence-meaning with something that is in some sense "relatively less problematic". And while it might seem to rob a semantic theory of interest if it avoids any such identification, that is not so, for there is still the task of finding meanings for subsentential units which compose together to result in the meanings of the sentences that they form. In fact, we get a pure form of the idea that the meaning of a subsentential unit is its contribution to the determination of the meanings of the complete sentences in which it occurs. And there are plenty of cases, some the focus of this book, in which the contribution is obscure.

One version of the non-structuralist approach is algebraic in nature (Bealer 1989, 1994). But there is another version, whose appeal rests on its very lucid *function-argument* model of meaning-composition. In Section 1, we wrote $x(y)$ for the composition of meanings x and y. This notation is silent about what composition consists in, and is consistent with it just being juxtaposition. But juxtaposing two meanings does not guarantee that they will compose together: the meanings have to be, in some sense, "suited" to each other. The function-argument model supports a clear account of what suitedness consists in for x and y: one meaning is a function that allows certain inputs ('arguments') and disallows certain others, and the other meaning is one of the allowed inputs. In the notation $x(y)$, x is the function and y is the argument or input.

This model can be applied to extensions, where it gives rise to what is known as the simple theory of types; it can be applied to intensions, producing higher-order intensional logic; and it can be applied to hyperintensions, where it produces what in (Thomason 1980) is dubbed 'intentional logic', and will be called 'hyperintensional logic' here (Thomason's system distinguishes (10a) and (10b), which our variant does not; see further n. 12, page 159). Our focus is on hyperintensional logic, but rather than leap in at the deep end, we start with a review of the function-argument model for extensions; readers familiar with the ideas can skip Section 1 of the next chapter.

2

A Brief Guide to Type Theory

1 EXTENSIONAL TYPE-THEORY

The organizing principles of the simple theory of types are: (i) sentence-meanings are truth-values, (ii) the meaning of a name is its referent, and (iii) the meanings of other basic constituents of sentences are to be assigned in such a way that when functions are applied to arguments as the structure of the sentence dictates, the final output is a truth-value. The overall approach is compatible with a wide range of syntactic theories,[1] but for purposes of illustration here, the simplest phrase structure grammar will suffice.

1.1 *Intransitive verbs*

The sentence 'Tom sleeps' consists in a proper name combined with an intransitive verb. According to (i) and (ii) above, the meaning of the name is an individual, and the meaning of the whole sentence is its truth-value. The meaning of 'sleeps' must therefore be a function which, given an individual i as input, produces a truth-value b ('boolean') as output. There is no other candidate that will work, given the prior choices of meanings for the name and the sentence.

---

[1] Usually, type-theoretic semantics is allied with categorial syntax; see (Carpenter 1997) for a thorough account. But type-theoretic semantics or an equivalent can also work with various versions of Chomskyan syntax; see (Partee 1973; Cooper and Parsons 1976; Authier and Reed 1999:81–101; Larson and Cho 2003:234).

In the preceding paragraph, we did not state the specific meanings of 'Tom', 'Tom sleeps', and 'sleeps', but only the *type* of meanings they possess: an individual, a truth-value, and a function from individuals to truth-values. Type-theoretic semantics assigns types of meaning to syntactic categories of expression. So the semantic type for the category *name* is *individual* (*i*), the semantic type for the category *sentence* is *truth-value* (*b*), and the semantic type for the category *intransitive verb* is *function from individuals to truth-values*, written *i↦b*, or, to save space, *ib*. We can represent the process of assigning types in 'Tom sleeps' in the following way:

(1) a. [[Tom] [sleeps]].
    b.
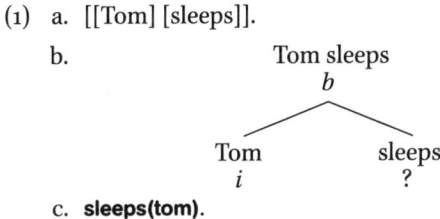
    c. **sleeps(tom)**.

In (1a) we parse 'Tom sleeps' into its constituents, and in (1b) we show this parsing as a binary-branching tree, with given semantic types entered. The problem is to replace the query with a semantic type that will combine, either as function with argument or as argument to function, with the type at its sister node, to produce the type at the parent node. Since the type at the sister node is not that of a function, the query must be replaced with a function type and only *ib* fits the bill.

The formula **sleeps(tom)** in (1c) belongs to a type-theoretic language $\mathcal{L}_x$ ('extensional') in which order of symbols is function-left-argument-right. **sleeps(tom)** is said to be *well-typed* because the type of **tom** is correct as an input for the type of **sleeps**. **tom(sleeps)** would be ill-typed, since it makes the meaning of **sleeps** the input to the meaning of **tom** (since the meaning of **tom** is not a function, **tom** cannot take inputs). At least, **tom(sleeps)** is ill-typed granted our initial decision that ⟦Tom⟧ is of type *i*. If instead we had decided from the outset that intransitive verbs have meanings of type *ib*, had left the type of names open, and wanted **tom(sleeps)** as the semantic representation, we would be faced with the following problem:

(2)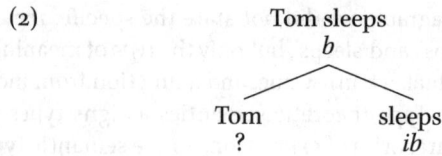

Since ⟦sleeps⟧ is to be the input and is of type *ib*, and the output is to be of type *b*, ⟦Tom⟧ itself must be a function from functions of type *ib* to truth-values. A function whose inputs are of type *ib* and whose output is of type *b* has a type that is written $(i{\mapsto}b){\mapsto}b$, or, to save space, $(ib)b$. With this assignment for ⟦Tom⟧, **tom(sleeps)** is well-typed; and now **sleeps(tom)** is ill-typed, because although **sleeps** is a function, it takes inputs of type *i*, not type $(ib)b$. Just from the point of view of representing composition of meanings, there is little to choose between these two semantics for 'Tom sleeps'. But we prefer (1b) because of its more intuitive choice of type for proper names.

1.2 *Transitive verbs*

The general strategy just illustrated is to parse sentences in ways that can be displayed by binary-branching trees, and assign types to expressions so that, for any two sister nodes (nodes on the same level), one of them has the type of a function whose output is of the type at the parent node, and the other has the type of inputs to that function. This determines the type of transitive verbs.

(3) a. [$_S$[$_{NP}$ Tom] [$_{VP}$[$_V$ chases] [$_{NP}$ Jerry]]].
b.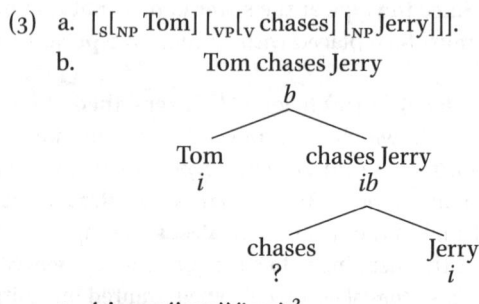
c. **(chases(jerry))(tom)**.[2]

---

[2] The source of the example, for those unfamiliar with it, is the *Tom and Jerry* cartoon series: Tom is a cat, Jerry a mouse, the former perennially scheming to catch the latter, and losing every time to the mouse's ingenuity or good luck.

A Brief Guide to Type Theory

In (3a) we parse 'Tom chases Jerry' into *labelled* constituents, a sentence consisting in a NOUN PHRASE and a VERB PHRASE, where the VP is further broken down into a transitive verb 'chases' and its object NP 'Jerry'. The meaning of the VP 'chases Jerry' must be of type *ib*, since that is what is required to combine with ⟦Tom⟧ and produce *b* at the top node. So the type of ⟦chases⟧ must be something that produces outputs of type *ib* like ⟦chases Jerry⟧. The input is of type *i* (namely, ⟦Jerry⟧), so the type of ⟦chases⟧ has to be *i(ib)*. The formula (3c) reflects order of application of functions, from the bottom up in the tree. First we apply **chases** of type *i(ib)* to **jerry** of type *i* to obtain the function **chases(jerry)** of type *ib*. Then **chases(jerry)** is applied to **tom** to get a truth-value. The parentheses around **chases (jerry)** in (3c) are not strictly necessary, for if we know that

(4) **chases(jerry)(tom)**

is well-typed, it cannot be **chases(jerry(tom))**. This is because **jerry** is not a function, so **jerry(tom)** is ill-typed. In general, we try to strike a balance between minimizing ambiguity and minimizing clutter in type-theoretic formulae. But in specifying a semantic type we fully parenthesize, so that the specification is unambiguous.

1.3 *Binary truth-functions*

Familiar two-place sentential connectives are accommodated in a binary-branching framework as follows:

(5) a. [_S[_STom sleeps] [_{CO-ORP}[_{CO-OR}or] [_STom chases Jerry]]].

b. Tom sleeps or Tom chases Jerry
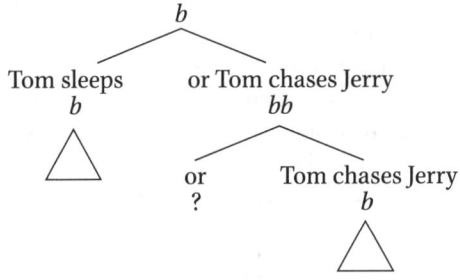

c. **(or(chases(jerry)(tom)))(sleeps(tom)).**

The parsing in (5a) breaks 'Tom sleeps or Tom chases Jerry' into a sentence 'Tom sleeps' and a co-ordinated phrase 'or Tom chases Jerry' headed by the co-ordinator 'or'. Since ⟦Tom sleeps⟧ is of type b, ⟦or Tom chases Jerry⟧ is the function, and it must be of type bb, since it is to accept an input of type b from its sister and produce an output of type b for its parent. ⟦Tom chases Jerry⟧ is also of type b, so the type of ⟦or⟧ must accept an input from the left of type b and produce an output at the parent node of type bb; hence ⟦or⟧ is of type $b(bb)$, and $b(bb)$ may replace the query in (5b). (The triangles in (5b) indicate that further analysis is being suppressed, in this case because it is given in previous examples.)

The formula (5c) accurately transcribes the bottom-up function-application sequence indicated in (5b): at the final step, the function **or(chases(jerry)(tom))** applies to the argument **sleeps(tom)**. However, this involves *prefix* positioning of **or(...)**, which makes formulae harder to understand than *postfix* positioning. So although (5c) is the official notation, we use postfix positioning as a notational variant, wherever it aids intelligibility. Thus in addition to (5c),

(6) **sleeps(tom) or chases(jerry)(tom)**

is also acceptable.

1.4 *Common nouns and adjectives*

For simplicity, we treat a common noun such as 'cat' as having the same semantic type, ib, as an intransitive verb: ⟦cat⟧ is a function which maps an individual x to ⊤ if x is a cat, and to ⊥ if x is a not a cat. For 'Tom is a cat' we then have the semantics **cat(tom)**.[3]

A common noun is the simplest example of a *nominal*. Complex nominals can be formed by prefixing adjectives to nominals. Semantically, adjectives may be classified into four groups. First, there are *intersective* adjectives, so-called because the extension of a compound nominal $a\!\!\hat{\;}n$ formed by prefixing an intersective a to a nominal n is the intersection of the extensions of a and n: $^{\vee}(a\!\!\hat{\;}n) = {^{\vee}a} \cap {^{\vee}n}$. For example, 'black' appears to be an intersective, since it

---

[3] This is not uncontentious, since we are just ignoring 'is' and 'a'. See (Partee 1986) for discussion of the relationship between G and 'is a G'.

seems the extension of 'black cat' may be obtained as the intersection of the extensions of 'black' and 'cat'. Consequently, intersectives support both adjective detachment and nominal detachment: all black cats are cats, and all black cats are black. They also support compounding: anything black and a cat is a black cat. (See also the discussion of 'pet fish' under (2) on page 5.) Intersectives are extensional: if a is intersective, and n_1 and n_2 are nominals such that $^\vee n_1 = {^\vee n_2}$, then $^\vee(a\widehat{\ }n_1) = {^\vee(a\widehat{\ }n_2)}$.

The most common adjectives are *subsective*. If a is subsective and n is a nominal, then $^\vee(a\widehat{\ }n) \subseteq {^\vee n}$. But unlike intersectives, a subsective cannot be regarded as a monadic predicate of things. 'Large' and 'typical' are illustrative. 'Large' is not intersective, otherwise 'Jerry is a large mouse' and 'all mice are animals' would entail 'Jerry is a large animal' (use detachment twice and compounding). And 'typical' is not a monadic predicate of objects, since there is no such thing as being typical, or atypical, *simpliciter*. If a is subsective, the extension of $a\widehat{\ }n$ is determined in part by a parameter, often for *standards*, usually given by n. Thus a large mouse is something that is both (i) a mouse and (ii) large *for* a mouse (one needs (i), since on its own, 'Jerry is large for a mouse' could be used to argue for the hypothesis that Jerry is a small rat). (i) guarantees nominal detachment: any large mouse is a mouse. Some subsectives, like 'large', are perhaps extensional; others, like 'famous', are non-extensional.

Non-extensional adjectives, though, need not be subsective. Some, such as 'forged', are *privative*, which means they form nominals $a\widehat{\ }n$ which apply only to things to which n does *not* apply: a forged Picasso is not a Picasso (but see Partee 2003 for scepticism about this). Other non-extensionals, such as 'alleged', prefix to a nominal n to form a nominal $a\widehat{\ }n$ which can be true of an object that n is true of, and of an object that n is untrue of: an alleged thief may or may not be a thief.

We assign types to intersectives and extensional subsectives as follows. A nominal such as 'mouse' has a meaning of type *ib*, and nominals such as 'white mouse' and 'small mouse' both have meanings of type *ib*. Hence, 'white' and 'small' accept input of type *ib* (e.g., **mouse**) and produce output also of type *ib*. So they are themselves of type (*ib*)(*ib*); hence **white(mouse)** and **small(mouse)** are both well-typed. (As for the differences between intersectives and extensional subsectives, see the proposal in note 6, page 27.) In the notation '**small(mouse)**', we suppress the parameter for standards (see also note 5, page 73).

1.5 Quantified noun phrases

Another major category of expression noted in Section 1.2 is *quantified noun phrase*. The type for QNP's is easily determined.

(7) a. [$_S$[$_{(Q)NP}$ Some cat][$_{VP}$[$_V$ sleeps]]].

b. Some cat sleeps
           b
      ╱   ╲
   Some cat   sleeps
      ?   *ib*

c. **(some(cat))(sleeps)**.

In (7b), we parse 'some cat sleeps' into a QNP and a VP enclosing an intransitive verb. For ⟦some cat⟧ the tree offers us a choice. One possibility is that ⟦some cat⟧ is the argument to ⟦sleeps⟧, and so is of type *i*, like ⟦Tom⟧ in (1b). The other is that it is the function, and so is of type (*ib*)*b*, like ⟦Tom⟧ in (2). (7c) shows that we have chosen the model of (2). ⟦Some cat⟧ is the function, so it accepts an input, such as ⟦sleeps⟧, of type *ib*, and produces an output of type *b*, giving it the type (*ib*)*b*.[4] The most obvious reason to treat ⟦some cat⟧ as the function rather than the argument is that if it were the argument, it would have to be an individual to combine with ⟦sleeps⟧; but 'some cat', unlike 'Tom', does not refer to an individual. So we would have to change the type of ⟦sleeps⟧ too.

'Some cat' is itself a complex expression. We parse it into a *quantificational* DETERMINER 'some' and a common NOUN 'cat', producing:

---

[4] In Section 1.2 we said that the extension of a QNP is a set of sets, e.g., the extension of 'some cat' is the set of all sets that include at least one cat. A set of sets of individuals and a function of type (*ib*)*b* are identical under the standard identification of sets with their *characteristic functions*. Given a domain D, a subset X of D may be identified with the function chr_X that sends all elements of X to ⊤ and all other elements of D to ⊥. A set of individuals, for instance {*x*: *x* is a cat}, is the function chr_{cat} of type *ib* such that $chr_{cat}(x) = ⊤$ iff *x* is a cat. In the same way, {*Y*: some cat is in *Y*} is the function $chr_{some\ cat}$ of type (*ib*)*b* such that $chr_{some\ cat}(Y) = ⊤$ iff some cat is in *Y*.

[$_{NP}$[$_{DET}$some] [$_N$cat]]. Suppose we take the type of common nouns to be *ib*, which allows us to represent 'Tom is a cat' as **cat(tom)**. Then ⟦some⟧ has to accept inputs of type *ib*, such as ⟦cat⟧, and, according to our discussion of (7), must produce outputs of type *(ib)b*, such as ⟦some cat⟧. In that case, 'some' and other quantificational determiners have meanings of type *(ib)((ib)b)*.

1.6 *The lambda operator*

No new issues are raised by the use of QNP's with transitive verbs, so long as the QNP is the syntactic subject. For instance, 'some cat chases Jerry' is just **(some(cat))(chases(jerry))**, where **chases(jerry)** is of type *ib*, as in (3), and is therefore a legal argument for **some(cat)**, which is of type *(ib)b*, as just discussed. But when the QNP is the syntactic object, there is a problem. We cannot represent (8a) as (8b),

(8) a. Tom chases some mouse
    b. **(chases(some(mouse)))(tom)**

because **chases(some(mouse))** is ill-typed. According to our analysis of (3), **chases** is of type *i(ib)*, and so needs an input of type *i*, such as **jerry**. But here its input, **some(mouse)**, is of type *(ib)b*.

One standard solution to this problem is to implement the type-theoretic version of the first-order logic paraphrase of (8a) as 'some mouse is such that Tom chases it'. The pronoun 'it' corresponds to an individual variable and is assigned an individual in first-order semantics, so we should be able to represent it type-theoretically by a variable of type *i*, say **x**. However,

(9) **(some(mouse))(chases(x)(tom))**

will not do either, because **some(mouse)** requires an input of type *ib*, which **chases(x)(tom)** is not. An expression with free variables has the type that results when the variables are assigned meanings from their types. Since **x** is of type *i*, the type of **chases(x)(tom)** is therefore *b*, because **chases(x)(tom)** stands for a truth-value when **x** is assigned an individual (⊤ if **x** is assigned Jerry, ⊥ if **x** is assigned Spike). So in (9), **some(mouse)** gets an input of type *b* instead of the required *ib*.

What we need is a way of converting a formula of type *b* into a term for a function of type *ib*. The reader is probably familiar with one way of converting a formula into a term, namely, *set abstraction:* from the formula $\phi(x)$, we can form the term $\{x: \phi(x)\}$, which stands for the set of all x such that ϕ is true of x. Now we want to convert the formula **chases(x)(tom)** into a term for a function, not a set, and an analogous device, *lambda abstraction* (λ-abstraction) allows us to do this. We write $\lambda x.\phi(x)$ for the function f such that $f(\alpha) = \top$ iff $[\phi(x) = \top$ when α is assigned to 'x']; in other words, $\lambda x.\phi(x)$ is the function f that sends those individuals of which ϕ is true to $\top$ and all other individuals to $\bot$. So we can write (10a), which may be read rather long-windedly as in (10b):

(10) a. **λx.chases(x)(tom)**
 b. the function f such that for any α of the type of '**x**', $f(\alpha) = \top$ iff **chases(x)(tom)** = $\top$ when α is assigned to '**x**'.

(10b) says **λx.chases(x)(tom)** is a function that maps those individuals which Tom chases to $\top$, and those individuals he does not to $\bot$. Thus

(11) a. **(λx.chases(x)(tom))(jerry)** = $\top$.
 b. **(λx.chases(x)(tom))(spike)** = $\bot$.

λx.chases(x)(tom) is therefore of type *ib*, and so is suitable as an argument to **some(mouse)**. Thus for (8a) we have arrived at

(12) **(some(mouse))λx.chases(x)(tom)**

which is well-typed, since the argument to **chases** is **x**, which is of type *i*, and the argument to **some(mouse)** is, as we just said, of type *ib*.

(12) may be well-typed, but are we sure it means that Tom chases some mouse? This depends on the semantics of $\mathcal{L}_x$: we have to set it up so that (12) is true iff for at least one mouse, **λx.chases(x)(tom)** = $\top$ when that mouse is assigned to **x** (see (21d) below). We can think of **λx.chases(x)(tom)** as an extensional representation of the *property* of being chased by Tom (of being an x such that Tom chases x). (12) is then somewhat analogous to **cat(tom)**, in which the subject Tom is an individual and we predicate the property of being a cat of this individual. In (12), the property of being chased by Tom is the subject, and we predicate something expressed by **some (mouse)** of that property. Since **some(mouse)** is predicated of a property, it itself is a property of properties. So (12) says that the property of being chased

by Tom has the **some(mouse)** property. We understand this in turn to mean that the property of being chased by Tom has the property of being a property of some mouse. So it *is* a property of some mouse. Hence some mouse is an *x* such that Tom chases *x*, the intuitive meaning we are after.

A property of individuals is sometimes called a *first-order* property. Correspondingly, a property of properties of individuals is a *second-order* property. Generalizing from (12), then, our semantics for QNP's makes them second-order properties.

Finally, we should correct a misleading impression that may be left by our discussion of λ-abstraction and example (10). We considered only the introduction of the lambda operator to bind an *individual* variable, and the formula in (10) on which abstraction is performed is itself of type *b*. But λ-abstraction is much more widely applicable. We assume that we have variables of every type, that is, for each type, there are variables which are assigned meanings of that type and no other, and whose syntactic distribution is the same as *constants* of the type (if **P** is a variable of type *ib*, then it can occur wherever **mouse** can). So in addition to the term **some(mouse)** we also have **some(P)**, which, like **some(mouse)**, is of type $(ib)b$ (because **some(P)** has a meaning of type $(ib)b$ when **P** is assigned a value of type *ib*, such as ⟦**mouse**⟧). And we can apply λ-abstraction to **some(P)** to obtain λ**P.some(P)**. This is a term for a function of type $(ib)((ib)b)$: it accepts an input of type *ib*, such as ⟦**mouse**⟧, and produces an output of type $(ib)b$, such as ⟦**some(mouse)**⟧; in fact, λ**P.some(P)** is the $\mathcal{L}_x$-semantics of the determiner 'some'. Hence a more general account of λ-abstraction in $\mathcal{L}_x$ is as follows:

(13) For **v** a variable of type t_1 and $\phi(\mathbf{v})$ a formula of type t_2 in which all occurrences of **v** are free, $\lambda\mathbf{v}.\phi(\mathbf{v})$ is a term for the function f of type $t_1 \mapsto t_2$ which is such that, for any α of type t_1, $f(\alpha) = \beta$ iff ⟦$\phi(\mathbf{v})$⟧ = β when ⟦**v**⟧ = α.

Using (13), the function f for λ**x.chases(x)(tom)** comes out as in (10b), since, for example, f(Spike) = ⊥ because ⟦**chases(x)(tom)**⟧ = ⊥ when ⟦**x**⟧ = Spike. In this application, $t_1 = i$ and $t_2 = b$. And the function f for λ**P.some(P)** outputs QNP-meanings when given common-noun meanings. For example, if g is the function that maps all and only mice to ⊤, that is, g = ⟦**mouse**⟧, then the function f = ⟦**λP. some(P)**⟧ maps g to h = ⟦**some(mouse)**⟧. (13) ignores some syntactic complexities (see Carpenter 1997:42–4), but it is adequate in this context.[5]

1.7 Type shifting and systematic ambiguity

So far we have assigned to expressions the types that we calculated were appropriate for them, without raising the question whether or not these types *exist*. This question is answered by the following rule:

(14) If t_1 and t_2 are types, then $t_1 \mapsto t_2$ is a type.

Of course, this produces vastly more types than we have much use for: there is little call, for, say, $((b(ib)))(ii)$. We summarize the type assignments we have made so far in this table:

(15) *Table of categories and types:*

Category	Examples	Type
Name (singular NP)	**spike, tom, jerry**	i
Sentence	**(chases(jerry))(tom)**	b
Intransitive verb	**sleep, bark, run**	ib
Common noun	**dog, cat, mouse**	ib
Extensional adjective	**black, German, small, typical**	$(ib)(ib)$
Quantified NP	**some(dog), every(cat), many(mice)**	$(ib)b$
Quantificational determiner	**some, every, three, most, many, few, none**	$(ib)((ib)b)$
Binary truth-function	**and, or, neither…nor**	$b(bb)$

---

[5] A fully general version of (13) would also have to make allowance for free variables in **λv.**ϕ**(v)**, and for the special case where there is no occurrence of **v** in ϕ, as for example in **λx**^{i}**.true**, which maps every individual to ⊤.

In the table, types are given for categories of $\mathcal{L}_x$-expressions, but we take those categories in natural language to have the same types. So far as the specific words and phrases of a natural language are concerned, though, we do not assume that there is a *unique* corresponding expression of $\mathcal{L}_x$. We noted in the discussion of (1) and (2) that 'Tom' in 'Tom sleeps' could be construed as having the type $(ib)b$ in place of the simpler i, and we do not rule out in advance that there may be purposes for which this $(ib)b$-semantics is desirable. But in $\mathcal{L}_x$, every expression has a unique type. So we might require two individual constants in $\mathcal{L}_x$ for 'Tom', **tom**^{i} and **tom**$^{(ib)b}$. Then either **sleeps(tom**^{i}**)** or **tom**$^{(ib)b}$**(sleeps)** would be a well-typed semantics for 'Tom sleeps'. The meaning of the constant of simpler type determines the meaning of the higher-type constant in either of the following ways:

(16) a. ⟦**tom**$^{(ib)b}$⟧ is such that for any function g of type ib, ⟦**tom**$^{(ib)b}$⟧$(g) = \top$ iff $g(⟦\textbf{tom}^i⟧) = \top$.
b. **tom**$^{(ib)b}$ = λP.P(**tom**^{i}).

'Tom' interpreted as ⟦**tom**$^{(ib)b}$⟧ defined either way is said to have had its type *raised* or *shifted* from i to $(ib)b$ (see Partee 1986).[6]

tom^i and **tom**$^{(ib)b}$ differ only with respect to superscript. Because each primitive expression of $\mathcal{L}_x$ has a unique type, this kind of difference is common. In interpreting sentences of natural language type-theoretically, we are at liberty to take certain appearances at face value. In first-order logic, logical connectives are restricted to connecting sentences (open or closed). But in natural language, they can connect expressions of various categories. Thus, in 'Tom sleeps and snores', 'and' appears to connect two intransitive verbs. One option is to deny appearances and treat 'Tom sleeps and snores' as the result of some kind of transformation of 'Tom sleeps and Tom

---

[6] We suppress superscripts wherever possible. Unless otherwise stated, all expressions of $\mathcal{L}_x$ are well-typed, and have the simplest available type if unsuperscripted. So we can just write **tom(sleeps)**, since these assumptions determine that **tom** is of type $(ib)b$. Type-shifting allows us to distinguish intersective from subsective adjectives. At the end of Section 1.4 we assigned both groups the same type $(ib)(ib)$, but this fails to explain why only intersectives support adjective-detachment and compounding. One way of distinguishing the two groups is to take the use of (say) 'large' as a nominal modifier to be *non-derivative*, while regarding the modifier use of 'white' as derivative upon its use as a predicate of type ib: **white**$^{(ib)(ib)}$**(P)** $\stackrel{\text{df}}{=}$ λx.**white**^{ib}**(x) and P(x)**.

snores', but it is not easy to state this transformation in general form (try replacing 'Tom' with 'some cat'). An alternative is to include in $\mathcal{L}_x$ not merely the connective **and** of type $b(bb)$, but an **and** for each case where we want to allow direct non-sentential conjunction. Taking 'sleeps and snores' to be such a case, the corresponding $\mathcal{L}_x$ expression is **(and(snores))(sleeps)**. Here **and** takes input of type *ib*, **snores**, and produces the function **and(snores)**. **And(snores)** must itself be of type $(ib)(ib)$, since it has to accept **sleeps** and produce a function of type *ib* that maps Tom to ⊤, since Tom sleeps and snores. So this **and** is **and**$^{(ib)((ib)(ib))}$. Effectively, then, we regard the English 'and' as *systematically ambiguous*, shifting its type according to its context of occurrence.

Reverting to postfix notation, we would then have the sequence of equivalents (17a)–(17e):

(17) a. Tom sleeps and snores.
  b. **(sleeps and**$^{(ib)((ib)(ib))}$ **snores)(tom)**.
  c. λx.**(sleeps(x) and**$^{b(bb)}$ **snores(x))(tom)**.
  d. **sleeps(tom) and**$^{b(bb)}$ **snores(tom)**.
  e. Tom sleeps and Tom snores.

(17b) is the proposed semantics of (17a). The subsequent steps in (17) explain why (17a) and (17e) are equivalent. (17b) leads to (17c) since **and**$^{(ib)((ib)(ib))}$ is fixed by **and**$^{b(bb)}$:

(18) **and**$^{(ib)((ib)(ib))}$**(Q)(P)** = λx.(**and**$^{b(bb)}$**(Q(x)))(P(x))**

where **P** and **Q** are variables of type *ib*. (18) says the functions on each side are the same (deliver the same output for the same input) and is an instance of a more general scheme of *boolean co-ordination* (Carpenter 1997:178–182; van Benthem 1995:26–7). According to (18), **and**$^{(ib)((ib)(ib))}$**(sleeps)(snores)** must be the function which maps to ⊤ exactly those individuals α assigning which to **x** makes **and**$^{b(bb)}$**(Q(x))(P(x))** true. It is because of (18) that the ambiguity of 'and' is systematic: there is a single flexible conjunction concept rather than a coincidental use of 'a'ˆ'n'ˆ'd' for two quite different concepts, since 'and' performs the same operation in each type.

(17d) is obtained from (17c) by the operation of λ-*conversion*. We may *reduce* or *convert* a term of the form λν.φ(ν)(τ), such as (17c) or the ones in (11), by deleting the displayed occurrence of λν and substituting τ for every occurrence of ν in φ(ν). (This is legitimate only if τ and ν are of the same type; also, since τ may be arbitrarily complex, conditions have to be imposed to prevent "accidental capture" of variables; see again Carpenter 1997:50–51.) By contrast, no valid principle produces (19a) from (19b):

(19) a. **(some cat)λx.(sleeps(x) and snores(x)).**
b. **(some cat)λx.sleeps(x) and (some cat)λx.snores(x).**

So the inclination to think of (17a) as resulting from a *syntactic* transformation of (17e) is probably semantics-based.

1.8 Interpretations of $\mathcal{L}_x$

To define an *arbitrary interpretation* of $\mathcal{L}_x$, we choose a non-empty domain D_i of individuals, and use the domain $D_b = \{\top, \bot\}$ of truth-values. Further domains are given by the following rule:

(20) If $t_1 \mapsto t_2$ is a type, then there is a domain $D_{t_1 t_2}$ consisting in all functions which (i) accept as input exactly the members of D_{t_1} and (ii) produce as output some member of D_{t_2}.

Primitive $\mathcal{L}_x$-expressions of a given type are assigned *semantic values* (meanings) drawn from the domain of their type. The semantic values of more complex expressions are calculated recursively. (13) gives the rule for lambda-terms, and the only other syntactic operation is that of function-argument concatenation. Here the rule is the obvious one that if $\alpha(\beta)$ is well-typed, then $[\![\alpha(\beta)]\!] = [\![\alpha]\!]([\![\beta]\!])$.

In the case of expressions related by type-raising or boolean coordination, the one of simplest type gets assigned a meaning directly and the meanings of the others are derived (*cf.* (18)). There are also rules specific to logical constants such as **not, and, some** and **every**:

(21) a. $[\![\textbf{not}]\!]$ is the function f in the domain D_{bb} such that $f(\top) = \bot$ and $f(\bot) = \top$.
b. $[\![\textbf{and}]\!]$ is the function f in $D_{b(bb)}$ such that (i) $f(\top) =$ the function g in D_{bb} such that $g(\top) = \top$ and $g(\bot) = \bot$; and (ii) $f(\bot) =$ the g in D_{bb} such that $g(\top) = \bot$ and $g(\bot) = \bot$.

c. ⟦**every**⟧ is the function f in $D_{(ib)((ib)b)}$ such that, for any g and h in D_{ib}, $(f(g))(h) = \top$ iff for every x in D_i such that $g(x) = \top, h(x) = \top$.
d. ⟦**some**⟧ is the function f in $D_{(ib)((ib)b)}$ such that, for any g and h in D_{ib}, $(f(g))(h) = \top$ iff for some x in D_i such that $g(x) = \top, h(x) = \top$.[7]

In the *intended* interpretation of $\mathcal{L}_x$, the domain D_i is the set of actual individuals, and the primitive expressions are assigned the extensions of their natural-language counterparts, so we can use the latter in defining the former. For example, on the intended interpretation of $\mathcal{L}_x$, the semantic value of **sleeps** is the function f in the domain D_{ib} such that for any x in D_i, $f(x) = \top$ iff x is asleep.

2 HYPERINTENSIONAL SEMANTICS

As discussed in Section 1.3, extensional type-theory is an inadequate framework for natural language semantics because it allows for only two sentence-meanings, $\top$ and $\bot$, assuming classical logic. The most common way of repairing this is to move to intensional type theory, where the leading idea is to use a sentence S's possible-worlds profile as its meaning: for each possible world w, S is either true or false at w, so S's profile is a set of pairs such as

(22) $\{\langle @, \top\rangle, \langle u, \bot\rangle, \langle v, \bot\rangle,...\}$.[8]

$\top$ is the truth-value of S. $\bot$ is the truth-value S would have had if things had gone as they do in u, $\bot$ is the truth-value S would have had if things had gone as they do in v, and so on. This framework is a distinct improvement over its extensional counterpart, which identifies the meanings of any two semantically unrelated contingent truths, such as 'snow is white' and 'grass is green'; using profiles, we get different meanings, assuming there is at least one world where 'snow is white' and 'grass is green' have opposite truth-values.

The notion of intended interpretation for this semantics requires

---

[7] If g is ⟦**dog**⟧ and h is ⟦**barks**⟧, this clause says ⟦**(some(dog))(barks)**⟧ = $\top$ iff for at least one individual x such that ⟦**dog**⟧$(x) = \top$, ⟦**barks**⟧$(x) = \top$ also.

[8] See also (7) on p. 9 for discussion of the possible-worlds profile of a predicate.

us to take some sort of realist attitude towards ways things could have gone (see, e.g., Salmon 1989): the real meaning of **sleeps(tom)** is that function which, for each way w that things really could have gone, produces ⊤ if Tom would have slept had things gone that way, and otherwise produces ⊥. This may seem an extravagant idealization, if grasp of meaning is to be identified with grasp of such a function. Worse, the problems noted in Section 1.5 remain. For instance, 'there are infinitely many numbers' and 'there are infinitely many prime numbers' have different meanings, but the same, constantly true, possible-worlds profile, so their meanings are wrongly identified in intensional type-theory.

An example Lewis (1972) uses to advertise the virtues of intensional type-theory, the adjective 'alleged', brings out a related difficulty. 'Alleged' is non-extensional, but like all adjectives, it 'takes a common noun to make a new, compound, common noun; and the intension of the new common noun depends on the intension of the original common noun in a manner determined by the meaning of the adjective' (Lewis 1972:182). Construed as a claim about meanings, this is unobjectionable: the meaning of 'alleged thief' depends on the meaning of 'thief', for 'alleged thief' and 'alleged cheat' mean something different precisely because, and to the exact extent that, 'thief' and 'cheat' mean something different. But the meaning of 'alleged thief' does not in any relevant sense depend on the *intension* of 'thief'. As Lewis says (1972:174), the intension is "something that determines which...things, if any...['thief']...applies to in various possible states of affairs". But if that is constitutive of the meaning of 'thief', then the meaning of 'thief' makes no contribution to the meaning of 'alleged thief'. For the composition operation that produces the meaning of 'alleged thief' is entirely insensitive to the details of the possible-worlds profile of 'thief': the profile does not *differentially* explain any aspects of the resulting complex meaning, not even its intension.[9] Consequently, even if 'thief' and 'cheat' had

---

[9] For differential explanation, see (Peacocke 1979:55–89). This objection persists even if we regard 'alleged thief' as the output of the kind of transformational component Lewis envisages, with something like 'an x alleged by someone to be a thief' in the base; for the intension of 'thief' is just as compositionally inert in the meaning of this phrase. For discussion of similar problems, see (van Benthem 1986:147–50).

the same intension$_{pw}$, there would be no reason to expect 'alleged thief' and 'alleged cheat' to have the same intension. While Lewis is surely right that meaning determines extension at different possible worlds, that cannot be constitutive of the meaning of 'thief', but must simply be a property of it.

For these reasons, we make a more radical departure from the extensional theory, and employ the *intentional* theory of (Thomason 1980). In this semantics we do not make any theoretical identification of sentence-meanings with some sort of logical entity or construction: we simply take sentence-meanings as given, and try to determine the contribution of a sentence's components to its overall meaning. This leads to a type-theoretic semantics for a language $\mathcal{L}_m$ in which the type b of truth-values is displaced by the type m of sentence-meanings. Thus types for the various categories in the table in (15) can be obtained by replacing b with m. For example, the intransitive verb **sleep** is of type im. Intuitively, when presented with the input ⟦**tom**⟧, ⟦**sleep**⟧ produces the output ⟦**sleeps(tom)**⟧, that is, the *meaning* (not the truth-value) of 'Tom sleeps'. The QNP **some(cat)** is of type $(im)m$, and the $\mathcal{L}_m$-sentence **(some(cat))(sleeps)** is of type m. The meaning of this sentence is the one obtained when ⟦**some(cat)**⟧ is applied to ⟦**sleep**⟧. For sentential 'and', we have ⟦**and**⟧, a function of type $m(mm)$, and for sentential negation, we have ⟦**not**⟧, a function of type mm. The expressions with the types just described are the *direct* translations into $\mathcal{L}_m$ of the eponymous English.

The type b is still needed, to ensure that $\mathcal{L}_m$-terms have the logical behaviour of the concepts they are supposed to express. To this end, Thomason (1980:50) introduces an operator $^\cup$ of type mb, which assigns a truth-value to each sentence-meaning. Adding extensional counterparts of the direct translations of logical connectives, he then imposes meaning-postulates to constrain the direct translations themselves. For example, adding $\forall^{(mb)b}$, $\neg^{bb}$, $=^{b(bb)}$ and $\wedge^{b(bb)}$ to $\mathcal{L}_m$, we have the postulates

(23) a. $\forall^{(mb)b}\lambda x^m.{^\cup}\textbf{not(x)} =^{b(bb)} \neg{^\cup}\textbf{(x)}$.
  b. $\forall^{(mb)b}\lambda x^m.\forall^{(mb)b}\lambda y^m.{^\cup}\textbf{and(y)(x)} =^{b(bb)} \wedge({^\cup}\textbf{y})({^\cup}\textbf{x})$.

The $\forall^{(mb)b}$ of (23a) produces a truth-value, given as input a function from sentence-meanings to truth-values. $\lambda x^m.{^\cup}\textbf{not(x)} =^{b(bb)} \neg{^\cup}\textbf{(x)}$ is such a function, mapping each sentence meaning μ to the truth-value that the formula $^{\cup}$**not(x)** $=^{b(bb)} \neg ^{\cup}$**(x)** has when μ is assigned to **x**. That formula is postfix for $=^{b(bb)}(\neg^{\cup}$**(x)**$)(^{\cup}$**not(x)**$)$, where $=^{b(bb)}$ is the identity function for truth-values, the f such that (i) $f(\top)$ = the function g such that $g(\top) = \top$ and $g(\bot) = \bot$; and (ii) $f(\bot)$ = the function g such that $g(\top) = \bot$ and $g(\bot) = \top$. So $=^{b(bb)}(\neg^{\cup}$**(x)**$)(^{\cup}$**not(x)**$)$ comes out true iff $\neg^{\cup}$**(x)** and $^{\cup}$**not(x)** are the same truth-value. Thus (23a) says that we assign meanings to $^{\cup}$ and **not** so that whatever meaning is assigned to **x**, that meaning's truth-value is the opposite of the truth-value of the meaning **not(x)**. For short, (23a) says that $^{\cup}$ and **not** are *truth-functionally appropriate*. In the same way, (23b) says that $^{\cup}$ and **and** are truth-functionally appropriate. (There need not be a *unique* way of guaranteeing truth-functional appropriateness.)

In an interpretation of $\mathcal{L}_m$ there are three basic domains, a non-empty domain D_i of individuals, the domain $D_b = \{\top, \bot\}$ of truth-values, and a domain D_m of sentence-meanings containing at least two elements. The hierarchy of domains is generated by (20), and the notions of arbitrary and intended interpretation for $\mathcal{L}_m$ are much as they are for $\mathcal{L}_x$. With the aid of $^{\cup}$ we can define a notion of consequence or semantic entailment, symbolized $\vDash$, as follows:

(24) If Δ is a set of (closed) $\mathcal{L}_m$-sentences and α is an $\mathcal{L}_m$-sentence, then $\Delta \vDash \alpha$ iff for every interpretation $\mathcal{I}$, $[\![^{\cup}\alpha]\!]_\mathcal{I} = \top$ if $[\![^{\cup}\delta]\!]_\mathcal{I} = \top$ for every δ in Δ.[10]

It is the option of having distinct sentence-meanings for the same intension that solves the problems with 'alleged'. First, adjectives in $\mathcal{L}_m$ are functions from nominal meanings to nominal meanings, since they combine with nominals to form more complex nominals. So adjectives have type $(im)(im)$, corresponding to $(ib)(ib)$ in $\mathcal{L}_x$. To record the fact that the nominal to which 'alleged' attaches makes a contribution to the meaning of the resulting nominal (recall 'alleged thief' versus 'alleged cheat') we impose the following requirement:

(25) a. for every f and g in D_{im}, $[\![$**alleged**$]\!](f) \neq [\![$**alleged**$]\!](g)$ if $f \neq g$.
b. **every(λP.every(λQ.alleged(P) unequal alleged(Q)**
   if P unequal Q)).

---

[10] See (Muskens 2005) for an interesting variant of Thomason's system that uses a mapping r from propositions to worldsets in place of $^{\cup}$.

Both statements in (25) require ⟦**alleged**⟧ to be one-one: if given nominals have different meanings, then the nominals resulting from prefixing 'alleged' to the given ones also have different meanings. (25a) has the form of an admissibility condition on interpretations, while (25b) is an $\mathcal{L}_m$-sentence that functions as a meaning-postulate: we only allow interpretations $\mathcal{I}$ such that $⟦^\cup(25b)⟧_\mathcal{I} = \top$. The effect is the same.[11]

However, conformity with (25) is not a special feature of hyperintensionals like **alleged**. For example, one expects the same behaviour of **not**^{mm}: if **P** and **Q** differ in meaning, so should **not(P)** and **not(Q)**.[12] The hyperintensionality of 'alleged' is rather a consequence of our making *no more* requirements of ⟦**alleged**⟧. Contrast the subsective 'notorious'. We will want the analogue of (25), but we will also want to enforce subsectivity:

(26) a. for every f in D_{im} and x in D_i, $⟦^\cup⟧[(⟦\text{\textbf{notorious}}⟧(f))(x)] = \top$ only if $⟦^\cup⟧(f(x)) = \top$.
b. **every[λP.every[λx.P(x) if (notorious(P))(x)]]**.
c. **(notorious(cat))(tom)** $\vDash_a$ **cat(tom)**.

The entailment relation $\vDash_a$ of (26c) is the restriction of the general relation given by (24) to interpretations which are admissible in (26a)'s sense of assigning an appropriate semantic value to **notorious**, or equivalently, in the sense of verifying the meaning-postulate (26b).[13]

Further development of hyperintensional semantics will occur where and when it is needed. However, because exchanging direct translations into $\mathcal{L}_x$ for direct translations into $\mathcal{L}_m$ involves only

---

[11] In (25b), **unequal** is of type $(im)((im)m)$, and **if** is of type $m(mm)$. **P** and **Q** are of type im, so the scope of λ**Q** is of type m. The λ**Q**-term itself is therefore of type mm, requiring the inner **every** to be of type $(mm)m$. Consequently, the scope of λ**P** is of type m, so by the same reasoning, the outer **every** is also of type $(mm)m$. For each type t we impose universal quantifier-like behaviour on the **every** of type tm using the extensional quantifier ∀ of type tb and the following meaning-postulate: $^\cup$**every**(λ$v^t.\phi$) = ∀(λ$v^t.{}^\cup\phi$). See (1.3) in (Thomason 1980:51).

[12] For more discussion of this point, see (Anderson 1980:223–4).

[13] Instead of (26a,b) we might try a conjunctive strategy ('F and notorious for an F') like the one for intersectives in note 6, p. 27; but it is unclear what non-derivative, more basic type there is for **notorious** in 'notorious for an F'.

exchange of isomorphic types for the same formulae – m just takes over the role of b – it turns out that much of our discussion can be conducted in the context of $\mathcal{L}_x$. The semantic problems that demand treatment in $\mathcal{L}_m$ prove not to be the usual ones discussed in theories of non-extensionality.[14]

---

[14] Fox and Lappin (2001:188–9) object that Thomason's system leaves unspecified the relationship between equivalence and identity in the type m. For example, if we take equivalence to be mutual entailment, (24) will tell us that **p and q** is equivalent to **q and p**, but not whether they are the same proposition. However, *if* there is a fact of the matter about whether or not **p and q** and **q and p** are the same proposition (and facts for other comparable issues) then among the admissible interpretations of $\mathcal{L}_m$ there will be an intended interpretation, and in it, **and(q)(p)** and **and(p)(q)** either always will, or sometimes will not, evaluate to the same element of D_m, depending on what the fact of the matter is.

For a more general critical discussion of type-theory as a semantic tool, see (Bealer 1989). One issue Bealer raises (p. 180) concerns 'transcendental' predicates and the generalizations we make with them, such as 'every entity is identical to some entity'. The point is that 'entity' and 'identity' cannot be assigned a specific type if the sentence is to mean what we (are supposed to) mean by it. To this I would respond that the problem is a special case of a more general problem about any model-theoretic semantics, that the metalanguage recognizes entities that are not within the range of the object-language's purportedly universal 'every' (for example, assuming a standard set-theory, such entities as the domain of discourse itself, or the property of being an element of the domain). Combine this with the shifting, context-dependent nature of the domain of discourse. Then 'every entity is identical to some entity' adverts to some contextually given hierarchy of types, all of whose elements become the individuals D_i of a new hierarchy, and 'entity' is the constantly true function of the new type ib. Someone may complain that this new hierarchy is now replete with entities not within the range of the object-language's 'every entity', so we still have not assigned to 'every entity is identical to some entity' the intended meaning. But to meet this complaint, we would have to abandon model-theoretic semantics – hardly a response Bealer would favor – or adopt a 'deviant' set theory.

3

Intensional Transitives

We now turn to the main topic of this book, the semantics of intensional transitive verbs (ITV's), like the 'fear' in (10a) on p. 12. 'Fear' is *transitive*, or has a standard transitive use, since it has a standard use in which it takes a direct object (it also has a standard use in which it takes a clausal complement, either finite, as in 'fear that the door is open', or non-finite, as in 'fear to open the door'). And 'fear' is *intensional*, or at any rate *not extensional*, because of the non-equivalence of (10a), 'Lex Luthor fears Superman', and (10b), 'Lex Luthor fears Clark Kent', on page 12. In this chapter we will classify ITV's and exhibit some problematic aspects of their behaviour. In the next, we will describe and criticize elements of the account of ITV's that is the main rival to the one to be developed here.

1 A TAXONOMY OF INTENSIONAL "TRANSITIVES"

ITV's can be grouped in certain ways by similarities of meaning and behaviour; the table on the next page is fairly inclusive. Items in it marked with an asterisk are not, strictly speaking, transitive verbs, but intransitive verbs that take prepositional phrase (PP) complements. They are usually grouped with strict transitives because they form verb phrases that are near-synonyms to ones with strict transitives, and in which the complement of the preposition is the direct object of the strict transitive ('{seek/look for} an explanation').

(1) *Table of intensional transitive groups.*

VERBS OF...	EXAMPLES
Absence	avoid, lack, omit
Anticipation	allow* (for), anticipate, expect, fear, foresee, plan, wait* (for)
Calculation	calculate, compute, derive
Creation	assemble, bake, build, construct, fabricate, make (these verbs in progressive aspect only)
Depiction	caricature, draw, imagine, portray, sculpt, show, visualize, write* (about)
Desire	hope* (for), hunger* (for), lust* (after), prefer, want
Evaluation	admire, disdain, fear, respect, scorn, worship (verbs whose corresponding noun can fill the gap in the evaluation 'worthy of _' or 'merits_')
Requirement	cry out* (for), demand, deserve, merit, need, require
Search	hunt* (for), look* (for), rummage about* (for), scan* (for), seek
Similarity	imitate, be reminiscent* (of), resemble, simulate
Transaction	buy, order, owe, own, reserve, sell, wager

To illustrate. According to the definition of 'extensional' on page 11, if the search-verb 'seek' is extensional then co-extensive complements to it should produce co-extensive VP's. 'A unicorn' and 'a gorgon' are co-extensive, since the set of all sets containing at least one unicorn is the same set as the set of all sets containing at least one gorgon, namely, the empty set. So 'seek a unicorn' and 'seek a gorgon' should be co-extensive. But they are not: there have been unicorn-seekers who were not gorgon-seekers, and vice versa. (Contrast 'find': there have been no unicorn-finders who were not gorgon-finders, and vice versa, nor will there ever be.)

However, this argument does not show that 'seek' is intensional in the possible-worlds sense we defined on page 11; it may rather be hyperintensional. Yet 'intensional' is the standard terminology for the verbs in the table in (1), though some are certainly hyperintensional if any verb is. To permit this standard usage, we will allow a sense of 'intensional' that simply means 'not extensional', thereby including the hyperintensional. When 'intensional' occurs in 'intensional transitive' or in the acronym 'ITV', we take it in this sense. Uses of 'intensional' in the possible-worlds sense defined on page 11 will therefore be labelled 'intensional$_{pw}$' to avoid any confusion.

Most other groups of intensional transitives are like 'seek', at least when the complement is an expression of type i, such as a proper name. For instance, assuming Stevenson's fiction to be fact, none of 'expect', 'caricature', 'want', 'admire', and 'resemble' combines with 'Jekyll' to produce a VP co-extensive with the one that results when it combines with 'Hyde'. With requirement verbs, however, intuitions tend to vary. Suppose that 'water' and 'H_2O' are terms for the same substance. The case of someone who is thirsty but otherwise content with life having the mistaken belief that H_2O is a lethal poison, suggests that wanting water and wanting H_2O are two different things. But it is hard to see how *needing* water could be a different thing from *needing* H_2O: whoever is dehydrated needs water, and *ipso facto* needs H_2O, regardless of what beliefs they hold. 'Need' is sensitive just to objective features of the needy, not to how they represent their condition to themselves. So 'need' is not hyperintensional.

On the other hand, there is the example of Max the theatre impresario (Larson 2002:232), who may truly be said to *need more singers* but not *need more dancers*, even if it happens that all who sing, dance, and vice versa. Hence 'need' is not extensional either: it is intensional$_{pw}$, disallowing interchange of complements that are accidentally co-extensive. Needing more singers would imply needing more dancers only if the *property* of being a singer were the same property as that of being a dancer.

But there is also a sense in which, if the singers and the dancers are the same people, then if Max needs more singers, he does in fact need more dancers. There even appears to be a sense in which someone who wants water *does* want H_2O, even if they would not put it that way because they believe that H_2O is a lethal poison. We can accommodate this by allowing that ITV-phrases such as 'wants water' and 'needs more singers' are capable of being *extensionally construed*. We will not at this point try to say exactly what this amounts to in their semantics; we merely note the possibility of the reading (see Section 8.3, for an account).

The problems we have just mentioned for ITV's arise in a parallel way for *propositional attitude* verbs. These are psychological verbs which take clausal complements with which complete propositions can be associated, and which can be used to assert a relation between a subject and a proposition (here and henceforth, 'proposition' is used as an alternative to 'sentence-meaning', not in the narrow sense of 'set of possible worlds', for which we will use 'proposition$_{pw}$').[1] For example,

(2) Perseus believes that gorgons can be found in Crete[2]

claims that Perseus stands in the believing relation to the proposition he would express with his version of 'Gorgons can be found in Crete'. And just as seeking a gorgon seems to be a different thing from seeking a unicorn, so believing that gorgons can be found in Crete seems to be a different thing from believing that unicorns can be found in Crete. In view of this parallel with propositional attitude verbs, we refer to psychological ITV's as *objectual* attitude verbs.

The hyperintensionality of psychological objectual attitude verbs goes hand in hand with that of propositional attitude verbs. The

---

[1] Many of the verbs in the table in (1) can take clausal complements, and in some cases can be used to ascribe propositional attitudes when they do (e.g., 'need to drink some water' does not, but 'want to drink some water' does, ascribe such an attitude).

[2] Since the gorgon myth will be one of our running examples, I remind the reader that: a gorgon is a petrifying snake-haired female humanoid; in the Greek myth there were three; two of them, Euryale and Stheno, were the daughters of gods and therefore immortal; one, Medusa, was mortal, having been turned into a gorgon by Athena in a fit of jealousy; and King Polydectes challenged Perseus to bring him Medusa's head as a ruse to sidetrack him while Polydectes tried to seduce Perseus's mother.

Even by the standards of Greek mythology, the gorgon myth is strange, and has provoked a vast interpretative literature – feminist, Freudian, Jungian, Lacanian, and others; see, e.g., (Wilk 2000), (Garber and Vickers 2003). I regret to report that this literature sheds very little light on the logico-semantic problems that are our concern here.

main argument for hyperintensionality in attitude verbs concerns the role of attitude ascriptions in the explanation of action: one set of ascriptions may explain an agent's action, while another derived from the first by substitutions based on true identities may fail to explain the same action. For example, we can explain Lex Luthor's attempts to conceal himself by the fact that he believes that Superman is nearby and fears Superman. If belief that Superman is nearby is the same thing as belief that Clark Kent is nearby, then his attempts to conceal himself should be equally well explained by the fact that he believes that Clark is nearby and fears Superman. But this explanation seems deficient. And an explanation in terms of the fact that he believes that Superman is nearby and fears Clark is just as deficient, for the same reason: more is needed to combine the attitudes in each of these derived pairs into a motive for what Lex does. Hence propositional attitude verbs are hyperintensional if and only if (psychological) objectual attitude verbs are.

2 RELATIONAL VERSUS NOTIONAL READINGS

It is plausible that a correct account of the difference (or appearance thereof) between, say, admiring Jekyll and admiring Hyde, should transfer straightforwardly to accounting for the difference (or appearance thereof) between having the attitude of belief towards the proposition that Jekyll is admirable and having the attitude of belief towards the proposition that Hyde is admirable. However, there is a second phenomenon characteristic of propositional attitude verbs and almost all ITV's, concerning which I shall argue that parallel theories are not to be expected. There is an ambiguity in

(3) Perseus believes that three gorgons can be found in Crete

and a superficially similar-looking ambiguity in

(4) Perseus is looking for three gorgons in Crete.

The ambiguity in (3) is brought out by the following paraphrases:

(5) a. Three gorgons are such that Perseus believes they can be found in Crete.

b. Perseus believes the proposition that three gorgons can be found in Crete.

The two readings of (3) in (5) articulate an ambiguity for which there are many labels in the literature: *de re/de dicto*, wide scope/narrow scope, relational/notional, specific/unspecific, to name some. The ambiguity was originally investigated by Quine (1956), who introduced the terminology 'relational/notional'. According to (5a), there are three gorgons (in the domain of discourse) to whom Perseus is *cognitively related* in believing that *they* can be found in Crete (he need not believe they are gorgons). According to (5b), Perseus merely has the *notion* that some triple or other of gorgons can be found in Crete.[3] This ambiguity is not present in all languages, but that is because in some, the different meanings are marked syntactically in different ways (Enç 1991:4).[4]

In equivalent language, (5a) says there are three *specific* gorgons such that Perseus believes they can be found in Crete – perhaps he has three beliefs, that Euryale can be found in Crete, that Medusa can be found in Crete, and that Stheno can be found in Crete. By contrast, (5b) requires him to believe a certain proposition expressible with the QNP 'three gorgons', though there need be no gorgon in the domain of discourse such that he believes that it can be found in Crete. Also, if Perseus has the three singular beliefs just mentioned, and assuming the Perseus myth to be factual, then in the relational sense he believes *every* gorgon can be found in Crete, for every gorgon is such that he believes it can be found in Crete. But on a notional reading there is no reason for him to have the belief that every gorgon can be found in Crete – he may not yet know that the

---

[3] I note here the scepticism of (Pietroski and Hornstein 2002) that (5a) is a possible literal meaning for (3). Given cases like 'somebody loves nobody' it is arguable that not every instance of multiple quantification with distinct quantifiers generates a scope-ambiguity, and Pietroski and Hornstein's proposals about the governing principles suggest to them that only (5b) is available for (3). I will not take a position on this because (a) it is not clear how their considerations apply to ITV's, and (b) our main concern is with the surviving notional readings.

[4] The reason that (5b) is unambiguous while (3) is ambiguous is that 'three gorgons' is embedded in the noun phrase 'the proposition that...'. Such NP's are known as "islands", in or on which embedded QNP's cannot acquire characteristics that justify a (5a)-type reading; see (Hornstein 1995:28–30).

jealous Athena has turned Medusa into a gorgon, or he may believe that there are many more gorgons elsewhere.[5]

Though some scepticism has been expressed in the literature about the distinction, by Quine himself (1979) and others (see Dennett 1982), the examples do seem to mark an undeniable contrast. This is so even with definite descriptions: someone who believes that Kim is a spy believes that the shortest spy is a spy, if (i) Kim is in fact the shortest spy, and (ii) we construe the ascription in the style of (5a), as saying that the shortest spy is such that the subject believes him to be a spy. On the other hand, if the subject instead believes (a) there is some non-zero but finite number of spies, and (b) no two spies are the same height, then by logic alone, the subject may conclude that the shortest spy is a spy. There is an intuitive sense of 'about' in which the first belief is about Kim and the second is not. For example, if Kim had not existed, the first case would not even be possible, while the second case would be unaffected. It would be surprising if the apparent contrast in these pairs turned out to evaporate on closer investigation (it would be unsurprising if there turned out to be borderline cases).

The ambiguity in (4) is superficially similar to that in (3) and may be brought out in what seems to be the same way:

(6) a. Three gorgons are such that Perseus is in Crete looking for them.
b. Perseus is in Crete, looking for three gorgons, though no particular gorgons.[6]

(6a) is true if Perseus is in Crete, looking for Euryale, Medusa and Stheno. (6b) is true if he is in Crete, searching with the intention of finding three gorgons, without there being any particular three he intends to find. The contrast here was famously captured in Quine's

---

[5] It is less clear that there is a comparable ambiguity in (2), with its bare plural 'gorgons'. We can distinguish between (i) 'he believes gorgons can...' and (ii) 'gorgons are such that he believes they can...', and in (ii) 'gorgons' has a 'some gorgons' reading on which it follows from (5a). But if 'gorgons' is interpreted univocally as a term for a kind of creature, there is no specific/unspecific contrast in meaning.

[6] There is also an attachment ambiguity in (4): is Perseus in Crete, or is it that he is looking for gorgons who are themselves in Crete? I have chosen the former reading.

comment on '$(\exists x)(x$ is a sloop and I want $x)$' as a regimentation of 'I want a sloop': 'if what I seek is mere relief from slooplessness, [this regimentation] gives the wrong idea' (1956:185).[7]

It should be emphasized that, while most of the examples of the ambiguity in the literature involve existential QNP's like 'a sloop' and 'three gorgons', notional readings are easy to get with other quantificational determiners like 'no', 'the' (as just noted) and 'every'. If Perseus is looking for a gorgon, but no particular one, 'Perseus is looking for no gorgon' has a true and a false reading (the true reading occurs in 'he isn't looking for Euryale, Medusa or Stheno, so he's looking for no gorgon'). If he is looking for a mortal gorgon and believes the proposition that exactly one gorgon is mortal, then 'Perseus is looking for the mortal gorgon' is notionally true. (The same sense is apparent if you are driving around a large, unfamiliar airport car-rental lot, looking for the exit.) And if Polydectes had challenged Perseus to bring him the head of *every* gorgon, whoever and however many they may be, Perseus would have been looking for every gorgon, though not for any particular gorgons (in just the sense that the police may be looking for everyone who witnessed the incident).[8]

According to (5), the ambiguity in (3) is a scope ambiguity, the crucial difference between (5a) and (5b) being that in the former, but not the latter, 'believes' is within the scope of 'three gorgons'. But it is far from obvious that the ambiguity in (4) is a scope ambiguity, though (6) may seem to represent it as such. The difficulty is in seeing how 'three gorgons' is to function as a quantifier in (6b)'s 'looking for three gorgons'. In the first-order framework on which many

---

[7] Quine (1979:273) writes of his earlier distinction, 'I now think the distinction is every bit as empty, apart from context, as...that of knowing or believing who someone is'. This is unconvincing. It may not be very helpful to say that wanting a sloop is relational only if you know which sloop you want, but it would anyway be incorrect to cast an explanation of the notional/relational contrast in such psychological terms, since this would leave non-psychological instances of the contrast unexplained (suppose your navy *needs* a sloop). In Section 6.4 we articulate the distinction in terms of modal variation, or the lack thereof, in the themes of certain events or states. See also (Kaplan 1986:258–60).

[8] These cases are problematic for the property-theoretic account of Zimmerman (1993); see his discussion at pp. 175–6. I understand from him that notional 'every' is easier to hear in some languages than in others.

approaches to natural language semantics are based, the semantics of quantifiers allows only one way for them to figure in the evaluation of formulae in which they occur. A quantifier Q is indexed with a variable (or "trace") v, and is prefixed to a formula $\phi(v)$ to form the more complex formula $(Qv)\phi(v)$. The truth-value of $(Qv)\phi(v)$ is then determined by assigning objects to v and evaluating $\phi(v)$ for truth or falsity across the assignments. For instance, (6a) requires for its truth that there be three gorgons such that, when each is assigned to 'x', then 'Perseus is in Crete looking for x' is true. But this paradigm cannot be straightforwardly applied to (6b), in which 'three gorgons' seems to be provided as an *argument* to 'look' in the prepositional phrase 'for three gorgons', and does not have any formula $\phi(v)$ within its scope; contrast (5b), where 'three gorgons' plays its usual quantificational role. So in (6b) the idea that the quantifier has narrow scope is inapplicable, since attempts to put it in such a position will produce ill-formedness (though readers who teach symbolic logic will be very familiar with the student who symbolizes 'Sue met Bill' as 'Msb', and then offers 'Ms($\exists x$)' for 'Sue met someone').

Clearly, the relational/notional ambiguity we have introduced in this section is not the same *phenomenon* as the substitution-resistance in ITV complements noted in section 3.1. Might the two phenomena nevertheless have the same semantic explanation, most likely in terms of occurrence outside versus within the scope of an intensional expression? We have just noted that there is no straightforward way of getting the required narrow-scope semantics for (4). There is a less straightforward way, but when we examine it in detail in Chapter 4, it will be found wanting.

The behaviour of 'need' is also a problem for a single-explanation approach, since with it we find a relational/notional ambiguity but no hyperintensionality. Moreover, it may even be that we can have a relational/notional ambiguity unaccompanied by intensionality$_{pw}$, as the case of verbs of absence suggests. If Max omits a singer from his cast, and the singers and the dancers are the same people, it appears to follow that he has omitted a dancer, his intentions notwithstanding. If a certain faculty committee lacks a mathematician and the mathematicians on the faculty are all and only the holders of NSF grants on the faculty, then it follows that the committee lacks an NSF grant-holder. But 'omitted a dancer' and 'lacks a faculty mathematician' in such contexts would be naturally interpreted notionally.⁹ These examples are not conclusive, since the hyperintensionality mechanism may be present in these sentences, but somehow rendered ineffective (see Parsons 1997:370). Presumably a similar claim will have to be made for cases where substitution-resistance is possible but there is no relational/notional ambiguity: any intensional verb used with a proper name, or evaluative verbs, which allow for substitution-resistance, but do not support notional readings with existential QNP's (see further Section 4.5). So if a single-mechanism account is to be developed, it will need more than a few epicycles to square with the data.¹⁰

In what follows, we will instead take seriously the appearance that the mechanism responsible for the relational/notional ambiguity occurs independently of the conditions that make for substitution-resistance (see also Fodor 1979; Recanati 2000:267–70; Zimmerman 2001:516–20). In order to keep these matters separate, therefore, we will assume that the notional VP's we discuss, if they are not extensional as such, are at least being *construed* extensionally, unless otherwise indicated.

---

⁹ I do not place too much weight on these supposed extensional cases of the relational-notional ambiguity, since it could be maintained that at some level of analysis, 'lack' unfolds into 'not have' and 'omit' into 'not include', or something more complicated with the same essential structure. Then '*x* omits a singer' on one notional construal is (roughly) **not(some(singer))λy.includes(y)(x)**. We apply 'notional' here since there is no particular singer who has not been included, but the semantics is unproblematic, since both readings raise 'a singer' to adjoin to an extensional formula, and differ only over the position of 'not'. However, the decompositions that this account is based on are controversial. For example, if 'lack' decomposes into 'not have', why do the two differ *vis à vis* support for negative-polarity 'any'? See (Higginbotham 1989, sec. 3 *ad fin.*) for further discussion.

¹⁰ Other grounds for classification as intensional transitive besides those mentioned so far are proposed in (Moltmann 1997:43–50), but some of them strike me as suspect. For instance, 'appointed' and 'hired' are said to be ITV's, on the grounds that 'John appointed/hired an assistant' has an intensional reading not equivalent to 'some (person who is already an) assistant was appointed/hired by John'. This reading is not a notional, 'no particular' reading, though it is undeniably intensional (hiring a singer is not the same thing as hiring a dancer even if ∨singer = ∨dancer). But its intensionality arises from the covert presence of 'as': 'John appointed/hired someone *as* an assistant' ('walks/quacks like a duck' prefers notional construal without 'walk' and 'quack' being intensional).

3 EXISTENCE-INDEPENDENCE

Substitution-resistance and a relational/notional ambiguity are two "marks" of intensionality. A third is that of *existence-independence*. This is illustrated by (6b), 'Perseus is...looking for three gorgons, but no particular ones'. Perseus can be looking for gorgons, though there are none, but if we replace 'looking for' with an extensional verb such as 'tracking', 'observing', or 'slaying', it is contradictory to add 'though there are none'. But before we conclude that existence-independence is a product of the same mechanism as accounts for notionality, we should note that it occurs with proper names: Perseus, a real person, may seek Medusa, even though there is no such creature. If so, existence-independence is less closely related to notionality, unless we were wrong in the previous section to say that the use of proper names rules out notional readings.

But it seems right to say that intelligible names make for specificity. Suppose that there is a well-developed lore about gorgons, who are mythical but mistakenly believed to be real, and that it is Medusa whom Perseus wishes to find. Then we should not say that he does not seek a particular, or specific, gorgon; he can be quite specific about the one he is looking for.

It will be replied to this that *his being* specific is one thing, there being a specific gorgon another. For if there is a specific gorgon Perseus seeks, then there is a gorgon Perseus seeks. But *ex hypothesi*, there are no gorgons.

However, this objection fails to take note of a contrast between the real and the mythical that is in play in such examples. The name 'Medusa' can be used to stand for a creature of myth, an actual but abstract object that would not have existed if no such myths had developed: Medusa is *actual*, but not *real*. Speakers can denote the abstract object with this name even though they think they are speaking of a physical thing.[11] In the myth, however, the abstract object in question has the property of being a physical thing. This requires a certain flexibility of "transrealm identity" that may make the situation somewhat disanalogous to that of merely possible

---

[11] Salmon (2002) argues that such a view of mythical objects is required to explain how we understand Hob-Nob sentences (Geach 1967). See further (Robertson 2003).

objects, but it is not incomprehensible, so far as I can tell. Perseus is one who uses the name 'Medusa' and refers to an abstract object with it. It is for this reason that we are inclined to say that Perseus is looking for a specific gorgon. There is no specific real gorgon that Perseus seeks, but there is a specific mythical one.[12]

The upshot of this is that existence-independence in ITV-proper name combinations is only independence of the physical, concrete world. The existence-independence of notional readings is rather different, for there do not even have to be specific gorgons in the abstract domain of mythical entities for it to be true that Perseus seeks a gorgon – the gorgon myths could have been completely general and plural, with no individual gorgons sufficiently characterized in them. If Perseus seeks a gorgon in this case, he is acting under an intention to find a gorgon, an intention he can have even if there are no specific mythical gorgons. It follows that a correct semantics for notional readings of quantified VP's cannot involve the assignment of an object from either the real, concrete, part of the domain, or the intentional, mythical part. And it seems likely that one mechanism is responsible for both notionality and the more radical existence-independence that it allows.

4 NON-RELATIONAL, ANTI-RELATIONAL, NOTIONAL

As it is usually presented in the literature, the relational/notional distinction is expressively exhaustive, in the sense that, absent other ambiguities, there are only two propositions that the likes of (3) and (4) can express. Moreover, it seems that notional and relational readings are contrary, given explicit 'no particular' riders: if Perseus seeks

---

[12] On this view, 'Medusa was turned into a gorgon by Athena' is true as normally understood because it is normally understood to be implicitly prefaced by 'in the myth'. Those under the misapprehension that the myth is factual intend no such qualification, so their statement should be evaluated (as false) with respect to the historical course of events. With respect to this course of events, 'Medusa is a creature of myth' is true. What of 'Medusa does not exist'? This ought to have a reading which is false because it denies that a certain mythical character was created. But we never hear it that way, since the use of 'Medusa' with determinate reference conflicts with not having been created. Instead we hear it as denying that Medusa is a spatio-temporal inhabitant of the real world; this is the gist of "she doesn't really exist".

a gorgon, but no particular one, then he does not seek a particular gorgon, and if he seeks a particular gorgon, it is false that he seeks a gorgon, but no particular one. (Both attributions may be false, since he may seek something else entirely, or nothing at all.)

Each claim in the previous paragraph, expressive exhaustiveness of the two readings and their contrariety, may be challenged. First, contrariety. Qualification is needed because Perseus may be conducting a single search, which is for Medusa and *also* for some other gorgon (but no particular one). What notional-relational contrariety amounts to is that one and the same search cannot be both for a particular gorgon, *and nothing and no-one else*, and also for a gorgon (no particular one) *and nothing and no-one else*.

As for expressive exhaustiveness, there is some reason to think that a third reading exists, one that implies neither 'particular' nor 'no particular'. The Norton Simon Museum has in its permanent collection a painting by the 17th-century Italian artist Guercino, entitled *The Aldrovandi Dog*. When it is on exhibit, the painting is accompanied by a wall-label which states 'this is surely the portrait of a specific dog'. But the curators give little justification for this claim, and if another expert claims that the portrait is probably of no dog in particular, Guercino having simply painted one from imagination, her case would be defensible.

Yet even though the parties disagree, there is something on which they can agree: that Guercino painted a dog. However, if a relational proposition ('painted a particular dog') and a notional (better: antirelational) proposition ('painted a dog, but no particular one') are the only two available for 'Guercino painted a dog' to express, there is no such proposition as one they agree on. The problem is not restricted to depiction verbs. Someone who sees Perseus making preparations for what is unmistakably a gorgon-hunt (the mirrored shield, the special pouch, and so on), but has no evidence whether or not Perseus is hunting a specific gorgon, can surely justifiably assert 'Perseus is going hunting for a gorgon'. It seems that in both cases, there is something we can say that is *non-committal* on 'particular' versus 'no particular', perhaps conveyed in the painting case by 'Guercino painted a dog, but *not necessarily* a particular dog'.

If non-committal readings do *not* exist, then the 'no particular' rider in

(6b) Perseus is in Crete, looking for three gorgons, though no particular gorgons

is merely an *articulation* of notional content, whose role is to make it clear that it is the notional reading that is intended. But if there *are* non-committal readings, a 'no particular' rider is just an extra conjunct (as it appears to be, since it is usually introduced by 'though' or 'but'). In this case the conjunct makes for a conflict with the relational reading that would not be there otherwise, unless understood from context. By analogy, inclusive disjunction is non-committal as to whether exactly one disjunct is true or both are. And the rider 'but not both' which can be attached to an inclusive disjunction plays a truth-condition-altering role similar to that of 'but no particular one(s)', on the hypothesis of a non-committal reading.

Against the hypothesis of non-committal readings, it may be argued that when the experts agree that Guercino painted a dog, all they are really agreeing about is that Guercino painted a dog, *either a particular one or not*. However, postulating literal disjunctive content seems more like a consequence of rejecting the non-committal reading that one is willing to swallow despite its phenomenological implausibility, than an independent intuition about the meaning of (5b). Of course, such a disjunction could be used to confirm that a non-committal reading is intended. In the same way we can add 'maybe both' to an inclusive disjunction to confirm the inclusiveness, without supposing that modality and conjunction are part of the literal content of $p \vee q$.

Another question about non-committal readings concerns how their semantics is represented. With clausal verbs there is a problem, since if the analogy with disjunction is to be preserved, the non-committal reading of

(8) Perseus believes some gorgon can be found in Crete

has to follow from

(9) Medusa is a gorgon and Perseus believes that Medusa can be found in Crete

even if Perseus does not have the concept *gorgon*. This is because (9) entails the relational reading of (8), and by the analogy with disjunction, the relational reading of (8) entails its non-committal reading. But in the semantics of a putative non-committal reading of (8), 'some gorgon' has to be within the scope of 'believes', or else we get a relational reading,[13] and it may seem that putting it there implies possession of the concept *gorgon* on Perseus's part, which we just said to be unnecessary. Thus non-committal readings appear to have inconsistent features.

But issues about concept-possession concern only substitution-resistant readings. These disallow removing predicates expressing concepts believers grasp and replacing them with at most intensionally$_{pw}$ equivalent ones they lack, as we can illustrate from the case of William III, the seventeenth-century English king who hoped to avoid a war with France but didn't hope to avoid a nuclear or non-nuclear war with France.[14] An *extensionally construed* propositional ascription (he *did* hope to avoid a nuclear or non-nuclear war) *can* have predicates within the scope of the attitude verb for concepts the subject does not grasp, and still be understood as not implying a relational reading (there is no specific nuclear or non-nuclear war he hoped to avoid).[15]

For the complements of ITV's, the availability of a non-committal reading depends on the semantics we propose, so further discussion of the matter will have to be delayed. But to anticipate, it will turn out, on the proposal to be developed here, that there is a natural candidate for the semantics of such a reading, which to some extent confirms its existence: if a proposition is available to be expressed, why would it remain unexpressed? At any rate, when it matters, we will be careful to note whether what we are saying applies only to *anti-relational* readings (readings with a 'no particular' rider) or to all *non-relational* readings (anti-relational and non-committal). Perhaps it would be best to drop the term 'notional' and work only with

---

[13] Recall that on the view currently being explored, a compulsory notional reading requires an extra conjunct to the effect that there is no gorgon such that Perseus believes...it...

[14] (Stalnaker 1984:88) is the source of the example, though not the moral.

[15] It follows that substitution-resistance (SR) is not just a matter of scope. The "hidden indexical" account of SR we will endorse in Chapter 8 implies this.

'anti-relational' and 'non-relational', but since Quine introduced 'notional' to contrast with 'relational', we will continue to use it for both non-relational and anti-relational readings. And so far as possible, we will try to carry the discussion along in a way that is neutral on the existence of non-committal readings.[16]

---

[16] Note that a *reading* is non-relational if it is not relational. This is consistent with the *circumstances that make it true* being ones that also make the associated relational reading true.

4

Propositionalism

The discussion of the previous chapter intimates that the central problem raised by intensional transitive verbs is that of accounting for notional readings of verb phrases they head, in particular, for vp's in which the complement of the ITV is a quantified noun phrase. If first-order logical formalisms are unusable given the *overt* structure of intensional transitive vp's, two strategies suggest themselves. One is to use higher-order logical formalisms, which is what we will end up doing. But the other, to be examined in this chapter, is to uncover enough *covert* material in the vp to allow the explicit QNP to function as a first-order quantifier.

1 THE QUINEAN STRATEGY

The idea of uncovering covert material was originally proposed by Quine in connection with search verbs (Quine 1956, 1960). For (1a), Quine (1960:154) suggests (1b) as the notional reading and (1c) as the relational reading:

(1) a. Ernest is hunting lions.
    b. Ernest is endeavouring that some lion is such that Ernest shoots it.
    c. Some lion is such that Ernest is endeavouring that Ernest shoots it.

Quine's general claim is that (*loc. cit.*), 'just as looking for is endeavouring to find, so hunting is endeavouring to shoot or capture'. Thus the strategy is to replace the ITV 'hunt' with the clausal 'endeavour' and draw the notional/relational contrast in terms of whether the direct object of 'shoots' is within the clause, as in (1b), or whether it quantifies in from above, as in (1c). Since the complement of 'endeavour' is a 'that'-clause, and 'that'-clauses are usually taken to denote propositions (though of course this is not Quine's view of them), I refer to the strategy illustrated here as *propositionalism*: the logical form problem for notional readings of intensional transitive VP's is solved by assimilation to the case of verbs whose semantic complement is a complete proposition, and whose corresponding syntactic complement provides an allowable position for a first-order QNP.

Some tweaking of (1b) is necessary. First, as Kaplan observes (1986:276, n.5), (1a) can be true while (1b) and (1c) are false if Ernest has lost track of the fact that he is Ernest (granted that 'is endeavouring that' induces substitution-resistance). We need to replace the inner 'Ernest' with 'he himself' (on that assumption).[1]

Secondly, Quine's claim that 'hunting is endeavouring to shoot or capture' contains an ambiguity that conceals a problem which arises for propositionalism about several groups of intensional transitives: the likely clausal paraphrases are all materially inadequate. Assume that Quine means that in each paraphrase of a hunt-ascription, either 'shoot' or 'capture' may be used (this is borne out by (1b), which does not use 'shoot or capture'). Then no-one who is told (1a) *understands* it unless they know whether it is an intention to shoot or an intention to capture that the speaker is attributing to Ernest (the speaker can perfectly coherently suppose *Ernest* hasn't decided yet,

---

[1] This is to get the effect of Castañeda's 'he*'; see (Castañeda 1968), also (Peacocke 1981; Chierchia 1989), and, of course, Frege on Dr. Lauben (Frege 1967:25–6) (Chierchia says (pp.24–5) that the Italian adjective 'proprio' in an attitude context always expresses recognition of personal ownership, so that the subject would have to use 'my' or 'my own' in an accurate expression of his attitude in English). In addition to 'he himself', Kaplan also suggests (1986:267) that something needs to be included in (1b) about recognizing that one's goal has been achieved: seeking an *F* is not just trying to find an *F*, but rather trying to find an *F* that one recognizes to be an *F*. If this is correct, it puts searching beyond the abilities of conceptually unsophisticated creatures. For more about this point, see p. 102ff.

which means nothing is to be gained by claiming that the implicit verb varies from context to context).[2] This suggests there should be a disjunction of verbs in the clause. But what disjunction, exactly? Perhaps Ernest intends to *spear* any lion he finds. Or set a pack of dogs on it. Perhaps he intends to wrestle it to the ground (and then strangle it, or not – *killing* is optional). If understanding (1a) involves implicit grasp of a hidden disjunction that covers all such outcomes of successful hunting, our understanding of (1a) would be *partial* in a way it is surely not.[3]

In (Quine 1956), hunting is endeavouring to *find*, but as Partee points out (1974:97), we cannot paraphrase all search verbs in terms of endeavouring to find, since they are not all synonyms (*cf.* 'hunt' and 'rummage about'). To get round this we could paraphrase 'hunt' as 'try to find by hunting', 'rummage about' as 'try to find by rummaging about', and so on. Perhaps 'try to find by hunting' means something along the lines of 'try to bring about a finding resultant upon a hunting'. But there is a clear danger here that the problem of accounting for notional readings will not be solved: hunting for a lion, but no particular one, would be trying to bring about one's finding of a lion resultant upon one's *hunting of a lion* (no particular one).

Another idea (Larson *et al.* 1997; Parsons 1997:381; Larson 2002: 233) is to replace the volitional 'try' with the search verb itself: hunting for a lion is hunting to find a lion, rummaging about for a pen is rummaging about to find a pen, and so on. The proposition that there is an *F* which so-and-so finds is the semantic complement of

---

[2] A more detailed contextualist proposal might be formulated on the model of contextualist accounts of possessives (see the account in Partee 1997). "John's book" may mean the book John wrote, the book he purchased, or the book he brought. So one semantics for the possessive NP is 'the book that John stands in relation R to', where the value of R is provided by context. But in this case, there is an intuition that someone who rejects the question "What do you think of John's book?" on the grounds that John hasn't written any books, genuinely *misunderstands* the question if what was meant was "What do you think of the book John brought?" By contrast, even if your assumption that Joe-Bob is looking for an alligator in order to kill it is wrong – he only intends to wrestle with it – we would not say that you *misunderstand* 'Joe-Bob is looking for an alligator'. (Thanks to Isidora Stojanovic for discussion that led to this note.)

[3] Some kind of higher-order existential quantification over ways of concluding a hunt successfully might be suggested; I consider an analogous proposal for depiction verbs in Section 4 of this chapter (see (16b), p. 63).

the ITV in notional readings. This is the best propositionalist account of search verbs, but there are still doubts about material equivalence. The infinitival 'to find...' is presumably a purpose clause. Thus looking to find is looking *in order* to find. Suppose you go whale-watching and are told that a flock of gulls hovering above the ocean is a likely sign of a whale. As you scan the sky with your binoculars, you are looking for a flock of gulls in order to find a whale. It follows from this that you are looking in order to find a whale – we have simply deleted information about *what* you are looking for. But looking in order to find a whale is the proposed account of looking for a whale. So, when you are scanning the skies *above* the waves, you are looking for a whale. This seems wrong, especially if contrasted with a case where it is right, because the kind of whale you are looking for is known for spectacular breaching.

But these points are insufficient to justify wide-ranging rejection of propositionalism. For one thing, they only concern search-verbs, which is just one of the ten groups of ITV listed in the table on page 37. If propositionalism were successful with most of the other groups, one would be inclined to classify problems with search verbs simply as hurdles that will eventually be cleared in the execution of the programme. So we should consider some other groups.

2 VERBS OF REQUIREMENT AND DESIRE

A strong case for propositionalism about requirement and desire verbs is made in (den Dikken *et al.*, 1996; Larson *et al.*, 1997), citing work by McCawley and others. Their proposal is that a desire verb such as 'want' means 'want to have' or 'want to get', *mutatis mutandis* for 'need'.[4] One ground for this might just be that

(2) a. Walter wants a bigger boat.
    b. Walter wants to have a bigger boat.[5]

---

[4] Sometimes 'have' is appropriate, sometimes 'get'; see (Harley 2004) for a possible explanation of why one can be favoured over the other.

[5] Walter Kornbluth is the hapless though ultimately heroic researcher who, in the movie *Splash!*, seeks a mermaid, but at least at the outset, no particular one, though he later comes to seek a particular mermaid, Madison.

seem synonymous – apparently, the difficulties described in the previous section for getting materially adequate propositional paraphrases of search VP's do not arise with desire verbs. But that by itself does not justify positing a hidden 'to have' in (2a), since two sentences can be synonymous while having distinct semantic structures. However, den Dikken *et al.* give two arguments for the plausibility of an implicit 'to have' in (2a), involving attachment ambiguity and propositional anaphora. These are illustrated by the following:

(3) a. Walter will want a bigger boat tomorrow.
    b. Walter wants a bigger boat, but his budget won't allow it.

and the parallel examples based on (2b),

(4) a. Walter will want to have a bigger boat tomorrow.
    b. Walter wants to have a bigger boat, but his budget won't allow it.

It is ambiguous whether (4a) says that tomorrow, Walter will want to have a bigger boat, or whether it says that at some future time, say later today, Walter will want it to be the case that tomorrow he has a bigger boat. Only on the second reading is 'tomorrow' used to specify part of the content of the desire. But (3a) is ambiguous in exactly the same way. However, the reading on which 'tomorrow' is used to specify part of the content of the desire seems to need 'have' or 'get' or a full clause for 'tomorrow' to attach to. So there must be an implicit 'have' or 'get' in (3a).

Similarly, the 'it' in (4b) can be variously resolved, but by far the most plausible reading anchors it to the clause 'to have a bigger boat', which has the meaning Walter expresses with 'I have a bigger boat'. But (3b) is naturally understood in the same way, confirming the implicit presence of a clause.[6]

---

[6] Other supposed evidence for a hidden 'have' is less persuasive. For example, citing Ross, Larson *et al.* (1997:1.2) note that ITV's such as 'want' show the same disjointness effects with certain abstract nouns as does 'have': both 'I have my co-operation' and 'I want/expect/demand my co-operation' are odd, and the oddness is removed if the co-reference is removed, e.g., 'You have my co-operation'. But the same disjointness effect is present with verbs where a 'have' clause is not independently grounded, for instance, 'I earned/bought my co-operation'.

To these two pieces of evidence we can add a third, an especially striking form of attachment to a hidden verb: adverbial modification which is unintelligible if applied to the explicit verb. For example,

(5) Walter needs a bigger boat quickly

makes little sense if 'quickly' is understood to modify 'need' or any other explicit material. An utterance of (5) would normally be taken to mean that Walter needs to get a bigger boat within a period of time which, measured from the reference time, is quickly over. In this example and the others, the verb is apparently transitive, but the way we interpret the sentences seems to invoke the proposition that Walter gets or has a bigger boat.[7]

A fourth piece of evidence for an implicit clause is from verb-phrase ellipsis. In both of

(6) a. Walter wanted a bigger boat before anyone else
 b. Walter wanted to have a bigger boat before anyone else

the ellipsis can be resolved in two ways (the same two). In the first way, both sentences in (6) say that a certain want arose in Walter before it arose in anyone else. In the second resolution, (6b) says that he wanted to be the first to have a bigger boat. And despite the absence of an explicit 'to have' in (6a), it does seem that this reading is available for it as well.

Two questions are raised by the propositionalist case made in this section. First, is propositionalism the only way of explaining the evidence adduced? And second, are requirement and desire verbs (also verbs of expectation, as in note 7) an idiosyncratic special case, or are they indicative of a generally successful approach to ITV's? In the rest of this chapter, I will argue that propositionalism is not generally successful, and *en passant* I will canvas alternative explanations of the four pieces of evidence for propositionalism about requirement and desire verbs just set out.[8]

---

[7] A comparable case may be made for propositionalism about verbs of anticipation. 'They will plan a summit attempt this afternoon' has the same ambiguity as (3a) and invites the same explanation in terms of a hidden 'to have/make'. 'She expects me promptly' makes a lot more sense if the adverb 'promptly' modifies an implicit 'to be there' rather than the explicit 'expects'.

3 SEARCH VERBS

Partee (1974:98–9) observes that transitive search verbs in notional VP's do not generate attachment ambiguities analogous to (3a), while clausal paraphrases behave like (3b):

(7) a. Walter will look for a bigger boat by dawn.
     b. Walter will look to find a bigger boat by dawn.

(7a) has only the reading which says that the looking will take place by dawn, whereas (7b) has a reading, not shared with (7a), which does not *say* the looking will take place by dawn, but does say that Walter's purpose will be *to find a bigger boat by dawn* (this reading says dawn is the deadline, and isn't available for (7a)). This difference between (7a) and (7b) is puzzling if we follow (Larson *et al.* 1997; Larson 2002) and propose the same syntactic account of (3a) and (7a).[9]

How does propositionalism about search verbs fare with the three other considerations that support it for desire verbs, namely ellipsis, propositional anaphor, and anomalous modification? It has problems with ellipsis, where there is another missing-reading issue like that in (7a), affording a second contrast with the behaviour of desire

---

[8] One problem for propositionalism about verbs of anticipation is that the implicit material can vary from case to case with the same verb. Expecting a bus may be expecting one to arrive or expecting to get one (DeCarrico 1983). But within the former sense, is it expecting a bus to *arrive* or to *appear*? If you are staring into the distance when you say "I'm expecting a bus", we might prefer 'appear' (which neither entails nor is entailed by 'arrive'). But in the absence of such clues, the propositionalist has to say that full understanding of your "I'm expecting a bus" by the audience is not available. Den Dikken *et al.* (1996:336) try to quantify this problem away, in effect construing "I'm expecting a bus" as "I'm expecting some event involving a bus to occur". But "I'm expecting a bus" is not made true if what you expect is a bus to *depart*, though in that case you expect some event involving a bus to occur.

[9] Transitive search verbs certainly give rise to *some* attachment ambiguities, but there is no reason to think that the different readings involve a contrast between positioning some modifier within and positioning it outside a purpose clause. For example, 'Walter is looking for a boat in the harbour', would be true if Walter is in a helicopter above the harbour, scanning the latter for a boat. But it would also be true if Walter is in the harbour, looking out to sea for a boat. In the first sense, 'in the harbour' circumscribes the area of his search, in the second, it gives his location. There may also be a third sense, in which 'boat in the harbour' is a complex nominal, like 'boat in good condition'.

verbs (recall (6), page 57). For each of

(8) a. Walter looked for a mermaid before anyone else
    b. Walter looked to find a mermaid before anyone else

there is a reading that says he was the first to look, but only (8b) has a reading that implies he was {looking/trying} to be the first person to find a mermaid.

There also seems to be no prospect of propositional anaphor with 'find'-propositions. 'Walter will look for a mermaid, if the course he sails facilitates it' only has a reading on which 'it' refers to his looking for a mermaid, but 'Walter will look to find a mermaid, if the course he sails facilitates it' has an extra reading, on which 'it' refers to his finding a mermaid.

As for peculiar adverbial modification (recall (5), page 57), if 'find' is implicit with search verbs, it ought to be available for modification. And since searches tend to be temporally extended while findings are quasi-instantaneous, it should not be too hard to produce a modifier that is natural with 'find' but unnatural with search verbs (*cf.* manner adverbs like 'ruthlessly', 'hopefully', and 'inefficiently', which are unnatural with 'find' but natural with search verbs). It seems that phrases expressing deadlines give modest support to propositionalism if we avoid the interpretation of the deadline as being on when the search must start. It would be dogmatic to insist that

(9) Walter seeks an answer immediately

cannot be understood as saying that he seeks to find or get an answer, with the immediate future as the deadline on the finding or getting. But to my ear, this is a secondary use of 'seek', as the greater naturalness of 'get' over 'find' indicates. If (9) is the best evidence we have for propositionalism about search verbs, the case is weak.

However, it would be possible to argue that propositionalism *is* the correct semantics for search verbs, and only seems incorrect because of idiosyncrasies of these verbs which prevent attachment ambiguities, propositional anaphor, and alternative ellipsis resolutions from arising. For example, (Den Dikken *et al.* 1996) attempts to explain the lack of attachment ambiguity in the likes of

(10) Walter will look for a bigger boat tomorrow

by the fact that 'if you seek something... and you obtain the object as the result of your search, the time of your obtaining the object must overlap with the time of your search' (p. 1047). Hence there is no seek today/find tomorrow reading of (10).

But this misses the point, which is that (10) lacks a reading in which 'tomorrow' specifies a time when the bigger boat is to be found, while

(11) Walter will look to find a bigger boat tomorrow

has such a reading: on this reading, if he looks, but doesn't find a bigger boat *tomorrow*, a failure has occurred, while (10) has no reading which implies a failure has occurred in this situation, merely that it has been unsuccessful *so far*.

Second, the impossibility of looking today with the intention of finding tomorrow could at best explain why it might be unsuccessful to try to *elicit* an ambiguity in (10) by reference to a scenario in which the seeking occurs today but is governed by an intention to find tomorrow. And it would then be equally unsuccessful to try to elicit the ambiguity of (11) in this way, so the point cannot explain the difference between (10) and (11): if a reading for (10) is ruled out on conceptual grounds, the reading should fail for (11) on the same grounds, yet (11) *is* ambiguous.

Third, even granting the impossibility of looking today with the intention of finding tomorrow, there is a distinction between a reading being necessarily false and its just not being there. Necessary falsehood is as much as the point delivers.[10]

(Larson 2002) offers another explanation of the lack of ambiguity in the likes of (7a), relying on a claim of Wurmbrand's that the

---

[10] It is unclear to me that every 'seek today/find tomorrow' reading *is* necessarily false, since there is the option of an extensional construal of 'tomorrow'. If Walter will seek today in order to find on the day before the voyage, as he would put it, and the day before the voyage is not, as he thinks, today, but is in fact tomorrow, then he will seek today in order to find tomorrow. Such substitutions are acceptable in error-attributions; e.g., if he wrongly thinks the voyage is on the first working Monday of the month, which is tomorrow, 'he thinks the voyage is tomorrow' is acceptable, extensionally construed.

German 'versuchen' ('try') 'resists an independent temporal specification in its complement' (p. 239). Thus

(12) Hans versuchte Maria in zwei Monaten in Wien zu besuchen.

('Hans tried to visit Maria in Vienna in two months') is disallowed. Assuming that what goes for 'try/visit' also goes for 'look/find', a 'look today/find tomorrow' reading of (10) is excluded. But Hans might be trying to get his unreliable time machine to work, so that he can jump two months into the future to visit Maria; thus the English for (12) is not so anomalous (German speakers tell me (12) isn't either). Secondly, as before, this point does not distinguish (10) from (11). And there is also the option of extensional construal of 'in two months', analogous to that made in note 10.

If there are no attachment ambiguities, there will be no peculiar modification phenomenon, since the unpeculiar reading will not be available. But one might still expect to find propositional anaphor and multiply-resolvable ellipsis. However, we do not find them. So the case for propositionalism about search verbs is unconvincing.[11]

4 DEPICTION VERBS

What kind of clausal complement might psychological and physical depiction verbs such as 'imagine' and 'draw' take? 'Imagine' can take 'that'-clauses, but this is a non-imagistic use of the verb, to which imagistic uses do not reduce,[12] while physical depiction verbs do not even have a use in which they take 'that'-clauses. On the other hand, many paintings are naturally said to depict states of affairs, so a

---

[11] Another problem for propositionalism involves pseudo-cleft constructions. (i), *What Walter wants is a bigger boat*, has two paraphrases that uncover a hidden 'get', viz., (ii), *what Walter wants to get is a bigger boat*, and (iii), *what Walter wants is to get a bigger boat*. Presumably (iii) is the propositionalist version, and seems required for (iv), *what Walter wants is a bigger boat by noon*. But the corresponding paraphrase of (v), *what Walter seeks is a bigger boat*, viz., (vi), *what Walter seeks (for) is to find a bigger boat*, makes little sense.

[12] In conversation, Barbara Partee remarked that she could not imagine a five-dimensional cube, but could imagine that p for propositions p mentioning a five-dimensional cube so-conceptualized.

proposition describing the state should be available. One thinks of, say, Yekaterina Zernova's 1937 masterpiece of socialist realism, *Collective Farmers Greeting a Tank*,[13] for which we have the proposition, in reporter's present, that some collective farmers greet a tank.

Other types of picture, for example, portraits, are less obliging, but (Larson *et al.*, 1997; Larson 2002) propose that 'for verbs of depiction, the transitive form typically corresponds to a *small clause* construction containing an overt subject and a bare predicate' (Larson 2002:234). For example, for (13a) we have (13b):

(13) a. Max visualized a unicorn
      b. Max visualized [$_{SC}$ a unicorn in front of him]

where 'in front of him' is the bare predicate (Larson 2002:233).

However, the bare predicate cannot be as specific as 'in front of him', for two reasons. (i) (13a) is true if Max is rather visualizing a unicorn below him (what would it be like to ride a unicorn?). Concomitantly, information about perspective is not required to understand (13a). (ii) It seems that whatever the bare predicate, postulating one will mishandle negation. In the case of (13), obviously "Max didn't visualize a unicorn" doesn't mean "Max didn't visualize a unicorn in front of him".

Call the problems described in (i) and (ii) the *specificity* problem and the *negation* problem respectively. We could ameliorate the specificity problem by replacing 'in front of him' in (13b) with 'spatially related to him', but the negation problem would still stand, since "Max didn't visualize a unicorn" does not mean "Max didn't visualize a unicorn spatially related to him" either. The latter may guarantee the former for reasons from the philosophy of mind (see Noordhof 2002), but the need for such considerations shows that there is no *semantic* equivalence between the two. And such a small clause is clearly incorrect for physical depiction verbs: a self-portrait is not a portrait of the artist in front of himself.

The specificity problem is also addressed by the proposal in (Par-

---

[13] '...the approaching machine gets a dewy-eyed welcome from the country folk, who doff their caps and offer flowers' (*The New York Times*, 4th. November 2003, B5). I do not know if there is a curatorial dispute about whether Zernova depicted a specific tank, or specific farmers, or a specific occasion of greeting.

sons 1977:376) which equates (14a) and (14b):

(14) a. Mary imagined a unicorn.
b. Mary imagined a unicorn to be.[14]

The general idea is that with depiction ascriptions with transitive verbs, the subject-verb-object form has undergone what Parsons calls 'Hamlet ellipsis'. But the long form is rather unhappy when the verb is a physical depiction verb ('draw a unicorn to be'?) and it still seems that the negation problem is unresolved. If "Mary didn't imagine a unicorn to be" implies "Mary didn't imagine a unicorn", that would be for reasons drawn from considerations about mental imagery, and therefore ones which would not transfer to physical depiction verbs. Worse, the equation in (14) appears to be materially inadequate with physical depiction verbs. For there could be a drawing entitled 'Mary imagining a unicorn' in which it is clear that the depicted unicorn is supposed to be a figment of Mary's imagination. So a unicorn is drawn, but not drawn to be.

Hamlet ellipsis also generates a mismatch of readings, as in

(15) a. Mary imagined a unicorn yesterday.
b. Mary imagined a unicorn to be yesterday.

Both have the reading according to which the imagining occurred yesterday. But (15a) has a reading which means that Mary imagined a unicorn as one would have been yesterday (which, we may suppose, was a great day for unicorns) while (15b) does not have this reading. And (15b) has a reading which means that Mary imagined the existence yesterday of a unicorn (as opposed to existence the day before) while (15a) does not have this reading.

A sure solution to the problem is to quantify specificity away:[15]

(16) a. Mary imagined a unicorn.
b. For some way of being, Mary imagined a unicorn being that way.

---

[14] Parsons prefers this formulation to 'Mary imagined there to be a unicorn', which is better English than (14b), because it has 'less structure' (1977:376). My objections apply to both.

[15] Parsons mentions this as an option but doesn't say in any detail why he rejects it.

This may also solve the negation problem, if we can ensure that the 'not' of 'did not imagine' comes to have scope over 'for some way of being' in the semantics of "Mary didn't imagine a unicorn", *and* explain why that is the only possibility (there being no reading of "Mary didn't imagine a unicorn" corresponding to the quantifier having scope over the negation). It still seems to me, however, that 'there is no way of being such that Mary imagined a unicorn being that way' does not *mean* "Mary didn't imagine a unicorn", though it might, for Berkeleyan reasons, guarantee it.

The quantificational account also has a problem with the collective/distributive distinction. Suppose Mary imagines five unicorns. Does this mean that there is some way of being she imagines applying to them collectively, for example, being in a row? Or is it that for some way of being F, she imagines five unicorns x such that Fx? There are no "senses" of 'Mary imagines five unicorns' reflecting this distinction, so we must pick one. A collective predication formalism will be more complex, maybe incredible, if applied to (16a). But of course, 'Mary imagines five unicorns' could be true because she *does* imagine five in a row. The propositionalist might insist that whenever a collective ascription is true, some distributive ascription is also true, perhaps as trivial as 'Mary imagined five unicorns self-identical'. But this makes some philosophical assumptions about the nature of mental imagery, and so is again a poor candidate for semantic equivalence.

5 VERBS OF EVALUATION

The case for hyperintensionality in verbs of evaluation, such as 'fear', 'disdain', and 'worship', is as good as that for hyperintensionality in propositional attitude verbs: fearing Superman and fearing Clark cannot be the same thing if fearing that Superman is nearby and fearing that Clark is nearby are different things. And even if Ahura Mazda and Allah are the very same god, worshipping Ahura Mazda is as different from worshipping Allah as sacrificing to glorify Ahura Mazda is different from sacrificing to glorify Allah.

However, it is sometimes said that verbs of evaluation do not permit notional readings of quantified noun-phrase complements (e.g.,

Almog 1998:56). If you worship a Greek goddess, or fear a hydra-headed monster, then generic readings apart, there must be a specific Greek goddess, or hydra-headed monster, whom you worship or fear.[16] So the propositionalist may not have to worry about this group of verbs: if there is no relational/notional ambiguity, there is no need to posit hidden clausal structure to explain it.

But actual propositionalists do not take this way out; rather, they regard *any* non-quotational non-extensionality as indicating a concealed clause with which a proposition is to be associated (Parsons 1997:369–70; Larson 2002:258–60). By these lights, the substitution-failures noted two paragraphs back demand a propositionalist semantics for 'fear' and 'worship'. Moreover, Den Dikken *et al.* (1996:339) say that for 'fear' at least, there is both a relational-notional ambiguity and attachment-ambiguity evidence for a hidden clause, as in the example

(17) John will fear a storm tomorrow.

This may mean that tomorrow he will fear that a storm will occur, or that in the future (perhaps this afternoon) he will fear that tomorrow a storm will occur.

This particular example does not establish the point, since it uses 'fear' as a verb of anticipation, expressing the idea of fearfully anticipating, rather than the evaluative 'fear', which lacks an anticipatory element. But using QNP's other than indefinites, we do seem to find notional readings. An example, due to Michael Jacovides (in discussion), is

(18) Perseus worships every god that lives on Mount Olympus.

We can imagine Perseus sacrificing some animal and reciting an incantation that begins (in translation) 'Oh all ye gods that live on Mt. Olympus...'. He cannot name any particular god who lives there, but is impressed by the address. This is not quite the same as saying that he worships *gods* who live on Mt. Olympus, in which there is a

---

[16] Generic readings express what happens as a rule, or what is normal, and occur with extensional verbs, e.g., 'drinks a whisky after dinner'. For various approaches to capturing generic meanings, see (Asher and Morreau 1995; Cohen 1999).

generic use of the bare plural, and which appears to allow for exceptions, which (18) does not.

However, this example may trade upon special features of 'worship' shared only with other verbs for activities that involve a linguistic and ritualistic element. In

(19) Churchill disdained a pedant, but admired every fluent writer

the first conjunct has a preferred generic reading, and can be true even if the odd pedant, although brought to his attention, escaped his disdain. That is, the disposition the generic reading attributes is only triggered *ceteris paribus*. Besides its relational reading, the second conjunct may also admit of a disposition-attributing reading, but it is hard to decide whether it is the form of words itself that permits the reading, or whether it is simply inherited by association from 'Churchill admired a fluent writer'. It is also hard to decide whether exceptions are permitted; they would be, despite the 'every', if the disposition-attribution had an implicit *ceteris paribus* clause, but it may be exactly the role of 'every' to exclude such a clause.

So the existence of notional readings with evaluative verbs is not clear-cut. But it is worth pursuing the question whether the apparently objectual attitude ascriptions we make with these verbs are plausibly propositional at an underlying level, especially if substitution-failure by itself is sufficient to require a propositional account.

Kaplan (1986:267) insists that no propositional attitudes can capture the psychological state of one who fears certain creatures, in the sense of having a phobia about them. To this, Den Dikken *et al.* (1996: 339) respond that 'fear' is not the appropriate verb for phobias: '…if, upon seeing a shark in an aquarium, Ctesias is gripped with fear…he is not afraid so much as phobic. Strictly speaking, he does not fear sharks…If you truly fear sharks, you fear that they will do something'. This seems to me to have a large element of the stipulative about it, but the main question is what the propositional analysis would be if you *do* 'truly' fear sharks. The difficulty is that introducing other material to make a complete clause will fall short of material equivalence, since the new material can displace the original object as the focus of the fear.

Obviously, fearing that sharks will do *something* is not sufficient for fearing sharks: I might fear that they will avoid me, thereby depriving me of the chance to display my shark-riding prowess to impressionable onlookers. But even fearing that sharks will do me some injury is not sufficient for fearing sharks, as other cases show: I may fear that my incompetent dentist will do me some injury, but not fear the dentist. Similarly, fearing *encountering* sharks is not sufficient for fearing sharks. I may fear encountering sharks because I believe they carry a nasty parasite, but I need not in that case be said to fear sharks. In the same way, I may fear encountering a certain person because I believe he has a communicable deadly disease, but this is not to say that I fear that person. In these propositional elaborations, the potential encounter and the potential injury become the focus of my fear, displacing the original objects.

A comparable anti-propositionalist case can be made for 'worship'. 'Worship' can be used in a primarily psychological sense, as when we say someone worships Maria Callas. In this sense, the case for hyperintensionality is as good as with any other attitude verb. But even if we stress the use for religious practice, invoking the rites and rituals characteristic of different forms of worship, the case is for anti-propositionalism is strong.[17]

Earlier (page 39) we argued for hyperintensionality from the role of attitude ascriptions in action-explanation. Suppose Ahura Mazda is Allah, and that z is a Zoroastrian who worships Ahura Mazda and who believes that mosques are the right places to worship Allah. If 'worship' permits substitution, then z worships Allah too. In that case, *ceteris paribus*, we would expect to find z sometimes worshipping in mosques. But z never even tries to enter a mosque, though he thinks he could if he wanted to (mysteriously, z never *wants* to enter any of the mosques he comes across). Here we have the same kind of predictive and explanatory failure of action-explanation as we had for 'fears', so the propositionalist is as obliged to produce a clausal account of one as of the other. Yet it is hard to see what such an account might be. The most likely candidate is a purpose clause, but worshippers can have a very wide range of purposes in worshipping.

---

[17] See further the discussion in (Montague 1960), where Hans Kamp is credited with raising the case of 'worship'.

They do not even have to believe the creed; they may just want to get the religious police off their backs.[18]

6 CONCLUSION

The conclusion our discussion suggests is that intensional transitives are a fractured class, with some groups amenable to a propositionalist account, while for others, propositionalism is incorrect. This is not elegant, but elegance is not an *a priori* constraint. The second conclusion we should draw is that if there is a uniform account, it will have to be non-propositional, since the problems for propositionalism that search verbs, depiction verbs and evaluative verbs present seem severe, while we have yet to see an argument that verbs like 'want', 'need' and 'expect' cannot be treated equally well in a non-propositional approach. The main challenge would be to explain the phenomena cited as evidence for propositionalism about 'need' and 'want' in a way that is compatible with their absence in the use of verbs in the other groups of ITV's.

---

[18] A propositionalist might claim that attributing worship of Allah does not, by itself, rationalize any particular behaviour, even given a framework of other beliefs, desires and intentions: worshippers must also *believe* they worship Allah. But this seems entirely *ad hoc*, and it is hard to see why the same principle would not apply to other attitudes such as fear, and to propositional attitudes, generating a regress: believing that Superman is nearby does not motivate Lex to hide unless he believes that he believes it, and so on.

5

Quantifiers and Characterization

Churchill once remarked that 'democracy is the worst form of government, except for all those other forms that have been tried from time to time'. Perhaps propositionalism is the worst semantics for intensional transitives, except for all the others. But at the start of Chapter 4, we noted that there is a higher-order alternative to propositionalism. It is championed most prominently in (Montague 1974) and we begin here with an outline of Montague's approach before arguing for a variant of it that employs ideas taken from (Davidson 1967) and (Goodman 1949, 1976).

1 QUANTIFIERS AS ARGUMENTS

In Montague Grammar, a sentence such as 'Perseus seeks every gorgon' may be formed in two ways. There is a *merging* operation, which simply concatenates 'Perseus' and 'seeks every gorgon'. And there is an operation called 'quantifying in', which, when applied to the NP 'every gorgon' and the sentence 'Perseus seeks it', produces 'Perseus seeks every gorgon' by *substituting* 'every gorgon' for 'it' in 'Perseus seeks it'. So we may obtain (1a) either from (1b) or from (1c):

(1) a. Perseus seeks every gorgon.
    b. merge('Perseus', 'seeks every gorgon').
    c. sub('every gorgon', 'it', 'Perseus seeks it').

The sentence-meanings compositionally determined by these two

70 *Attitude Problems*

syntactic construction processes are distinct, and are candidates for being the notional and the relational meanings of (1a), the notional arising from merging and the relational from quantifying in.

The semantics of the notional meaning is the result of Montague's adopting a higher-type solution to the problem of accounting for [$_{VP}$V QNP] phrases (recall Section 2.1.6, pp. 23–7). Standardly, the type of transitive verbs is $i(ib)$ and we use lambda abstraction to provide, say, **catch**, with an input of type i when "catch"'s syntactic complement is a QNP such as 'some mouse'. But Montague allows transitive verbs to accept inputs of type $(ib)b$, such as **some(mouse)**, *directly*. This means the verbs are themselves of type $((ib)b)(ib)$. So by contrast with our discussion of (8b) on page 23, **catch(some(mouse))** is well-typed, and is of type ib. Montague also assigned the type of QNP's to singular NP's, so that **tom** and **perseus** are of type $(ib)b$ (recall the discussion of **tom**^{i} and **tom**$^{(ib)b}$ on p. 27). Thus **tom** can take **catch (some(mouse))** as input. For our two English sentences, then, we have respectively the Montagovian semantics

(2) a. **tom(catches(some(mouse)))**
    b. **perseus(seeks(every(gorgon)))**

for the readings produced by merging.[1]

Montague presented his account in an intensional type-theory, not in the extensional language of (2), but the main difficulties are already present in (2). If merging produces anti-relational, 'but no particular one(s)' readings, it is hard to know what to make of (2a), since it is not possible to catch some mouse, but no particular one. Montague provides a meaning-postulate which guarantees that **tom** maps **catches(some(mouse))** to ⊤ iff for some mouse, the property of catching it maps Tom to ⊤. But when a meaning-postulate is applied

---

[1] I am making various simplifications here in addition to the extensionalization of the semantics. In Montague's formalism, an individual constant like **tom** is of type i, not $(ib)b$; but the name 'Tom' is translated not by **tom** but by **λP.P(tom)**, where **P** is of type ib. So 'Tom catches some mouse', if formed by merging 'Tom' and 'catches some mouse', means **(λP.P(tom))(catches(some(mouse)))**, with **λP.P(tom)** as a function of type $(ib)b$ and **(catches(some(mouse)))** as the ib-input; and this simplifies by λ-conversion to **(catches(some(mouse)))(tom)**. But if formed by substituting 'some mouse' for 'it' in 'Tom catches it', the rule is to abstract on the i-variable, say **z**, in the $(ib)b$-term translating 'it', say **λQ.Q(z)**. So we get **(some mouse)λz.(catches(λQ.Q(z)))(tom)**.

to a well-typed combination of antecedently meaningful expressions, it can only articulate *a priori* linguistic knowledge about the phrase, in this case an extensional VP. The problem is that (2a) is parallel to (2b), so if (2b) expresses 'no particular one', so must (2a). Then the meaning-postulate that **tom** maps **catches(some(mouse))** to ⊤ iff for some mouse, the property of catching it maps Tom to ⊤, actually *contradicts* the intrinsic meaning of (2a), if the latter expresses 'no particular one', since the postulate requires that there be a particular thing caught.

One might reply that all this objection shows is that (2a) expresses a meaning that is merely non-relational, or 'non-committal', in the sense of Section 3.4 (recall the common ground, that Guercino painted a dog, between those who say that *The Aldrovandi Dog* is of a specific dog, and those who say it is not). The meaning-postulate for **catch** then reflects the fact that the non-committal (2a) can only be true in situations in which a specific mouse is caught. However, this does not work: the non-committal reading has the gist 'not necessarily a particular one', yet it *is* necessary (*de dicto*) that if Tom catches a mouse, there is a particular mouse he catches.[2] So, while (2a) must, by compositionality, have some meaning as it stands, it remains obscure what that meaning is. The problem appears to trace to the choice of ((*ib*)*b*)(*ib*) semantics for transitive verbs.

This brings a more fundamental problem into view. For (1a), there is a non-committal meaning to be captured, one which is capable of being true even if there are no gorgons. Does (2b) really capture it? (2b) has a term for a property of properties as input to **seeks**, so its gist is not transparent. Where NP is singular, we understand '*x* seeks NP' to mean that *x* is in the seeking relation to the individual to whom NP refers. We cannot understand **seeks(P**$^{(ib)b}$**)(x)** in any different way, given that 'seek' is univocal with singular and quantified NP-complements. But to understand '*x* seeks QNP' in this way is to have *x* seeking the meaning of a quantifier (perhaps by looking it up in a dictionary). Montague assigned type (*ib*)*b* to singular terms as well,

---

[2] If the necessity were *de re* all would be well again, but saying that it is not necessarily a particular mouse Tom catches does not merely mean that it can be different mice in different worlds; it means something – something we are failing to pin down – internal to each world where this catching occurs.

but matters are hardly clarified by *extending* the scope of the puzzling property-of-properties semantics.[3]

It may be replied that all we need is to supplement (2b) with an account of *what it is* to stand in the seeking relation to the property of being a property of every gorgon, in the drawing relation to the property of being a property of a dog, and so on. We could say, for the former case, that it is a matter of acting under a certain governing intention, for instance, the intention that one find every gorgon (as opposed to the intentions, for each gorgon, that one find *it*). Or we could say, following the elaborations of Montague's account in (Moltmann 1997) and (Richard 2001) for search verbs, that it is a matter of the nature of the circumstances under which the search would end in success. For the drawing case, some account of depiction, such as that in (Peacocke 1987), could be roped in.[4] But while this would be all very well if the proposed semantics contained some theoretical primitive, there are no theoretical primitives in (2b). Why then do we need a philosophical gloss to explain its renderings of ordinary expressions? It seems that (2b) is something of a *tabula rasa*, and the philosophical gloss is there just to inscribe notional meaning on it by *fiat*.

If this complaint is justified, then (2b) brings us no closer to understanding how notional readings acquire their special truth-conditions. Still, given the problems of propositionalism, the idea that the QNP complements of ITV's have a role in notional readings that they cannot play in first-order logic is appealing. It is just that direct input to the verb is not the best implementation of the idea.

---

[3] Note that I am not objecting that the object-language sentence '*x* seeks every gorgon' is implied to be synonymous with the object-language sentence '*x* seeks the property of being a property of every gorgon'. These two OL sentences have distinct Montagovian truth-conditions. The issue is rather about the conception of truthmaker in play for the first sentence.

[4] According to Peacocke's account, a depiction of, say, a dog, is something which, when viewed in appropriate conditions, is presented in a region of the visual field experienced as similar in relevant respects (for instance, shape) to one in which it is possible for a dog to be presented.

2 EVENT SEMANTICS FOR ACTION VERBS

Search verbs fall into the category of action verbs, for which a seminal semantics was proposed in (Davidson 1967). In a simple-minded first order approach to verbs, arguments and adjuncts, we find arguments and adjuncts built into the relation the verb stands for. Thus 'Tom chased Jerry in the kitchen' would come out as something like 'Ctjk', involving a predicate $Cxyz$ for 'x chased y in (place) z'. This is unsatisfactory because there is no end of positions that would have to be provided, not all of which are always filled. Tom may, or may not, have chased Jerry in the kitchen *into* something, say a corner. Lacking information, we would have to say 'Tom chased Jerry in the kitchen' is ambiguous between a sense of 'chase' expressing chasing-into, and a sense without such a component. It would be better to allow the PP to express an independent and optional condition on some element introduced by the verb itself. Davidson argues that we can do this by discerning quantification over actions, or more generally, over events, in such verbs. So for (3a) we have (3b):

(3) a. Tom chased Jerry in the kitchen.
    b. For some event e, e was a chasing of Jerry by Tom and e was in the kitchen.

Here we quantify over token, unrepeatable, events, in this case a specific chasing of Jerry by Tom.[5]

In his influential elaboration of this approach, Parsons (1990: Ch.5) argues for further conjunctive articulation of phrases like 'e

---

[5] Adverbs as well as PP's can be event-modifiers. For example, although 'Tom chased Jerry furiously' has a reading in which 'furiously' is a subject-oriented adverb (Parsons 1990:64), i.e., 'Tom chased Jerry in a fury', there is also a reading on which it was the chasing, not Tom, that was furious. It is natural to treat such manner adverbs as predicates of events, e.g., 'e was a chasing of Jerry by Tom and e was furious'. But Davidson does not advocate this, because of the attributive nature of the predication: 'furious' in this context means 'furious for a chasing' (recall the discussion of subsective adjectives on p. 21). I follow Parsons (1990:45) in taking the point while noting that it is easily enough accommodated; Parsons suggests something like 'furious(e, P)' where P fixes the fury-standard. A subsective operator account of attributive adverbs is also possible: **(furious(chasing))(e)**. I will employ Parsons' idea, but like him, I will, for simplicity, suppress the parameter for standards.

was a chasing of Jerry by Tom' (see also Castañeda 1967; Davidson 1985). In part, this is because, in some cases, a verb-argument is optional, as when a dentist asks the patient to bite, and she does, but bites nothing: a three-place predicate 'e is a biting of x by y' will have trouble expressing this. Further articulation also allows us to make a connection with one strand of syntactic theory, in which verbs are said to assign *thematic roles*, or θ-roles, to their syntactic arguments (see Radford 1988:372–84; Huddleston and Pullum 2002:227–35). To articulate 'e was a chasing of Jerry by Tom', Parsons uses *semantic θ-roles*, which put individuals into certain role-relations with respect to particular events. For (3b) this leads to

(4) For some event e, e was a chasing and Tom was agent of e and Jerry was theme of e and the kitchen was location of e.

If someone bites but bites nothing, then for some event e, e was a biting and that person was agent of e; end of story.[6] Parsons uses the term "subatomic semantics" for analyses like (4), the contrasting "atomic" semantics being one which treats the transitive verb as a binary relation and in which no event-quantification is discerned.

(4) introduces the thematic roles *agent*, *theme* and *location*. There is some controversy in the literature over whether there are such things as semantic roles, and if so, how such roles as agent and theme are to be explained (see Dowty 1989; Parsons 1995; Schein 2002). If the treatment of intensional transitives to be given here has any appeal, that will be a consideration in favour of the existence of such roles, at least as logical constructions. As for explaining them, I will follow Parsons (1995:637–9) in avoiding substantive criteria, typical examples of which ('the theme is that which is affected by the event') are usually subject to counterexample. Instead, we use prepositional criteria: if e is *by x*, then x is agent of e, and if e is *of x*, then x is theme of e. So, to use Parsons' example, if you played the sonata,

---

[6] This argument for conjunctive articulation might be resisted on the grounds that all the patient does is make a biting motion; similarly, in response to Parsons' example that Brutus might have stabbed and missed (Parsons 1990:96), it may be insisted that he only made a stabbing motion – he stabbed at Caesar, but did not stab. This is not how we actually speak, but there are other considerations favouring articulation as well; see (Schein 1993:Ch. 5; Pietroski 2002:89–100).

you were agent of the playing and the sonata was the theme, since the playing was *by* you and *of* the sonata.

Other thematic relations include *source, goal, instrument,* and *benefactive,* associated with the prepositions 'from', 'to', 'with' and 'for' respectively. Prepositions often have multiple senses, however, and it will only be specific senses that indicate these relations. Thus 'for' can mean, among other things, 'for the benefit of' and 'on behalf of'. If I do something for you in the sense of on your behalf, that would not make you the beneficiary of my action. More generally, thematic roles express ways in which objects may enter into, or be participants, of events. In the case of beneficiary, this is admittedly a rather extended sense of 'participant'.

The event-based approach has illuminated many problems in semantics, among which are: the articulation of subtle ambiguities in various kinds of modifier (Higginbotham 1989); the semantics of plurality (Schein 1993); the explanation of unbound anaphora (Ludlow 1994); the semantics of scoping in 'because' conjunctions and attitude ascriptions (Kratzer 1998); the theory of focus (Herburger 2000); and the analysis of kinds of intensionality (Larson 2002). It also simplifies certain logical problems, which was one of Davidson's original motivations. For example, (3b) shows the adjunct-detachment inference from (3a) to 'Tom chased Jerry' to be essentially an application of *and*-Elimination, so no special 'logic of modifiers' is needed. Where detachment fails, as in 'Tom chased Jerry in a dream', we would not want a semantics like (3b) or (4) anyway, for there is no (real) event of chasing such that it is in a dream; rather, 'in a dream' is a modal operator with the event-quantifier in its scope. Dream-Elimination, however therapeutically desirable, would not be a sound rule for this operator.

3 ITV'S AS PREDICATES OF EVENTS OR STATES

If action verbs require event semantics, then, since search verbs are action verbs, some intensional transitives require event semantics. Thus our earlier example (1a), here reproduced as (5a), which has the relational atomic reading (5b), would acquire the sub-atomic event semantics (5c), or more formally in $\mathcal{L}_x$ or $\mathcal{L}_m$, (5d):

(5) a. Perseus seeks every gorgon.
   b. **(every gorgon)λx.seeks(x)(perseus)**.
   c. for some event e, e is a seeking, Perseus is agent of e, and for every x such that x is a gorgon, x is theme of e.
   d. **(some)λe.seeking(e) and agent(e)(perseus) and (every gorgon)λx.theme(e)(x)**.

(5c) represents one possible relational reading of (5a), the one that says there is a single seeking such that for every gorgon, the seeking is *of* (hence 'theme') that gorgon. By reversing the scopes of the quantifiers we would say that for each gorgon there is a seeking of it by Perseus. This latter version would be preferred for such examples as 'Perseus sought every gorgon, but no two at the same time'. The initial **some** in (5d) is a sortal existential quantifier for events. If e is the type of events, a subtype of i, this **some** is of type $(eb)b$.

Many search verbs are prepositional verbs, being accompanied by an explicit 'for' heading a PP adjunct, and 'of' cannot be used in the event paraphrase. So for (6a) we would have (6b):

(6) a. Perseus is looking for Medusa.
   b. **(some)λe.looking(e) and agent(e)(perseus) and for(medusa)(e)**.

Here **for** is a relation between events and individuals. We do not use the thematic role *goal*, because *goal* is associated with the preposition 'to', standardly expressing movement of the theme to the goal. There is no theme in (6a) and Perseus might be going in the opposite direction to the one in which Medusa is to be found.[7]

Some other categories of ITV are amenable to very similar event semantics. For instance, in selling his birthright to Jacob, Esau was agent of a selling with his birthright as theme and Jacob as goal (the selling was *to* Jacob). For other categories, events do not seem to be

---

[7] In the previous paragraph we allowed a single event to have multiple themes. If multiple agents are also allowed, a semantics like (6b) will be inadequate for (6a), since (6b) might be made true by an event with two agents and two themes, one of whom, Perseus, is looking for the other theme rather than Medusa (see further Schein 2002:272). Full accommodation of this point could take us rather far afield, so for the purposes of this monograph I shall simply stipulate that events have unique agents (in the case of collective events, a unique collective agent).

the right entity to employ. If Jacob wants Esau's birthright, he is not the agent of an event, but rather the subject, or experiencer, of a state. Parsons uses the term 'eventuality' to subsume both events and states, a usage we shall follow. 'Subject' will replace 'agent', but otherwise we shall use standard thematic relations where appropriate. For the example just given, we would say that Jacob is the *subject* of a state of desire *e* and *e* is *for* Esau's birthright.[8]

4 THE NOTIONAL AS NON-THEMATIC

The literature on event semantics has concerned itself mainly with extensional verbs. Their treatment seems to apply without extra complications to relational uses of ITV's (extensionally construed), as (6b) indicates. But how is the approach to be extended to notional readings of the likes of (5a)? In event-semantics terminology, it is characteristic of notional readings that the QNP complement of the ITV does *not* characterize a semantic theme for the event provided by the verb. Indeed, one might say that the oddity of Montague's account derives from its treating the QNP complement in notional readings as contributing a semantic theme of a peculiar sort, a property of properties.[9] What, then, is the QNP complement doing?

An interesting hypothesis can be found in Nelson Goodman's account of depiction verbs (Goodman 1949, 1976). According to Goodman, if we say that a picture is a picture of a man, but do not

---

[8] For scepticism that state sentences like "Jacob wants Esau's birthright" involve quantification over underlying states, see (Katz 2000). However, the kind of argument from logical consequence for quantification over underlying *events* in action sentences given in (Parsons 1990:13–14) can be duplicated for state sentences, despite Parsons' doubts (188–9). From (a) *Tristan is madly in love with Isolde for the moment*, we can infer a number of consequences by removing any combination of 'madly', 'with Isolde' and 'for the moment', and no combination of these consequences implies (a). This is quite well explained by the occurrence of separate state quantifiers in the separate consequences.

[9] Given Parsons' distinction between atomic and sub-atomic semantics, with event quantification restricted to sub-atomic semantics (1990:8–9), an irenic approach accepts the Montagovian (2b) as atomic-level semantics. But we are compelled to proceed to the sub-atomic level because of doubts about the intelligibility of the narrow-scope Montagovian formulations.

mean that there is a man of whom it is picture, we are *classifying* the picture as belonging to a certain kind (1976:23). To indicate classification, Goodman prefixes the nominal of the QNP adjectivally, so that 'picture of a man' becomes 'man-picture'. Goodman's idea here seems to be generally applicable to ITV's, so long as there is some entity to be classified, corresponding to the depiction in the case of depiction verbs. And of course, event semantics provides such an entity. To say that Perseus seeks a gorgon, but no particular one, would, in Goodman's terms, be to classify the *event of search* as a gorgon-search. To say that Walter needs a bigger boat is to classify his state of need as one of bigger-boat-need. And so on.

The obvious virtue of this account is that it is suggestive of how the verb and its complement NP could interact semantically without any entity associated with the NP being assigned a thematic role: no man who is theme of the picture, no gorgon the search is for, no bigger boat that Walter needs. But there are two problems with the details Goodman sketches.

First, it will not do to replace 'picture of a man' with 'man-picture', dropping the indefinite article. Suppose there are two dogs in a picture. 'The artist made a picture of two dogs' must be capable of notional construal, and must differ in meaning from 'The artist made a picture of one dog' in a way that is exactly accounted for by the difference in meaning between 'two' and 'one'. If the numerical determiners do not contribute to the classification, we are left with 'made two dog-pictures' and 'made one dog-picture', which are presumably appropriate only for 'made two pictures of a dog' and 'made one picture of a dog'. So the determiners must be part of the hyphenated phrase that does the classifying: what we want is 'the artist made a two-dog picture' and 'the artist made a one-dog picture'. By the same token, then, and for all its awkwardness, 'picture of a man', understood as a classification, should be 'a-man picture'. Extending this to other ITV's, we could, for instance, represent 'search for every gorgon' as 'every-gorgon search'.

Second, there is an obvious question about the hyphenated terms: what exactly is the semantic operation corresponding to the adjectivization of the QNP? According to Goodman, the hyphenated phrases are best considered 'unbreakable one-place predicates' (1976:22), but it is very hard to accept that the meaning of 'two-dog 'picture' is not built up from the meanings of 'two', 'dog' and 'picture'.[10] It is the structure, or mode of combination, that is unobvious. Goodman says that we can learn how to apply, say 'unicorn-picture', without first learning 'unicorn'; indeed, we may learn 'unicorn' *from* 'unicorn-picture' (*loc. cit.*, 24–5). But it is quite likely that this ability depends on what Fodor and Lepore call 'reverse compositionality' (2002b:59–60): the meanings of the parts of an expression are determined by the meaning of the whole expression exactly because the parts contribute their (complete) meanings to the whole and can be extrapolated from it in a unique way. So we can pick up 'unicorn' from 'unicorn-picture' and go on to use it competently, given that we understand the context 'ζ-picture'.

A proposal that takes compositionality more seriously is that the type of the QNP shifts in a uniform, productive way, from that of a restrictive quantifier to that of an adjective. One way in which this might happen is analogous to the way in which the type of 'and' can shift from sentential to VP conjunction, as we discussed in Section 2.1.7. But for 'and' we have the rule (18) on page 28, which shows how sentential 'and' determines VP-'and', while we have no comparable rule showing how quantificational 'two dogs' determines adjectival 'two-dog'. Generally, the change of type we are countenancing here lacks the "logical" nature of standard type-shifting principles.[11]

But type shifts can be governed by less topic-neutral principles, which is what seems to happen in already-familiar cases where a broadly existential QNP is adjectivized, such as 'no-fault divorce', 'one-woman university',[12] 'two-man bobsled', 'three-storey building',

---

[10] One argument Goodman gives for his 'unbreakable' thesis is that 'we cannot reach inside...and quantify over parts [of these hyphenated expressions]'. But even putting aside quantification over fictions, this is not so. You may, by coincidence, have drawn a picture of a mountain (no particular one) that looks like Everest. Then, for some *y*, you have drawn an a-mountain-that-looks-like-*y* picture.

[11] If we read the input-output arrow ↦ as a conditional, type-shifting principles can be codified in conditional logics which bear some similarity to systems of relevant implication because of their restrictions on conditionalization (↦-I). Expressions of one type can shift to another if the second type is entailed by the first in the logic. See further (van Benthem 1988; 1995, Chs. 3, 4).

[12] *The Chronicle of Higher Education* 6/25/04, A8. The "university" is a diploma-mill and the woman in question is its founder, owner, and sole employee.

'many-splendoured thing', and so on.[13] Language-speakers who understand these compounds in the normal way know a rule relating the adjectival usage to the more fundamental quantifier usage. In a simple case like 'three-storey building', we would have:

(7) **(three-storey)**$^{(ib)(ib)}$**(P**^{ib}**)** $\stackrel{\text{def}}{=}$ $\lambda x.P(x)$ and **(three(storeys))**$^{(ib)b}\lambda y.\text{has}(y)(x)$.

That is, a three-storey building is a building which has three storeys.

We might regard (7) as a principle that is employed as a rule of expansion in the compositional derivation of the meanings of sentences that contain 'three-storey building', so that in their semantics we find the conjunction on the right of (7). This is the easiest way of justifying the claim that 'three' and 'storey' occur with their normal meanings in 'three-storey building', but it does not generalize to more complicated cases very well, and does not suggest any explanation of the hyphenation that accompanies adjectivization of QNP's. An alternative is to ascribe semantic significance to the hyphenation, regarding it as a syntactic signal of the type-shifting that converts meanings of type $(ib)b$ to meanings of type $(ib)(ib)$. **Three-storey** is the standard way of writing the result of such a shift, and (7) may be viewed as a meaning-postulate for hyphenation. And since the type-shift is a step in the derivation of the meaning of **three-storey**, and this process routes through **three(storeys)**, the meaning of **three-storey** is derived here, as elsewhere, from that of **three** and **storey**, since the meaning of **three(storeys)** is so-derived. On the other hand, **three-storey** acquires its meaning as a whole directly from **three(storeys)**, which may be the truth in Goodman's 'unbreakable predicate' view.

For something sufficiently abstract that it covers the other examples as well, we generalize (7) to permit any existential determiner and any nominal in the QNP, and also existentially quantify **has** and

---

[13] Technically, I define 'broadly existential QNP' to be a QNP whose determiner is *intersective* in the sense of (Keenan 1987): Đ is intersective iff whenever A ∩ B = E ∩ F, Đ A is/are B iff Đ E is/are F. In the examples in the text, the determiners are also *cardinal*: whenever card(A ∩ B) = card(E ∩ F), Đ A is/are B iff Đ E is/are F ('many' is understood in a cardinal rather than proportional sense).

schematize the containing lambda term, resulting in the schema **(some(R))**... λy$_1$...λy$_n$...**R(y$_1$)**...**(y$_n$)(x)**... There would then be a question about whether understanding these phrases requires knowing the specific **R** in question, or only knowing an existentially quantified version. The case of 'one-woman university' and the information in note 12 is suggests that knowledge of the specifics of **R** is required for understanding, with the more abstract schema guiding but not providing full interpretation. So the type-shifting gets extended in an *ad hoc* way that interpreters have to work out.

'Two-man bobsled' is an intensional case with import for Goodman's formulations. A two-man bobsled is a bobsled *designed* to be run by two people, though not any particular two; or perhaps it is a bobsled such that in *every normal world* where it is operated, two people operate it. In these explanations of the QNP-as-modifier, 'two men' is within an intensional clausal context, which accounts for the unspecificity of 'two-man' in 'two-man bobsled'.

However, we should not allow explanatory clauses to become too recondite, since the material in the clause is the kind of thing we expect speakers to be able to produce to explain what they mean by a hyphenated use of a QNP as a nominal modifier. Thus we would not want an explanation of 'two-dog picture' that embodies a *philosophical analysis* of depiction; 'is a picture which depicts two dogs' will do to begin with, and suffices to rule out that we are talking about pictures on which artistic dogs collaborated. In this explanation, 'depicts two dogs' is non-committal, having what we will later refer to as the 'pure inventory' sense for depiction verbs: it may depict two particular dogs, or it may not.

Similarly, there is not much more we would want an explanation of 'three-gorgon search' to say than that it applies to an event iff that event is a search for three gorgons. Once again we use a QNP noncommittally in the explanation of its adjectival use, while making clear that we are not talking about searches *carried out* by three gorgons. But this distinguishes the examples with intensional transitives from 'two-man bobsled' and 'three-storey building', where the explanatory clauses make perfectly standard use of **two(men)** and **three(storeys)** as first-order quantifiers. By contrast, in ITV cases like 'three-gorgon search' and 'five-man picture', the explanations use the QNP's in exactly the way we are trying to shed light on. So this explanation of the type-shift looks circular in the current context.[14]

For search verbs we can get round this in ways already alluded to, using explanations that describe propositional intentions governing the search or, alternatively, the circumstances under which the search would end in success; in such explanations, the QNP's are used straightforwardly (we develop a successful-outcome account in Section 6.7).[15] For depiction verbs, we can give a more complex condition that compares the regions of the surface that five figures in the painting occupy with regions of physical space a man might occupy (*cf.* Peacocke's analysis summarized in note 4), though at this point we are in danger of moving away from speaker accessibility towards philosophical analysis.

So a possible proposal is that for (5a), repeated here as (8a), and on the one-search-for-all construal, we have the relational semantics (5d), here (8b), and the Goodmanian notional semantics (8c).

(8) a. Perseus seeks every gorgon.
 b. **(some)λe.seeking(e) and agent(e)(perseus) and (every gorgon)λx.theme(e)(x).**
 c. **(some)λe.((every-gorgon)(seeking))(e) and agent(e)(perseus)).**

((every-gorgon)(seeking))(e) is of type b because it applies a function of type eb, **(every-gorgon)(seeking)**, to an input of type e. **(every-gorgon)(seeking)** is of type eb because **seeking** is of type eb and **(every-gorgon)** is of type $(eb)(eb)$, coming from **every(gorgon)** by a type-shift.

But it is arguably an objection to (8c) that it uses a universal QNP

---

[14] One issue that I am ignoring in this discussion is whether **three(storeys)** *is* a standard first-order quantifier and **three** a determiner of the standard type. An alternative is that **three** is a plural adjective and **storeys** the set of sets of storeys (? of cardinality ≥ 2). **Three** then functions as a subsective that outputs the set of sets of storeys of cardinality ≥ 3 (or = 3, according to taste); see (Carpenter 1997:301) for details. So far as I can tell, nothing in my account of intensional transitives turns on which account of **three** I adopt, so I will stay with the simpler, if perhaps less realistic, determiner semantics for number-words.

[15] Are we allowing ourselves something here that we disallowed the Montagovian? No; in our current terminology, the main problem with the Montagovian approach was its seeming to make the quantifier-meaning the theme of the search. Examples like (8c) below bring out exactly why it is not.

as a modifier. In ordinary English one typically finds modifier uses of only those QNP's that occur naturally in existential contexts like 'there is/are' or 'there should be'. These include QNP's with numerical determiners, as occurred in our earlier examples ('one-woman university', etc.) and more generally QNP's with intersective determiners (defined in note 13 on page 80), but not QNP's with determiners such as 'every', 'most' and 'the'.

We might get round this by using prepositional phrases as the modifiers ('**(for two men)(bobsled)**'), though there may not always be a convenient preposition. Alternatively, we can replace the modifier approach with a theoretical primitive directly expressing Goodman's concept of classification, or, as I shall call it, *characterization*, that he uses to explain modification. Instead of writing **((every-gorgon)(seeking))(e)**, we say that *e* is *characterized by* the quantifier **every(gorgon)**. To do this we add a primitive **char** of type $((ib)b)(eb)$ to $\mathcal{L}_x$ (type $((im)m)(em)$ for $\mathcal{L}_m$). Then where a relational reading has a conjunct such as **(*det*(P))λx.theme(e)(x)**, the corresponding notional reading has **char(*det*(P))(e)**. This is to be read as '*e* is characterized by the property of being a property of [DetP]'. So as an alternative to (8c), we have something structurally closer to (8b):

(9) **(some)λe.(seeking)(e) and agent(e)(perseus) and char(every(gorgon))(e).**

Here we say that *e* is a seeking whose agent is Perseus and which is characterized by the property of being a property of every gorgon. We will use **char** in this way in all our accounts of notional readings.

There is nothing in (9) that settles whether there is a category of non-committal readings that are neither relational nor anti-relational but are consistent with both. However, if there is such a reading of (8a), (9) is a plausible semantics for it, since there is no obvious obligation to read **char(every(gorgon))(e)** as *entailing* that no particular gorgons are at issue. We could impose this by meaning-postulate, but such an anti-relational, 'no particular', reading, could be obtained at least as naturally by adding **and(no gorgon)λx.for(x)(e)** within the scope of **λe** in (9), preserving the appearance that 'but no particular ones' is a separate conjunct.

There is also the question of whether (9) allows us to maintain a distinction between the mechanism responsible for the relational/notional ambiguity and the one responsible for hyperintensionality (resistance to intersubstitution of terms for the same entity). In the intended interpretation of $\mathcal{L}_x$, any water search is an H_2O-search and vice versa, because water is H_2O. But the hidden-indexical mechanism for substitution-failure described in Chapter 8 can be added to $\mathcal{L}_x$, producing substitution-failure. However, in the more adequate framework of Thomason's $\mathcal{L}_m$, we can allow for substitution-failure *without* employing anything like a hidden-indexical mechanism. For we may take the elements of the domain D_m to be as fine-grained as sentence-meanings.[16] But we would still have to add **char** to the language of event-semantics before we would have the expressive resources to formulate notional readings. So in both $\mathcal{L}_x$ and $\mathcal{L}_m$, the mechanisms are distinct.

We argued in Section 5.1 that it is a cost of Montague's semantics that an everyday concept such as *seek* ends up taking a property of properties as an argument: it is hard to make much sense of this on our intuitive understanding of 'seek', and adding a philosophical gloss just stipulatively associates a sense with it. It is an advantage of the approach which (9) represents that no special expressive burdens are superimposed on everyday concepts: the philosophical gloss is rather applied to the theoretical primitive **char**. The sort of gloss that is required is best brought out by considering what we have to say about **char** in order to get sensible inferential behaviour out of intensional transitives. So it is to the logic of ITV's that we turn in the next chapter. But even as it stands, I would submit that (9) is more revealing of the difference between relational and notional readings of (8a) than any proposed scope ambiguity.

---

[16] A somewhat less fine-grained view of D_m is that its members are *states of affairs*. Then **char(some(water))** and **char(some(h₂o))** would be the same function from events to states of affairs, since water and H_2O are the same substance, hence same state-of-affairs constituent. In this case, substitution-resistance would again have to be achieved by a separate mechanism, such as hidden indexicality.

5 DERIVING INTERPRETATIONS

It is one thing to propose (9) as the semantics of 'Perseus seeks every gorgon', quite another to show that such a semantics can be compositionally assigned to the English sentence (though readers happy to accept that this can be done should now skip ahead to Chapter 6). The problem is how to get from a clause like 'Perseus seeks every gorgon', which has no overt event-quantification or indication of thematic roles, to a formula like (9), which displays these explicitly. One idea, developed in (Parsons 1995), is that thematic roles for the arguments of a verb are built into that verb's lexical entry. For example, for extensional 'find', we would have the entry λx.λy.λe.(finding)(e) and agent(e)(x) and theme(e)(y). 'Perseus found Medusa' would receive the interpretation that results from (i) applying this function to the input **perseus** and the result to the input **medusa**, then (ii) applying a rule δ of *default existential closure*. So we end up with the expected semantics **(some)λe.(finding)(e) and agent(e)(perseus) and theme(e)(medusa)**. For adjuncts as opposed to arguments, however, Parsons proposes a special rule of *lambda-conjunction* (λ&). For example, the adjunct 'in a cave', interpreted as λe.a(cave)(λx.in(e)(x)), would by λ& be conjoined with the verb and its arguments before δ is applied (Parsons 1995:651–2).

This scheme is not entirely ideal for our purposes, since our main claim is that relational and notional readings differ in that the first involve **theme** and the second **char**. So the lexicon should not impose **theme** on any ITV that supports notional readings. Additionally, Parsons' approach needs one distinction between arguments and adjuncts and another between optional and obligatory arguments. Agents, normally obligatory in the active voice, are optional in the passive ('Medusa was found [by Perseus]') so perhaps we also need separate entries for active and passive forms. In particular cases, intuitions may be uncertain about whether or not themes are obligatory with the active form.[17] And we need to be more explicit about

---

[17] There is some agreement that, e.g., 'eat' and 'drink' have non-obligatory themes (i.e., non-transitive uses, such as 'he eats and drinks far too much'). In (Parsons 1995) it seems to be taken for granted that 'devour' and 'destroy' must have a theme. But "he doesn't eat, he devours" and 'where Satan destroys, God rebuilds' show this is not so.

how terms for thematic roles such as instrument, source, goal, and so on, get into the interpretation of adjunct phrases. So we will make some (minor) changes in Parsons' account.

If the broad lines of the event-based approach to semantics that we are pursuing are correct, then someone who understands an English sentence must be capable of associating its NP's with thematic roles. This may be done by syntactic-semantic criteria, for instance, that the subject-term of an action verb is associated with **agent**. Or it may be by semantic criteria that do not presuppose the interpretations we are trying to derive.

This makes it plausible that the input to the process of compositionally deriving a meaning for a sentence includes information about thematic roles – a *thematic labelling*, we might call it. In the examples below, I employ essentially the natural deduction format of (Carpenter 1997) to demonstrate how one can progress from the input to the final interpretation. Recalling that a complex type is specified in the form $t_1 \mapsto t_2$, "logical" steps in such deductions can be carried out by Lambek-style $\mapsto$I and $\mapsto$E rules similar to Conditional Introduction and Elimination, along with a raising rule for quantifiers due to Moortgat. In addition, we use modified forms of Parsons' δ and $\lambda\&$. We simplify by (i) considering only sentences with simple syntax and (ii) abstracting from directionality in the style of (van Benthem 1995).

The simplest cases involve just singular NP's and extensional verbs, for instance, 'Perseus found Medusa', which is input as

(10) $|Perseus|_{agent}$ found $|Medusa|_{theme}$.

The derivation of the meaning of (10) proceeds as follows:

(11)

$$\frac{\mathbf{agent}^{e(ib)}\ [e^e]^{(1)} \quad |Perseus|_{agent}}{\dfrac{\mathbf{agent}(e)^{ib} \quad |perseus^i|_{agent}}{\mathbf{agent}(e)(\mathbf{perseus})^b} \mapsto E} \mapsto E \quad \text{Lx}} \quad \frac{\mathbf{theme}^{e(ib)}\ [e^e]^{(2)} \quad |Medusa|_{theme}}{\dfrac{\mathbf{theme}(e)^{ib} \quad |medusa^i|_{theme}}{\mathbf{theme}(e)(\mathbf{medusa})^b} \mapsto E} \mapsto E \quad \text{Lx}}$$

$$\dfrac{\text{found}}{\lambda e.\mathbf{finding}(e)^{eb}}\ \text{Lx} \quad \dfrac{\mathbf{agent}(e)(\mathbf{perseus})^b}{\lambda e.\mathbf{agent}(e)(\mathbf{perseus})^{eb}} \mapsto I^{(1)} \quad \dfrac{\mathbf{theme}(e)(\mathbf{medusa})^b}{\lambda e.\mathbf{theme}(e)(\mathbf{medusa})^{eb}} \mapsto I^{(2)}$$

$$\dfrac{\lambda e'.[(\lambda e.\mathbf{finding}(e))(e') \text{ and } (\lambda e.\mathbf{agent}(e)(\mathbf{per}))(e') \text{ and } (\lambda e.\mathbf{theme}(e)(\mathbf{med}))(e')]^{eb}}{(\mathbf{some})\lambda e.\mathbf{finding}(e) \text{ and } \mathbf{agent}(e)(\mathbf{perseus}) \text{ and } \mathbf{theme}(e)(\mathbf{medusa})}\ \delta \quad \lambda\&$$

Some comments are in order. (i) A leaf formula with brackets is a discharged assumption, and the numerical superscript shows which application of ↦I discharges it. The undischarged leaves in (11) all correspond to elements of (10), either individual words in the lexicon, whose interpretations follow by the rule Lx, or else role labels. By convention, role labels are carried down until they are removed by application of a functor headed by the formal term for the role in question. (ii) Parsons' rule of lambda conjunction is shorthand for application of the derived lambda terms of type eb to an assumed term of type e, followed by successive conjunctions of type $b(bb)$, then a lambda abstraction that discharges the assumptions. (iii) The rule of default existential quantification also embodies lambda conversions; so for instance, **(λe.finding(e))(e′)** converts to **finding(e′)**. Before abstracting, **e′** is changed to **e** throughout (to save space).

The next example, still with an extensional verb, illustrates the treatment of quantifiers and adjuncts. The raising rule μ for quantifiers permits the substitution of a term of type i for a QNP of type $(ib)b$ in the derivation of a term of type b. By μ, the i-term is then abstracted on, and the original QNP prefixed to the abstract.

(12) |Perseus|$_{agent}$ slew |every gorgon|$_{theme}$ with |a sword|$_{instrument}$.

(12) has a number of readings. On the following page we derive the interpretation that allows different slayings for different gorgons and different swords for different slayings. Other readings are obtained by applying the raising rule μ in different ways. Thus, instead of moving immediately from **instrument(e)(y)** to **(a(sword))λy.instrument(e)(y)** by μ, we could delay this application of μ until the last line of the derivation. We then get the reading that there exists a sword that Perseus used to slay every gorgon.

A double underscore indicates suppression of a sequence of steps that has been shown in full in a previous example. We also use some abbreviations for role labels ('ag' for 'agent', 'instr' for 'instrument', etc.) and to keep within the page margins, the following abbreviations for types: $r = e(ib)$, $det = (ib)((ib)b)$, $q = (ib)b$. As usual, we ignore tense, number, and similar irrelevant features.

(13)

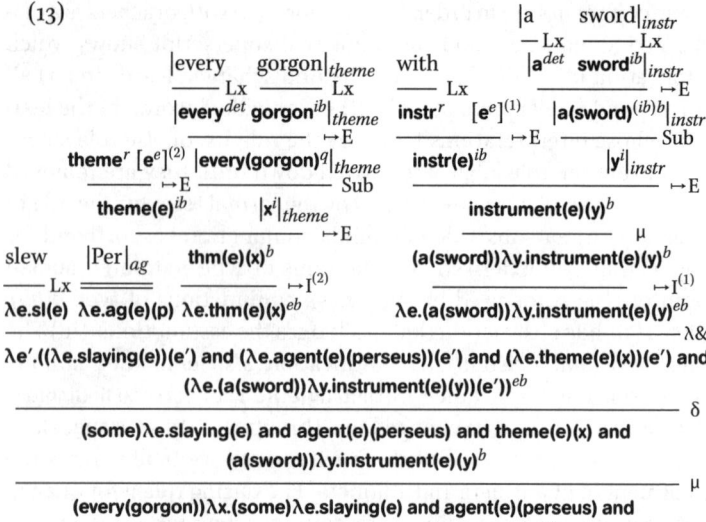

At the second line of this derivation we have directly assigned 'with' the lexical semantics **instrument**$^{e(ib)}$. Neither the verb meaning nor the fact that 'with' has a QNP complement themselves determine that 'with' means **instrument**$^{e(ib)}$, as is shown by the acceptability of replacing 'with |a sword|$_{ins}$' in (12) by 'with difficulty' or 'with a smile on his face'. Rather, it appears to be the combination of the lexical meaning of the verb and of the prepositional complement 'a sword' that narrows the field: swords are natural implements to use for slayings, and once 'gorgon with a sword' is ruled out as a phrasal constituent, **instrument**$^{e(ib)}$ has the field to itself. This process, a kind of trial-and-error method that settles on **instrument**$^{e(ib)}$ as the most plausible hypothesis, does not require prior grasp of the meaning of any phrasal constituent that already includes 'with'.

Our third example introduces an intensional transitive:

(14) |Perseus|$_{agent}$ seeks a mortal gorgon.

In accordance with our 'dethematizing' conception of notional readings, 'a mortal gorgon' has no theme label in (14), which, for the object position of an ITV, we take by default to mean that its function is to characterize. The proposed derivation is

Quantifiers and Characterization 89

(15)

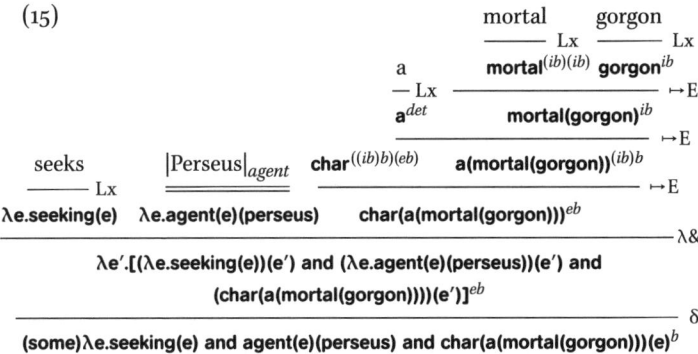

In this derivation there is one undischarged leaf, **char**, which corresponds to nothing explicit in (14). We could change this by using '*char*' as a label, but it seems sufficient to observe that grasp of the non-relational meaning of (14) depends on implicitly construing 'a mortal gorgon' as characterizing the seeking.

A final and perhaps more interesting example is

(16) Perseus sought and found a gorgon.

(16) has a weak pure relational reading ('sought a particular gorgon and found some gorgon') and a strong one ('sought a particular gorgon and found that gorgon'). But to my ear, it also has a mixed reading that can be true if Perseus was not seeking any particular gorgon. This requires 'a gorgon' to function as theme for 'found' while also characterizing the seeking. In (16), 'and' appears to conjoin **λe.seeking(e)**^{eb} and **λe.finding(e)**^{eb}, making it of type $(eb)((eb)(eb))$. When 'and' is of type $t(tt)$, we write it as **and**$_t$. It turns out that **and**$_{eb}$ will not do for the mixed reading of (16). Instead, we need **and**$_{qp}$, where $q = (ib)b$ and $p = ib$; that is, 'and' in the mixed reading of (16) co-ordinates functions from quantifiers to properties. In the derivation of the mixed reading to follow, we write $(qp)(qp)$ as **aa**. We also employ the standard unravelling principle for higher-type co-ordinations, known in this context as Simp(lification): **(and**$_{t_1 t_2}$**(φ))(ψ)** = **λx**^{t_1}**.and**$_{t_2}$**(φ(x))(ψ(x))**. So, for example, **[(and**$_{ib}$**(fierce**^{ib}**))(large**^{ib}**)](spike)**, in which 'large' and 'fierce' are directly conjoined, can be rewritten as **λx**^{i}**.[(and**$_b$**(fierce(x))**^{b}**)**^{bb}**(large(x))**^{b}**](spike)**. See also (18) on page 28.

90 *Attitude Problems*

(17)

$$\dfrac{\mathsf{char}^{q(eb)} \quad [\mathbf{Q}^q]^{(2)}}{\mathsf{char(Q)}^{eb} \quad [\mathsf{e}^e]^{(3)}} \mapsto \mathrm{E}$$

$$\dfrac{\mathsf{sought} \quad [\mathbf{x}^i]^{(1)} \quad \mathsf{char(Q)(e)}^b}{\lambda\mathsf{e.seeking(e)}^{eb} \quad \lambda\mathsf{e.agent(e)(x)}^{eb} \quad \lambda\mathsf{e.char(Q)(e)}^{eb}} \begin{array}{l}\mathrm{Lx}\\ \\ \mapsto\mathrm{I}^{(3)}\end{array}$$

(some)λe.seeking(e) and agent(e)(x) and char(Q)(e)^b
────────────────── ↦I$^{(1)}$

λx.(some)λe.seeking(e) and
agent(e)(x) and char(Q)(e)^p and   found...
────────────── ↦I$^{(2)}$ ═══════════════════

λQ.λx.(some)λe.seeking(e) and   and$_{qp}$ λQ.λx.(some)λe.finding(e) and
agent(e)(x) and char(Q)(e)^{qp} agent(e)(x) and Q(λy.theme(e)(y))^{aa}
── ↦E

λQ.λx.(some)λe.seeking(e) and agent(e)(x) and char(Q)(e)^{qp}
and$_{qp}$
λQ.λx.(some)λe.finding(e) and agent(e)(x) and λy.theme(e)(y)^{qp}
── Simp

λQ′.[λQ.λx.(some)λe.seeking(e) and agent(e)(x) and char(Q)(e)](Q′)
and$_p$
[λQ.λx.(some)λe.finding(e) and agent(e)(x) and Q(λy.theme(e)(y))](Q′)
── λ-conv

λQ′.λx.(some)λe.sk(e) and ag(e)(x) and char(Q′)(e)
and$_p$ a gorgon
λx.(some)λe.fd(e) and ag(e)(x) and Q′(λy.thm(e)(y))^{qp} a(gorgon)^q
── ↦E, λ-conv

λx.(some)λe.seeking(e) and agent(e)(x) and char(a(gorgon))(e)^p
and$_p$
λx.(some)λe.finding(e) and agent(e)(x) and (a(gorgon))(λy.theme(e)(y))^p
── Simp

λz.[λx.(some)λe.seeking(e) and agent(e)(x) and char(a(gorgon))(e)](z)
and$_b$
[λx.(some)λe.finding(e) and agent(e)(x) and (a(gorgon))(λy.theme(e)(y))](z)
── λ-conv

λz.[(some)λe.seeking(e) and agent(e)(z) and char(a(gorgon))(e)
and$_b$
(some)λe.finding(e) and agent(e)(z) and (a(gorgon))(λy.theme(e)(y))]
══

(some)λe.seeking(e) and agent(e)(Perseus) and char(a(gorgon))(e)
and$_b$
(some)λe.finding(e) and agent(e)(Perseus) and (a(gorgon))(λy.theme(e)(y))

6

Unspecificity and Inference

It is controversial whether there is such a topic as the logic of *propositional* attitudes. For if p and q are distinct complete propositions and R an attitude relation, then even if p entails q, it is not obvious why logic alone should compel everyone who stands in R to p also to stand in R to q (say if R is belief) or conversely (say if R is doubt). For example, even if Perseus believes the proposition that Medusa is a mortal gorgon and Stheno an immortal gorgon, it does not logically follow that he believes that Medusa is a mortal gorgon. It may *in fact* be the case that all who believe the conjunction believe the first conjunct, but that is a psychological effect, not a logical one: 'and'-Elimination is hard to resist.[1] In terms of a popular metaphor, logic alone does not guarantee that if a token conjunction is inscribed on a thinker's belief board, a second token of the first conjunct is also inscribed there. Perhaps the first conjunct must be *implicitly* believed. In that case, we can take ourselves to be discussing only explicit attitudes. This is actually a welcome restriction, as the idea of a logic of implicit propositional attitudes is rather unappealing,

---

[1] Peacocke makes a similar point in connection with ∃I: 'Belief in existentially quantified propositions is a *psychologically* determined consequence of recognition of the truth of singular instances...' (1999:181, my emphasis). Closure, explicit or implicit, under an introduction rule, is a risky hypothesis, but ∃I is a special case if we disallow vacuous quantification and factor out alphabetic variance. For an interesting discussion of closure under ∧I, see (Evnine 1999), esp. *c*. p. 219.

due to the obscurity of 'implicit'. But in either sense, closure of belief under logical consequence is *prima facie* unattractive. However, as we shall see in this chapter, closure principles for objectual attitudes are more defensible.

1 SIMPLIFICATION

Conjunction Elimination, or *Simplification*, may be at best a psychological closure principle for propositional ascriptions, but it is quite likely that Simplification in objectual ascriptions is underpinned by the very meaning of the ascriptions. This is illustrated in

(1) Perseus seeks a mortal gorgon and an immortal gorgon.
∴ Perseus seeks a mortal gorgon.

(1)'s premise has two relational readings and two notional ones. (1) is obviously valid relationally, assuming boolean 'and' (so that 'e is a seeking for objects x and y' is 'e is a seeking and e is for x and e is for y' – the non-boolean case is not to the point here).

One notional reading, (n1), is equally straightforward. According to (n1), the premise says that Perseus is agent of a seeking characterized by the property of being a property of a mortal gorgon and agent of a seeking characterized by the property of being a property of an immortal gorgon. And of course this entails the conclusion, understood in the same way, by one step of ∧-Elimination.

On the second notional reading (n2), the inference (1) says that if Perseus is the agent of a seeking that is characterized by the property of being a property of a mortal gorgon and an immortal gorgon, then he is the agent of a seeking characterized by the property of being a property of a mortal gorgon:

(2) **(some)λe.seeking(e) and agent(e)(perseus) and char[a(m(g)) and $^{x(xx)}$ (an(i(g)))](e) ⇒ (some)λe.seeking(e) and agent(e)(perseus) and char(a(m(g)))(e)**

where $x = (ib)b$. (2)'s correctness, if it is correct, is not a consequence of any built-in feature of our apparatus. Simply because **(char(Q and Q'))(e)** holds, nothing in our semantics compels **(char(Q))(e)** to hold. We should find some way of compelling it *if* the inference is correct,

Unspecificity and Inference 93

so two questions arise. The first is, if it is correct, how do we adjust our semantics to deliver it? And the second is, how do we ascertain independently whether the inference is correct?

Lacking a knockdown counterexample to (2) or to the schema **(char(Q and Q'))(e)** ⇒ **(char(Q))(e)**, the best we can do is assess what resources are needed to validate them. If it turns out that they come at a high price, or are awkward to implement, then we should conclude that our particular approach to the semantics of notional readings is hostile to the inferences.

In fact, there is a rather obvious general principle which validates Simplification. Suppose we write '$f ⊑ g$' to mean that for some type t, (i) f and g are both of type tb, and (ii) $g(z) = ⊤$ if $f(z) = ⊤$.[2] Then for the purposes of defining validity, we might replace arbitrary interpretations of $\mathcal{L}_x$ with models $\mathcal{M}$ satisfying the following condition on the **char** of $\mathcal{L}_x$ and $\mathcal{M}$'s domains of events ($D_e^{\mathcal{M}}$), individuals ($D_i^{\mathcal{M}}$), and properties of properties ($D_{(ib)b}^{\mathcal{M}}$):

(3) for any e in $D_e^{\mathcal{M}} ⊆ D_i^{\mathcal{M}}$, and any f, g in $D_{(ib)b}^{\mathcal{M}}$, if $[\![\mathbf{char}]\!]^{\mathcal{M}}(f)(e) = ⊤$ and $f ⊑ g$, then $[\![\mathbf{char}]\!]^{\mathcal{M}}(g)(e) = ⊤$.

This gives us a notion of admissible model, to which we can relativize other concepts, such as entailment. We would say that $\Delta \vDash_a \sigma$ iff for every admissible model $\mathcal{M}$, if $\mathcal{M}$ verifies every sentence in Δ, then $\mathcal{M}$ verifies σ. (2) and the schema **(char(Q and Q'))(e)** ⇒ **(char(Q))(e)** are correct in the sense of $\vDash_a$. For **(Q and Q')(F)** unfolds by the standard semantic account of **and**$^{x(xx)}$, where $x = (ib)b$, into Q**(F) and**$^{b(bb)}$ Q'**(F)**. So $[\![Q \text{ and } Q']\!] ⊑ [\![Q]\!]$. Hence by (3), if Q **and** Q' characterizes an event, so does Q. This is for any substituend of type $(ib)b$, so the "schema" is really a universally quantified principle.

But since (3) is a kind of 'closure under entailment' principle, it is natural to suspect that it will license more inferences than we want, even if it is restricted to particular types of events, such as searches, or states, such as desires. So we next investigate how (3) adjudicates some other inference patterns.

---

[2] f and g are the characteristic functions of sets X_f and X_g of items of the same type τ. So the condition $g(e) = ⊤$ if $f(e) = ⊤$ means $X_f ⊆ X_g$.

2 WEAKENING

There are other inference-types in the same family as (1), but which do not involve conjunction, or at least, not so explicitly. In all these inferences, a notional characterization of a search is weakened by making the characterization less informative.[3]

(4) a. Perseus seeks a mortal gorgon. ∴ Perseus seeks a gorgon.
b. Perseus seeks every gorgon. ∴ Perseus seeks every mortal gorgon.
c. Perseus seeks at least two gorgons. ∴ Perseus seeks at least one gorgon.

'Mortal' is intersective, so (4a) and (4b) are not all that different from (1), but the level of plausibility attaching to them does not seem to drop if we replace 'mortal' with a subsective such as 'typical'.[4]

The inferences in (4) are all valid, according to (3), since $[\![Q]\!] \sqsubseteq [\![Q']\!]$ in each of the three cases.[5] For example, in case (4a), we have $[\![\text{a(mortal(gorgon))}]\!] \sqsubseteq [\![\text{a(gorgon)}]\!]$; similarly in (4b) and (4c). Nevertheless, one may have one's doubts about their validity.

Part of the problem is that they do not appear to be compelled by

---

[3] Richard (2001:114) suggests that in cases where the agent seeks with the governing intention to find a specific thing, and is not looking for anything else, an 'exactly one' ascription is correct. Perhaps so, but the 'not looking for anything else' premise is crucial. 'Perseus seeks (the gorgon) Medusa' means the same in a situation where he seeks Medusa and Stheno and one where he is only interested in Medusa. So it cannot by itself entail 'Perseus seeks exactly one gorgon'.

[4] Of course, the inferences fail with other modifiers, such as privatives, and also with other ITV's, in particular, verbs of absence, which have the "reverse" polarity. If your art collection lacks a Picasso, it lacks a blue-period Picasso, but not vice versa (contrast (4a)). On the other hand, verbs of absence seem to support (1)-type inferences, e.g., lacking a Picasso and a Matisse seems to imply lacking a Picasso. But in this sense, lacking a Picasso and a Matisse means lacking a Picasso and lacking a Matisse; (3) is reversed for the reading with the gist "doesn't have both a Picasso and a Matisse", which is true of any collection that lacks a Picasso.

[5] Rather than rely on a meaning-postulate like (3) to underpin (4a), we could build the subset condition directly into the semantics. Thus 'Perseus seeks a mortal gorgon' would say that for some $Q \sqsubseteq [\![\text{a(mortal(gorgon))}]\!]$, Perseus is agent of a search characterized by Q (this adapts a proposal by Zimmerman (2004:18) for his own property analysis). Since $Q \sqsubseteq [\![\text{a(mortal(gorgon))}]\!] \sqsubseteq [\![\text{a(gorgon)}]\!]$, 'Perseus seeks a gorgon' follows. I do not take this line because of problems with disjunction; see section 6.3.

"notionalizing" codas such as 'but no specific ones' or 'but not necessarily a particular one'. Suppose Perseus seeks a mortal gorgon, but no specific one, and, to avoid irrelevant issues, doesn't seek anything else. Could it be false that he seeks a gorgon, but no specific one? The conditions of the example say that he is the agent of a search and that he is not searching for a specific mortal gorgon, and not searching for anything that is not a mortal gorgon. But it is still a step to the positive conclusion that he is searching for a gorgon, but no particular one.

Why might one want to resist this step? Reasons based on substitution-resistance are irrelevant here (if it helps, replace 'seek' with 'need' throughout (4)). Yet even putting these aside, the inferences in (4), especially (4a), may still seem problematic. One reason to doubt (4a) is the seeming plausibility of a certain way of explaining unspecificity, the *indifference* or 'any one will do' explanation. We find this in the following passage from Ian Rankin (*The Falls*, p. 105):

Rebus explained who he was. 'I want to speak to someone who was working at the hotel in nineteen ninety-five.' 'What's their name?' He smiled at her mistake. 'No, I mean, anyone will do.'

And the indifference explanation is implicitly endorsed by Lewis, when he writes about "'Lothario seeks a girl' in...the sense in which any old girl would do" (Lewis 1972:199; also Larson 1985:218).

According to the indifference explanation, (4a) is invalid, because the premise means 'Perseus seeks a mortal gorgon, any one would do', and the conclusion means 'Perseus seeks a gorgon, any one would do' (no it wouldn't – mortality is rather important here). However, the indifference explanation of unspecificity is a poor rival to the 'no particular/not necessarily a particular' explanation. This is in part because it cannot be applied to many ITV + QNP combinations that have unspecific readings. For example, 'Perseus seeks every gorgon, any ones would do' makes little sense, though 'Perseus seeks every gorgon, but no particular gorgons' is fine. And postfixing 'any one would do' to a depiction-verb phrase does not capture a notional sense, whatever the QNP complement of the verb.

A more devastating objection to the indifference explanation is that it implies a *sufficiency* thesis: if Perseus seeks a mortal gorgon, and any one would do, then his search ends successfully if he finds any mortal gorgon at all.[6] In other words, the indifference explanation makes it sufficient for a search for an *F* to end successfully that something falling under *F* be found. Besides threatening the very possibility of justified search-ascriptions, a sufficiency thesis validate *strengthening* inferences: if it is sufficient for a search for a gorgon to end successfully that some gorgon be found, it is sufficient that some immortal gorgon be found. Hence, if Perseus seeks a gorgon, he seeks an immortal gorgon. This is clearly incorrect.[7]

So these attacks on weakening inferences can be deflected (we respond to another in Section 6.4). But that is just an argument against an argument. Moreover, it is not only weakening inferences that (3) validates, and it is really (3) that is at issue. We consider a more difficult challenge for (3) in the next section.[8]

3 THE DISJUNCTION PROBLEM

Even if weakening inferences are valid, (3) appears to be the wrong generalization with which to validate them, as the examples in (5) show (propositionalists about 'need' should suspend their disbelief for the purposes of this discussion):

(5) a. Perseus seeks (either) a gorgon or a unicorn.
 b. Richard III needs (either) a horse or a donkey.
 c. The Duke owes the taxman (either) a million pounds or two of his stately homes.

a(gorgon) ⊑ (a(gorgon)) or (a(unicorn)) on any standard semantics for 'or', whether extensional or intensional$_{pw}$, and consequently, (5a) is predicted by (3) to be a consequence of 'Perseus seeks a gorgon'; similarly, (5b) is predicted to be a consequence of 'Richard III needs a

---

[6] It might be replied that context will always indicate some restricted group, any one of whom will do. But it is unclear how the contextual restriction is to be generated, and how it is transmitted in communication; see further (Forbes 2003:58).

[7] We can express indifference in English with free-choice 'any'. 'Perseus seeks *any* mortal gorgon' would be understood to mean that finding any mortal gorgon at all would end his search successfully; so it does not entail 'Perseus seeks *any* gorgon', though it is entailed by it. Such 'any'-NP's are a special case .

[8] Thanks to Diana Raffman for helpful discussion of the issues in this section.

horse', and (5c) to be a consequence of 'The Duke owes the taxman £1M'. But these predictions all seem incorrect. Each example in (5) has what we can call 'conjunctive force': (5a) says, roughly and in part, that bringing the search to a successful conclusion can be effected by finding a gorgon *and* can be effected by finding a unicorn; (5b) says, roughly and in part, that meeting the need can be effected by getting a horse *and* can be effected by getting a donkey; and (5c) says, roughly and in part, that discharging the debt can be effected by surrendering £1M *and* can be effected by surrendering two stately homes. But none of these conjunctive claims follows from premises that mention only gorgons, horses, and a million pounds, respectively. Richard III, for instance, would have been unlikely at Bosworth to offer an exchange of his kingdom for a donkey.[9]

A related problem is apparent in the following pair:

(6) a. Perseus seeks a gorgon.
    b. Perseus seeks a mortal gorgon or an immortal gorgon.

The quantifiers 'a gorgon' and 'a mortal gorgon or an immortal gorgon' are equivalent both extensionally (the same set of sets) and intensionally$_{pw}$ (the same set of sets at each world), but (6a) is true, granted (4a), while (6b) is false, given its conjunctive force (Perseus would prefer to *avoid* immortal gorgons). So the difficulty we face will not be remedied just by tinkering with (3), for (6a) and (6b) are *logically* equivalent in standard systems, not merely equivalent as a consequence of a special postulate like (3). We will see below how $\mathcal{L}_m$ solves this problem.

Our negative verdict on (3) depends on reading the examples in (5) with conjunctive force. It might be argued that this is not the only reading they have, and that there is a disjunctive reading which (3) gets right. We can bring out this alternative by attaching riders, as in

(7) a. Perseus seeks (either) a gorgon or a unicorn, and only he knows which.

---

[9] Though all our examples involve disjunctions of QNP's, the same problems arise with disjunctions of other categories, such as singular NP's, modifiers, and predicates. For example, 'Perseus seeks a gorgon that is either mortal or fast asleep' has a conjunctive reading that is not a consequence of either one-disjunct premise.

b. Richard III needs (either) a horse or a donkey, and it's quite clear which.
c. The Duke owes (either) one million pounds or two of his stately homes, and his accountant will tell him which.

It may even be that there is no problem at all with (3), if it is only the disjunctive readings in (7) that have a genuine disjunction of QNP-meanings in their semantics.

However, the opposite appears to be the case: *genuine* disjunctions of QNP's occur only in the readings with conjunctive force. The disjunctive reading of (5a), brought out in (7a), and available with or without 'either', is explicitly captured by the VP-disjunction 'Perseus seeks a gorgon or [*seeks*] a unicorn', which has no conjunctive force. The disjunctive readings in (7) seem to involve ellipsis, or some other mechanism with the same semantic effect.[10] The riders that force the disjunctive readings all involve verbs or operators taking 'that'-clause or propositional complements, since the riders themselves embed questions with propositional answer-sets (for (7a), {*that Perseus seeks a gorgon, that Perseus seeks a unicorn*}). The readings with genuine disjunctions of QNP-meanings in their semantics are ones with no elided verb, and these are just the readings with conjunctive force. What we need, then, is a replacement for (3) that does not allow the derivation of the statements in (5) from premises that say nothing about unicorns, donkeys, and stately homes; and, if at all possible, settles the status of the cases in (4) without further untoward consequences.

4 OUTCOME POSTULATES

To formulate possible constraints on **char** in a different style from (3), we employ the terminology we found ourselves naturally using to explain the conjunctive force of the cases in (5): for searches, the notions of finding and of success; for needs, the notions of getting and of meeting; for debts, the notions of paying and discharging. We

---

[10] The VP-disjunctions in (7) do not require a representation in which a second 'needs' is explicit, and is then interpreted: we can get 'needs' to distribute simply by type-raising. For details, see (Rooth and Partee 1982:356).

begin with non-compound QNP's. Then, after a general account of how 'or' comes to have conjunctive force, we formulate the constraints for compound QNP's.

Focusing on the case of search verbs, a first thought is that Perseus is searching for such-and-such iff his finding such-and-such is *sufficient* to make a success of his search. But as we already saw in Section 6.2, this validates strengthening inferences. Thus sufficient conditions for search-success do not stand in criterial relations to search ascriptions that justify their use to decide the logical status of (2) and weakening inferences. However, necessary conditions fare much better. If Perseus seeks a gorgon, then finding a gorgon is necessary for success. And if finding a gorgon is necessary for a search to be a success, it is arguable that the search must be for a gorgon, whatever else it may be for. So one way to proceed is to build something like the following equivalence into the semantics:

(8) a. Perseus seeks a gorgon.
    b. Perseus is agent of a search which is successful only if a gorgon is found.

Generalizing this will validate (2) and all the weakening inferences. For example, it will follow from his seeking every gorgon that he seeks every mortal gorgon, because if it is necessary for the success of a search that every gorgon is found, then it is necessary that every mortal gorgon is found.

A more regimented version of (8b) involves quantification over findings. However, examples like 'seek every gorgon' and 'seek three gorgons' remind us that a search for many things is not a success until they have *all* been found. It is too strict to require that they all be found in a single act of finding, so in the analogue of (8b) for 'Perseus seeks every/three gorgons', we will have to explain 'every/three gorgons are found' in a way that allows for two or three findings.

Secondly, there is nothing about (8b) which indicates that it is the finding that *makes* the search a success. We will probably avoid trouble if we include that. But if there are multiple findings, then the success-making relation is one which may hold in a given case between a *group* of findings and a search. Similarly, a need may be met by multiple gettings, and a debt discharged by multiple payments. We should not say that it is really the temporally last of the event-group that produces the effect, since, after all, it is getting *two* horses that meets a need for two, finding *three* gorgons that makes a search for three a success, and so on.

One option here is to introduce groups into our ontology, and allow groups of events as well as events to stand in (non-distributive) relations to events. But a simpler alternative in the present context is to treat multiple findings as constituting a single *course* of events, this latter being the success-maker for the search; to treat multiple payments as a single course of events, this latter being the discharger of the debt; and so on.[11] So while we can allow (8a) as a special case in which the course of events has a single member (we may as well identify the course with its member), plural cases make explicit use of the idea of an event being *part* of a course of events $\bar{e}$:

(9) a. Perseus seeks exactly three gorgons.
 b. **(some)λe.seeking(e) and agent(e)(perseus) and char((exactly(three))(gorgons))(e).**
 c. Perseus is agent of a search e such that □(for any $\bar{e}$ that makes e successful, for exactly three gorgons x, there is some e' which is part of $\bar{e}$ such that e' is a finding and Perseus is agent of e' and x is a theme of e').[12]

First, two minor points. For the verb 'need', the □ of (9c) is too strong if unrestricted. If Perseus needs a spear, getting an army of well-equipped spear-throwers to fight at his command would probably meet his need better than just getting a spear for himself. Various miracles would improve on that. For needs, □ is implicitly restricted to a range of worlds which are *realistic*, or the *most* realistic, given Perseus's circumstances (more on this in Section 6.5).[13]

---

[11] This is in effect a special case of the general approach to plurality developed in (Schein 1993).

[12] I am making some assumptions about the modal metaphysics of events, for instance that *de re* formulae with event-terms make sense ("Perseus's search would have ended earlier if..."), and that events' agents and sorts are essential to them.

[13] Moltmann (1997:26–7) appears to endorse a restriction to worlds where the extension of 'gorgon' is the same as it actually is. But assuming the myth to be fact, this would make it difficult to distinguish notionally seeking exactly three gorgons from notionally seeking every gorgon and from relationally seeking Euryale, Medusa and Stheno.

(9c) is supposed to be analogous to clauses like (5.7) on page 80, an analogy that would be more obvious if we had retained the letter of Goodman's modifier account of notional readings. That is, the idea is meant to be the kind of thing speakers could articulate under non-Socratic prompting, albeit with results in the style of (8b), not (9c), if asked what they meant by 'seeks three gorgons (but no particular/not necessarily particular ones)'.

(9c) makes use of two primitive concepts, that of being a *finding* and of making a search *successful*, which require further discussion. Finding a physical thing involves a perceptual relation, normally either of a visual or a tactile nature. This perceptual condition lets us stave off one type of objection to (9c) as an equivalent of (9a). The presence of an F may *guarantee* the presence of a G without a search for an F being a search for a G. But (9c) does not imply that a search for an F is a search for a G when there is such a guarantee, since merely the presence of a G along with an F does not entail that if an F is found, so is a G. This is because the G need not be *perceived* along with the F. Perhaps there are special cases where the G and the F must be perceived together, such as ones involving constitution. But there is still no counterexample to (9c), since it is not obviously wrong to say that whoever is looking for a stone statue of a discus thrower is looking for a piece of stone carved as a discus thrower.[14]

The other primitive in (9c) is that of a search being *made a success* by a finding or by some findings. Searches are successful when their agents find what they are looking for. So there is an implicit occurrence of 'looking for' in (9c), which may seem to threaten circularity.

---

[14] (9c) takes sides on whether a search e for exactly three is made a success by a course of events in which four or more are found. If four are found separately, we can always choose an $\vec{e}$ that is constituted of exactly three of the four findings; and it seems right, independently, to say that the first three findings constitute an $\vec{e}$ that makes e successful. But if two or more of the four are found simultaneously, and we agree that a simultaneous finding of two or more cannot in general be split into individual findings of each, then the $\vec{e}$ constituted by such findings will not satisfy (9c). But this is also intuitively acceptable. If the search is for *exactly* three, and four are found simultaneously, the search cannot yet be said to be successful: first, one of the four must be discarded. And if something prevents exactly one from being discarded, then the search is not a success, as far as this scenario goes (see also the discussion of 'at most' in Section 6.11).

But we are not trying to give a reductive analysis of the 'seeks' of (9a); the presence of 'search' in (9c) would already scotch that. (9c) only articulates what it is for a search to be for *this* thing or type of thing, rather than *that*.

If success involves finding, and Kaplan is right that we need an intensional sense of 'find' that involves recognition (note 1, page 53), then we have uncovered another reason to doubt weakening inferences: (i) seeking every gorgon does not entail (ii), seeking every mortal gorgon, if that requires (iii) recognizing that every gorgon has been found, to entail (iv), recognizing that every mortal gorgon has been found ('recognize' has scope over 'every' here). For it simply may not have occurred to Perseus that some gorgons are mortal.

Of course, it seems quite coherent to object to Kaplan that agents of searches can find what they are looking for without recognizing what they find *as* what they are looking for. But if Kaplan is right and the 'find' we want is intensional, this is just an ambiguity over whether or not intensional 'find' is used in a substitution-resistant way: the site of Troy may be such that Schliemann has found it, without Schliemann being in a position to assert 'Ich habe den Standort von Troja entdeckt!' However, this means we need not debate an alleged intensional sense of 'find', for at the moment we are only trying to explain substitution-permitting notional readings, so we would always use 'find' in a substitution-permitting way.[15]

5 POSSIBILITY AS CONCEIVABILITY

To be a candidate as an account of notional readings, it is crucial in (9c) that the modal operator □ have the objectual quantifier 'exactly three gorgons' within its scope. We can then claim to have explained the meaning of the notionalizing rider 'no particular one' in terms of *modal variation:* (9c) can hold, though at different worlds, different triples of gorgons can be the themes of findings in success-making courses of events. But such an account can run into trouble over

---

[15] Since the only mark of intensionality 'find' can bear is substitution-resistance – one cannot find an F but no particular F, nor can one find an F unless there are F's – it will be quite difficult to justify classifying 'find' as an intensional transitive, in view of the 'simple sentence' phenomenon discussed in Section 8.5.

cases where the modal variation is lacking, resulting in failure to distinguish a relational objectual attitude from a notional one.[16]

Compare a thirsty person, who seeks water, with an early chemist, who believes that there ought to exist in nature a substance whose chemical composition is two parts hydrogen to one part oxygen, and who is looking for such a substance. There is a specific substance the first subject is looking for – he is the agent of a search e which is for the substance water – but the second subject is not looking for any specific substance, simply for the one with a certain chemical composition. However, assuming that necessarily, a substance is water iff its chemical composition is two parts hydrogen to one part oxygen, the analogue of (9c) for 'the' or 'a' cannot distinguish these subjects, since each is agent of a search e meeting the following condition:

(10) $\Box$(for any $\bar{e}$ that makes e successful, for some/exactly one y whose chemical composition is two parts hydrogen to one part oxygen, there is some e' which is part of $\bar{e}$ such that e' is a finding and x is agent of e' and y is a theme of e').

So the thirsty subject is agent of a search that is characterized by the property of being a property of some substance whose chemical composition is two parts hydrogen to one part oxygen.[17]

This is not yet a counterexample, for we can avoid the false conclusion that there is no particular substance the thirsty subject is looking for if we insist on the non-committal construal of **char**-formulae. But it is too *ad hoc* to adopt this construal just to evade an objection. An alternative is to address the problem directly: in our current example we have unspecificity of attitude without any modal variation (because, in the standard terminology, the definite

---

[16] Though we will not pursue the issue, the role of modal variation is also manifest in the phenomenon of 'modal subordination', in which an anaphoric pronoun anchored by a notionally understood QNP is acceptable only if it occurs in an intensional context. We can have 'Perseus seeks a gorgon, but it must be mortal' but not 'Perseus seeks a gorgon, but it is mortal' if 'seeks a gorgon' is interpreted notionally. One explanation of this is that the modally subordinate 'it' is a descriptive pronoun in the sense of (Evans 1977), and 'it must be mortal' means 'necessarily, a mortal thing is theme of any finding that makes the search a success'.

[17] If we explained **for(x)(e)** (as in (6b), p. 76) in the same kind of way as (9c), then we would also have to say that the chemist is looking for a specific substance.

substance-description is *de facto* weakly rigid[18]). So we shall simply restore modal variation.

We can do this by interpreting □ as expressing quantification over *conceivable* ways for things to go, instead of metaphysically possible ones.[19] ◇p will mean 'conceivably, p' and □p will mean 'it is inconceivable that ¬p'. Conceivability can be many things, however.[20] If the metaphysically possible worlds are to be a subset of the conceivable ways for things to go, we should not say that 'conceivably, p' requires that a situation verifying p is capable of being *conceived of*, since there are no doubt many metaphysically possible situations that we cannot form conceptions of, at least if we hold human cognitive capacities fixed. The account of conceivability we will employ here is given by:

(11) ◇p iff p is logically possible and there is no evident conflict between p and what we know *a priori*.[21]

The logical possibility requirement allows us to retain our favourite modal logic, since we will not need to countenance the truth of ◇p in cases where p is logically impossible but its impossibility is hidden. Note that *logical* impossibility is all we are ruling out. For example, (11) allows for the case of a mathematician m who does not keep up with the news and seeks a counterexample to Fermat's Last Theorem, which he needs to complete the proof of a result he is trying to obtain. As this suggests, ◇ expresses agent-relative possibility. So when we apply the analysis of **char** to obtain

(12) □(for any $\bar{e}$ that makes e successful, for some y which is a counterexample to FLT, there is some e' which is part of $\bar{e}$ such that e' is a finding and m is agent of e' and y is a theme of e')

---

[18] In note 7 of Chapter 1 (page 12) we somewhat stipulatively made the term 'H_2O' a strongly rigid designator, so it is not simply an abbreviation of the description 'the substance with chemical composition...'.

[19] One model of a way for things to go is a set of propositions (Salmon 1989).

[20] Chalmers (2002:146) distinguishes 'maybe up to eight' types of conceivability. See also Yablo (1993; 2002).

[21] In Chalmers' taxonomy mentioned in the previous note, ◇, if defined by (11), expresses a "sub-sense" of *prima facie* negative primary conceivability.

the condition in parentheses has to hold of any world (logically consistent set of propositions closed under logical maximality) conceivable to the mathematician m in question, for whom there is no evident conflict between the thought m expresses with "I've found a counterexample to FLT" and what m knows *a priori*. Of course, this is still vague; for example, it does not say how much ratiocination is required before revealed conflicts can be classified as non-evident. But it is not worthwhile to try to be precise about this.

Why this notion of possibility, rather than some other? Its naturalness consists in its permitting roughly the right amount of world-to-world variation. Any use of modality in the manner of (12) will collapse some apparent differences, but that does not matter if those differences are *merely* apparent. Let W be a mathematician who grasps and accepts the proof of FLT. Then according to our account, W seeks a counterexample to FLT iff W seeks something that is simultaneously red all over and green all over. But this does not appear to be a problem, since both search ascriptions suffer from the same kind of unintelligibility *qua* ascription to W, even though, if they *were* true, the searches in question would have different governing intentions. Similar cases arise with non-psychological ITV's. For example, if x bets y an object that is simultaneously red all over and green all over, and loses, then x owes y an object that is simultaneously red all over and green all over, and so owes y an object that is simultaneously blue all over and yellow all over. This is the kind of case where one can shoulder-shruggingly allow the theory to say whatever it says.

It might be objected that desire verbs show (11) is too restrictive, resulting in analogues of (12) conflating distinct desires. Even if it is *a priori* and evident to a subject x that nothing is simultaneously red all over and green all over, isn't that compatible with x *wanting* something that is simultaneously red all over and green all over, without wanting something that is simultaneously blue all over and yellow all over? However, though the knowledge merely that there are no F's does not in general prevent people from wanting F's ('I wish we had a Star-Trek transporter'), the *inconceivability* for x of the existence of F's does call into question the intelligibility of attributing a desire for an F to x. This is consistent with allowing that if there *were* incompatibly coloured things, x would want one; we can evaluate counterfactuals with inconceivable antecedents.

Finally, it is reasonable to ask, in regard to requirement verbs, how (i) the condition of realism on the range of □ introduced after (9c) above, meshes with (ii) the current proposal that the range of □ include some worlds that are not metaphysically possible. The idea was, for example, that if your presence is suddenly required on the same day in a distant part of the country, what you need is a seat on the next flight out of town, not a Star-Trek transporter. On the other hand, if your presence is required in the next two hours, what you need is a direct supersonic connection. Only if your presence is required in, say, the next fifteen minutes, does it seem right to say that you need Star-Trek transportation. In this example there are certain relatively non-instrumental needs, involving being at a certain place within a specified amount of time; and there are various instrumental needs. The instrumental needs are for the disjunction of the least outlandish ways of meeting the (relatively) non-instrumental need. The non-instrumental need therefore imposes a rough similarity metric on worlds where it is met, and instrumental need-ascriptions are equivalent to outcome postulates in which the □ is restricted to the most similar worlds. This gives the evaluation of need-ascriptions a relativity absent in the case of desire and search verbs, but it does not appear to create any obstacles of principle to (11). We would probably want to adopt some general principles about similarity, for instance that if w and u are both metaphysically possible worlds and v is mathematically impossible, then each of w and u is more similar to the other than is u to either or vice versa (see further Nolan 1997 for this type of issue). But this still allows for the case of the ill-informed mathematician and his need for a counterexample to FLT.

We can abstract a schema from the various examples just discussed which displays a general account of what it is for an event of a given sort to be characterized by a property of properties:

(13) **(char(Q))(e)** iff □(for any $\bar{e}$ such that $R\bar{e}e$, for Q x, there is some e' that is part of $\bar{e}$ such that Fe' and x is a theme of e').

Here Q and Q are restricted to non-compound QNP's (ones formed with 'and' or 'or'). F is a schematic letter for an event-sortal and is replaced by 'finding' if e is a search, 'getting' if e is a need, 'surrendering' if e is a state of indebtedness, and so on, on a case-by-case basis. The schematic letter R is replaced by 'makes successful' if e is a search, by 'meets' if e is a need, by 'discharges' if e is a state of indebtedness and so on, on a case-by-case basis.

If the compositional semantics of objectual attitude ascriptions is presented *via* type-theoretic formulae such as (9b) on page 100, what exactly is the theoretical status of a principle like (13) governing **char**? On one view, clauses like (13) do not belong in the official semantics, any more than an account of 'two-man bobsled' as **(two-man) (bobsled)** needs extra parts with quantifiers over typical worlds. But when we come to explain the conjunctive force phenomenon that refutes (3) on page 93, some part of the theory will have to bestow conjunctive force on disjunctive QNP-complements of certain intensional transitives. So we can only give the whole semantic story for ITV's if the language in which their semantics is represented contains expressions for the concepts employed on the right-hand-sides of (9c) and (10) or that figure in the instantiations of (13).

This means we need the formal language to contain modal operators, and also such primitives as **part**$^{e(e\tau)}$, **successful**$^{e\tau}$, **meets**$^{e\tau}$, and so on (τ is b or m).[22] The most direct procedure is then to write instances of (13) as meaning-postulates, which will, of course, produce formulae of comical unreadability (the norm for meaning-postulates in type-theory). Fortunately, the formulations we have already arrived at, such as (9c) and (10), can be applied as they stand to answer our open questions about the logic of objectual attitude ascriptions. So we leave rewriting them as meaning-postulates to the enthusiast, and turn instead to the phenomenon of conjunctive force, which made us abandon the appealingly simple (3).

6 A THEORY OF CONJUNCTIVE FORCE

The presence of conjunctive force in 'or' is common across many

---

[22] For the addition of modal operators to $\mathcal{L}_m$, see (Thomason 1980:65–7). The type assignments to **successful** and **meets** are to allow, e.g., **e′ makes e successful** a subatomic semantics ('**e′** is agent, **e** theme, of a success-making'), but I will not pursue here whether applying event semantics to event-talk in the semantics is appropriate.

languages (e.g., French, German, Italian, Swedish, Finnish) and is not restricted to the complements of certain ITV's. Indeed, the ITV case has not been much noticed, though it has an interesting twist. More commonly noted cases of 'or' with conjunctive force include

(14) a. Perseus's sword is heavier than his shield or his helmet.
b. Perseus could have been a statesman or a philosopher.
c. Perseus prefers unicorns to gorgons or manticores.
d. If Perseus were to find a sword or a spear, he'd be happy.
e. Perseus is allowed to use a sword or a spear.

The conjunctive force in these cases is easily expressed by a De Morgan-style distribution. For example, the conjunctive import of (14a) is expressed by "Perseus's sword is heavier than his shield and heavier than his helmet"; that of (14b) by 'Perseus could have been a statesman and could have been a philosopher'; and that of (14d) by 'if Perseus were to find a sword he would be happy and if he were to find a spear he would be happy'. The twist in the ITV case is that no comparable distribution captures conjunctive force. For example, (5a), 'Perseus seeks a gorgon or a unicorn', does not mean 'Perseus seeks a gorgon and seeks a unicorn'. For this has him still seeking a unicorn even after he finds a satisfactory gorgon, though so far as (5a) goes, his search is over at that point. So we will need a less direct way of accounting for the examples in (5) within a general theory of conjunctive force.

One view of the cases in (14), which if applied to (5) might even allow us to rest content with (3), is that conjunctive force is not part of their *literal* meaning. Instead, the literal meaning of, at least, the modal examples, is exactly what standard modal semantics says it is. For instance, according to the Lewis-Stalnaker semantics for counterfactuals (Lewis 1973; Stalnaker 1968), (14d) entails neither that Perseus would be happy if he found a sword nor that he would be happy if he found a shield. The apparent entailment is really a matter of (generalized) conversational implicature, on the pragmatic story. When sincere speakers assert $(p \vee q) \;\square\!\!\rightarrow r$ (instead of just $p \;\square\!\!\rightarrow r$, or $q \;\square\!\!\rightarrow r$), their grounds are that $p \;\square\!\!\rightarrow r$ and $q \;\square\!\!\rightarrow r$.[23] But the audience

---

[23] An exception has to be made for the likes of 'if Perseus were to find a sword or a shield, he would find a sword'.

knows this, so $(p \,\square\!\!\rightarrow r) \wedge (q \,\square\!\!\rightarrow r)$ gets conveyed (see Loewer 1976: 529–31). And perhaps a similar argument is available for the other cases (see Kamp 1979).

It can often be hard to tell where semantic content ends and implicature begins,[24] and there may be no conclusive objection to the pragmatic view on offer here. But there are aspects of our examples which favour a semantic classification of conjunctive force. First, the counterfactual example is structurally the same as other conditionals, such as material and strict ones, where the conjunctive force is unquestionably semantic, in view of

(15) $(p \vee q) \rightarrow r \dashv\vDash (p \rightarrow r) \wedge (q \rightarrow r)$.

Second, our explanation of the effect of the riders in (7) in terms of invoking propositional answer-sets means that the riders are not implicature-cancellers. So the readings in (7) cannot be represented as the literal readings of the cases in (5), shorn of non-literal meaning they otherwise convey.

And third, there are examples involving small changes to the ones in (5) which have a large effect. We have already noticed that changing the QNP-disjunctions into VP-disjunctions in (5) eliminates conjunctive force (as in 'needs a horse or needs a donkey'). Changing (14b)'s 'could have been' to 'could become' retains conjunctive force, but substituting 'is going to be' removes it. Finally, if we put 'obliged' for 'permitted' in (14e), the result does not mean that he is obliged to use each (whether the form is $\square(p \vee q)$ or $(\square p \vee \square q)$). None of these changes in interpretation appears to be pragmatically triggered.

The undeniable advantage of the pragmatic account is that we get off lightly: if we treat conjunctive force as a *semantic* phenomenon, it looks like we acquire the obligation to revise standard modal logics to validate $\Diamond(p \vee q) \vDash \Diamond p \wedge \Diamond q$; and this is no small task (Loewer 1976:531–4; but see Dignum *et al.* 1996). However, there is an alternative semantic account of conjunctive force which explains it by assimilating the underlying forms of cases like (14) to (15)'s left-hand-side (Makinson 1984). For example, '*a* is heavier than *b* or *c*'

---

[24] There is a huge literature on the distinction. Recent work includes (Recanati 2003) and the papers in (Szabó 2005).

becomes 'for any x, if x is b or c then a is heavier than x'. By (15), this is equivalent to 'for any x, if x is b then a is heavier than x and if x is c then a is heavier than x'. So rather than create a logic which contains $\Diamond(p \lor q) \vDash \Diamond p \land \Diamond q$, we are proposing that the surface appearance of cases like those in (14) is misleading.[25] In their semantics, the disjunction moves to the front and provides values for a variable, with the overall import 'for any one$_x$ of these, ... it$_x$ ...'.[26]

Applying this general idea to the examples in (14) produces results along the following lines:

(16) a. (either x: x = Perseus's shield $\lor$ x = Perseus's helmet) [Perseus's sword is heavier than x].
   b. (either F: $F = {}^\wedge\lambda x.\text{statesman}(x) \lor F = {}^\wedge\lambda x.\text{philosopher}(x))$ [$\Diamond {}^\vee F(\text{Perseus})$].[27]
   c. (either K: K = gorgons $\lor$ K = manticores)[Perseus prefers unicorns to K].
   d. (either Q: $Q = {}^\wedge\lambda P.(\text{a}(\text{sword}))(P) \lor Q = {}^\wedge\lambda P.(\text{a}(\text{shield}))(P))$ [${}^\vee Q(\lambda x.\text{Perseus finds } x) \,\square\!\!\rightarrow \text{happy}(\text{Perseus})$].

---

[25] The idea of applying (15) in this way to the examples in (14) occurred to me before I came across Makinson's paper. Makinson focuses mainly on permission-statements, but he is clear about the wider applicability of his approach.

[26] How exactly does the 'any' universal quantifier emerge? (Rooth and Partee 1982: 359–60; Larson 1985:252–3) suggest, in connection with the example (i) 'if Mary is swimming or dancing, Sue is', that a hidden adverb of universal quantification, with the force of 'always' or 'as a general rule', is present (here they follow Heim 1983). But the conjunctive reading of (i) does not depend on reading (i) as the expression of something general: it may only be on this one occasion that Sue can be guaranteed to be doing exactly the same thing as Mary. It is also rather unclear why a generalization over, say, situations, should become a universal quantifier over properties.

[27] This and the following modal examples are in an informal version of the system of intensional$_{pw}$ type-theory in (Gamut 1991:117–25). All the modal examples have the (highly preferred) *de dicto* readings: we do not understand, say, (14b), as asserting that at some world, Perseus is a member of the set that contains all and only the statesmen of the *actual* world. To remind the reader, $[{}^\wedge\lambda x.\text{statesman}(x)]$ is a function which takes possible worlds as input and for each world w, produces (the characteristic function of) the set of statesmen of w as output. Hence F in (16b) is of intensional type, and cannot be applied to an individual such as Perseus at any world. But ${}^\vee F$ can be applied to Perseus at w, since at w it stands for the characteristic function of a set of individuals, those that are F at w.

e. (either Q: $Q = {}^{\wedge}\lambda P.(\text{a(sword)})(P)$ ∨ $Q = {}^{\wedge}\lambda P.(\text{a(spear)})(P)$)
   [it is allowed that ${}^{\vee}Q(\lambda x.\text{Perseus uses } x)$].

Here 'either' expresses a free choice between the alternatives, like free-choice 'any' for three or more options:

(17) a. Perseus could have been a statesman or a philosopher or a farmer.
   b. (any F: $F = {}^{\wedge}\lambda x.\text{statesman}(x)$ ∨ $F = {}^{\wedge}\lambda x.\text{philosopher}(x)$ ∨ $F = {}^{\wedge}\lambda x.\text{farmer}(x)$)[◇${}^{\vee}F(\text{Perseus})$].

It would be an extraordinary coincidence if the formulae in (16) and (17) were unreflective of the semantics of the English, since the same pattern captures conjunctive force in the full range of cases. It is not surprising that the disjunction is at the top, for a disjunction of NP's such as 'a statesman or a philosopher' should be able to move much like a non-compound quantified NP. One reading of the result of such movement is implicitly partitive, as in 'any of a statesman, a philosopher, or a farmer, is something Perseus could have been', which exactly captures the conjunctive force reading of (17a).[28]

Jennings (1994:167) complains that the sort of approach illustrated in (16) trades one mystery for another: we have an account of conjunctive force where it exists, but not of why it exists. It seems that in our contrasting pair (18a) and (18b),

(18) a. Perseus {is going to/will} capture Euryale or Stheno.
    b. Perseus could capture Euryale or Stheno.

there must be some property of the contexts which blocks a distributive reading of (18a) while allowing or requiring it for (18b). However, while it is a *good* question what this property is, it is not *our* question. The most pressing question for us is how, exactly, the explanation of conjunctive force we have given for the examples in (14) is to be applied to the ones in (5).[29]

---

[28] This explanation may seem to run into trouble with the phenomenon noted by Zimmerman (2000:258–9), that conjunctive force can be retained even when 'or' has widest scope, as in 'Perseus may use a sword or he may use a spear' ('may' of permission). However, the conjunctive reading vanishes if 'may' is replaced by 'is permitted to'. It appears that modal auxiliaries are special, allowing 'either of the propositions, *that...may/can/could...*, or *that...may/can/could...*, is true'.

7 CHARACTERIZATION BY COMPOUND QNP'S

The type-theoretic semantics of the examples in (5) are not themselves hard to state. We take (5a), here (19a), as illustrative:

(19) a. Perseus seeks a gorgon or a unicorn.
b. **(some)λe.seeking(e) and agent(e)(perseus) and char(a(gorgon) or a(unicorn))(e)**.[30]
c. Perseus seeks a gorgon or seeks a unicorn.
d. **λx.{[(some)λe.seeking(e) and agent(e)(x) and char(a(gorgon))(e)] or [(some)λe.seeking(e) and agent(e)(x) and char(a(unicorn))(e)]}(perseus)**.

(19b) is the default reading of (19a), and embodies the hypothesis that conjunctive force arises from a configuration in which **or** is within the scope of **char**. (19c) is an ∨-distributive reading of (19a) such as is prompted by a rider like 'we are not sure which'. (19d) is the semantics of (19c); its disjunction expresses 'x is the agent of a search for a gorgon or agent of a search for a unicorn'; this could be reduced to 'x is the agent of a search for a gorgon or for a unicorn', in which the disjunction would simply be **char(a(gorgon))(e)) or char(a(unicorn))(e)**. Comparing this with the disjunction in (19b), we see that (20a) does not entail (20b):

(20) a. **(char(Q))(e) or (char(Q'))(e)**.
b. **(char(Q or Q'))(e)**.

since the (19d)-reading is a consequence of 'Perseus seeks a gorgon' while the (19b)-reading is not. But whether (20b) entails (20a) is more involved, and requires that we settle on outcome postulates like (13) for QNP's formed with **and** or **or**.

---

[29] Say that a propositional context C (such as 'it is not the case that') is *downward entailing* (DE) iff $C(p)$ and $q \vDash p$ entail $C(q)$. It might be suggested that 'or' has a special 'negative polarity' sense in DE contexts, and this accounts for the behaviour seen in (5) and (14). But besides positing equivocation in the various De Morgan laws, this view faces the problem that in (14b), 'Perseus could have been...', ◊ is not DE.

[30] **or** forms a compound quantifier in this example, so it is of type $\alpha(\alpha\alpha)$ where $\alpha = (ib)b$. Its semantics is, in official prefix notation, **(or(Q'))(Q)** = $\lambda P.$**(or(Q'(P)))(Q(P))**, in which the second **or** is of type $b(bb)$, i.e., it is the standard truth-functor.

Conjunctive QNP's are straightforward:

(21) **(char(Q and Q'))(e)** iff $\Box$(for any $\bar{e}$ such that $R\bar{e}e$, for Q x, there is some e' which is part of $\bar{e}$ such that Fe' and x is a theme of e', and for Q' y, there is some e'' which is part of $\bar{e}$ such that Fe'' and y is a theme of e'').

So a search for every gorgon and two unicorns is something which cannot be made successful except by a course of events in which every gorgon is found and two unicorns are found.

However, the clause for disjunctive QNP's must have a component with no counterpart in (13) and (21). For in articulating the conjunctive force of (19a), 'Perseus seeks a gorgon or a unicorn', we said it has the partial content that making the search a success can be effected by finding a gorgon *and* can be effected by finding a unicorn. On the other hand, if this were the whole story, we would be unable to distinguish 'Perseus seeks a gorgon or a unicorn' from 'Perseus seeks a gorgon *and* seeks a unicorn': for if the former means that he is the agent of a search that finding a gorgon can make successful and finding a unicorn can make successful, then by distributing the event quantifier through, he is the agent of a search that finding a gorgon can make successful and of a search that finding a unicorn can make successful, which, by (21), verifies 'Perseus seeks a gorgon and seeks a unicorn'. It seems that for **(char(Q or Q'))(e)**, we need the special content that contributes the conjunctive force, but also a necessary condition in the style of (13) and (21): a search for a gorgon or a unicorn cannot be made successful by a finding unless that finding is of a gorgon *or* a unicorn ((21) has it that a search for a gorgon and a unicorn, or two searches, one for each, cannot be made successful except by findings of a gorgon *and* a unicorn).

To capture conjunctive force, we use the ideas in Section 6.6. A search for every gorgon *or* two unicorns is one that can be made successful either by *a course of events which has a finding of each gorgon as a part* (not necessarily different findings for different gorgons) or by *a course of events which has findings of two unicorns as parts*; and which cannot be made successful except in one or other of these ways. The requirement that the search *can* be made successful in one or other way is comparable to example (14b), whose conjunctive force is accounted for in (16b), repeated here as (22a,b):

(22) a. Perseus could have been a statesman or a philosopher;
b. (either $F: F = {}^\wedge \lambda x.\text{statesman}(x) \vee F = {}^\wedge \lambda x.\text{philosopher}(x))$ $[\diamond {}^\vee F(\text{Perseus})]$.

The full story for (19a), following (22b), is therefore:

(23) a. Perseus seeks a gorgon or a unicorn.
b. **(some)λe.seeking(e) and agent(e)(perseus) and char(a(gorgon) or a(unicorn))(e).**
c. for some seeking e such that Perseus is agent of e:
   (i) (either $G: G = {}^\wedge \lambda \vec{e}_0.$for some gorgon x, there is some e' which is part of $\vec{e}_0$ such that e' is a finding and Perseus is agent of e' and x is a theme of e', or $G = {}^\wedge \lambda \vec{e}_0.$for some unicorn y, there is some e' which is part of $\vec{e}_0$ such that e' is a finding and Perseus is agent of e' and y is a theme of e') $[\diamond(\text{for some } \vec{e} \text{ such that } {}^\vee G\vec{e}, \vec{e} \text{ makes } e \text{ successful})]$;
   and (ii) □(for any $\vec{e}$ such that $\vec{e}$ makes e successful, either for some gorgon x, there is some e' which is part of $\vec{e}$ such that e' is a finding and Perseus is agent of e' and x is a theme of e', or for some unicorn y, there is some e' which is part of $\vec{e}$ such that e' is a finding and Perseus is agent of e' and y is a theme of e').

Conjunctive force derives from part (i) of (23c), which says that for either of a certain pair of properties of courses of events, a course of events with that property can make e a success.[31] The first property is that of being a course of events with a part that is a finding of a gorgon by Perseus. The second property is that of being a course of events with a part that is a finding of a unicorn by Perseus. Notice that this does *not* say that finding a gorgon is sufficient for success, and finding a unicorn is sufficient for success; because of the ◇, we are only saying that *in some circumstances*, such findings are sufficient. Part (ii) of (23c) then imposes the necessary condition that distinguishes seeking a gorgon *or* a unicorn from seeking a gorgon *and* a unicorn.

The principle that we can extract from (23c) is

---

[31] As observed in n. 9 (p. 97), the disjunction problem arises in other categories. However, the approach of (24) is adaptable to such cases.

(24) **(char(Q or Q'))(e)** iff (i) (either $G: G = {}^\wedge\lambda\bar{e}_0$.for Q x, there is some e' which is part of $\bar{e}_0$ such that Fe' and x is a theme of e', or $G = {}^\wedge\lambda\bar{e}_0$.for Q' x, there is some e' which is part of $\bar{e}_0$ such that Fe' and x is a theme of e')[$\diamond$(for some $\bar{e}$ such that $^\vee G\bar{e}, R\bar{e}e$)]; and (ii) □(for any $\bar{e}$ such that $R\bar{e}e$, either for Q x, there is some e' which is part of $\bar{e}$ such that Fe' and x is a theme of e', or for Q' y, there is some e'' which is part of $\bar{e}$ such that Fe'' and y is a theme of e'').

(24) has two parts while (13) and (21) only have one, corresponding to part (ii) of (24). A more uniform alternative is to give (13) and (21) $\diamond$-clauses as well, so that (13), for example, would have a part (i) that says that there could be a course of events that makes the search successful in which there is a finding with a theme of a certain sort. However, there appears to be no reason why such uniformity is required, so we will not give this hostage to fortune. The disjunctive case is *sui generis*.

(24) settles our earlier question about whether (20b) entails (20a) and therefore whether (19b) entails (19d). Part (ii) of (24) blocks the inference: the conjunctive-force reading (19b) requires that at any world where the search is a success, it succeeds either by finding a gorgon or by finding a unicorn. But the disjunctive reading corresponds to a disjunction of (13)-style conditions: either, at every world, success is achieved by finding a gorgon, or, at every world, success is achieved by finding a unicorn. So in general, a conjunctive-force reading with **(char(Q or Q'))(e)** in its semantics does not entail the corresponding disjunctive reading with **(char(Q))(e)** or **(char(Q'))(e)** in its semantics.

And and **or** can be iterated, which occasions some complications in the story we have told so far. For example, we cannot apply (24) to the semantics of

(25) Perseus seeks a gorgon or a unicorn or a manticore

if we want the natural conjunctive-force reading according to which finding any one of the three can end his search in success. Applying (24) requires choice of one 'or' in the compound QNP as main connective, and this fails to produce the conjunctive-force reading. For example, from **char([a(gorgon) or a(unicorn)] or a(manticore))(e)**, (24) determines a meaning for (25) that makes (25) a consequence of 'Perseus seeks a gorgon or a manticore'. (24) must therefore be generalized to a schema with condition (i) on the right having the form (any $G: G = {}^\wedge\lambda e_0 \ldots Q_1 \ldots$ or ... or $G = {}^\wedge\lambda e_0 \ldots Q_n \ldots)[\diamond \ldots G \ldots]$.

This still derives the associated outcome condition directly from the semantic representation. But when an 'or' falls within the scope of an 'and', a preliminary transformation is required. For example, the conjunctive-force reading of

(26) Perseus needs a sword or a spear, and a shield

is not a consequence of 'Perseus needs a sword and a shield', but would be if we applied (21) directly to **char([a(sword) or a(spear)] and a(shield))(e)**. This suggests that outcome postulates should only be applied to arguments to **char** that are in a *normal form* consisting in alternations of conjunctions ('either a sword and a shield, or a spear and a shield' for (26)). So (21) ends up being applicable only to compound QNP's with no connective except **and**. Note, however, that we are not proposing any changes to the *semantics* of the likes of (25) and (26): the complications arise in deriving the right outcome condition for a given semantic representation.

Our approach explains what it is for an event to be characterized by a property of properties, in terms of outcomes. Earlier, we mentioned an alternative type of account of the conjunctive force of examples like (5a). According to this alternative, conjunctive force is traced to the contents of governing intentions. For instance, to seek a gorgon or a unicorn is to be the agent of a search governed by the intention *to find a gorgon or a unicorn*. 'Perseus intends to find a gorgon or a unicorn' has conjunctive force, and so contrasts with 'Perseus intends to find a gorgon or intends to find a unicorn'. But the conjunctive force cannot be articulated by distribution: to intend to find a gorgon or a unicorn is not to intend to find a gorgon and (to find) a unicorn, nor is it to intend to find a gorgon and intend to find a unicorn. We would have to explain the conjunctive force by *fulfilment* conditions: roughly, to intend to find a gorgon or a unicorn is to have an intention that can be fulfilled by finding a gorgon and can be fulfilled by finding a unicorn (and cannot be fulfilled without finding one or the other). This would then have to be complicated to handle the full range of QNP's. So we would end up with something similar to (24) but with one extra step on the route, the introduction of intentions. This makes the approach of (13), (21) and (24) more appealing, especially as it is not clear how to generalize governing intentions to the other cases in (5).[32]

8 COMPOUND COMPLEMENTS WITH SINGULAR TERMS

We can still use (21) and (24) in cases where the complement of the ITV is a co-ordination of two NP's at least one of which is of type i. For example, there is conjunctive force in both of

(27) a. Perseus seeks Medusa or Stheno.
b. Perseus seeks Medusa or an immortal gorgon.

According to (27a), there is a way of making his search successful that involves finding Medusa and a way that involves finding Stheno; according to (27b), there is a way that involves finding Medusa and a way that involves finding an immortal gorgon. The conjunctive force in (27a) lends it an element of notional meaning that a pure disjunctive reading lacks, in that we can coherently append 'but no particular one of the two' to (27a).

As for the semantics, generalized co-ordination requires that the co-ordinated expressions be of the same type, and we assume that the lowest possible type is preferred. So (27b) indicates that the type of a name can be raised to that of an individual quantifier – in $\mathcal{L}_x$, $(ib)b$. For a name such as 'Medusa', the corresponding quantifier is **λP.P(medusa)**, which is a function of type $(ib)b$. For any property of type ib assigned to **P**, this function outputs the truth-value of the sentence **P(medusa)** under that assignment. That is, **λP.P(medusa)** maps a property to ⊤ iff that property is a property of Medusa (recall the discussion of (16) on page 27).

We take the same line with (27a), since a disjunction of expres-

---

[32] Propositionalism is in the same boat. Explaining the conjunctive force of 'trying/searching to find a gorgon or a unicorn' will lead the propositionalist to a version of (24). And there will be the same problem of explaining why some propositional entailments persist in the scope of ITV's, e.g., (2), while others do not, e.g., (6a) and (6b) (page 97).

sions of type i is uninterpretable without more apparatus. So the semantics of 'Medusa or Stheno' is $\lambda P.P(\text{medusa})$ or $\lambda P.P(\text{stheno})$. This disjunction is a function of type $(ib)b$ that maps an input to ⊤ iff the input is a property of at least one of Medusa or Stheno. And since we do not want to make a property of properties into a *theme* of a seeking, the full semantics for (27a) employs **char** (this explains why (27a) has a notional meaning):

(28) (some)λe.seeking(e) and agent(e)(perseus) and char(λP.P(medusa) or λP.P(stheno))(e).

If we express the right-hand side of (24) type-theoretically, applying its part (i) tells us that whether **G** is (29a) or (29b), we have (29c):

(29) a. $^\wedge\lambda e_0$.finding(e_0) and λP.P(medusa)(λx.theme(e_0)(x)).
 b. $^\wedge\lambda e_0$.finding(e_0) and λP.P(stheno)(λx.theme(e_0)(x)).
 c. ◊(some)$\lambda e'$.$^\vee$G(e') and e' makes e successful.

If **G** is (29a), applying (29c) and standard simplifications produces

(30) ◊(some)$\lambda e'$.finding(e') and theme(e')(medusa) and e' makes e successful.

(30) is exactly what we mean by 'there is a way of making *e* successful that involves finding Medusa'. Instantiating (29c) with (29b) gets us 'there is a way of making *e* successful that involves finding Stheno'; and part (ii) of (24) will deliver the correct necessary condition, that any way of making *e* successful involves finding Medusa or Stheno.

9 APPLYING THE POSTULATES

(13) settles the status of the weakening inferences in (4) on page 94: they are all valid. If Perseus is agent of a search *e* for a mortal gorgon, then (13) implies that in any world u, if *e* is successful in u, it is made successful by a finding of a mortal gorgon. Since every finding of a mortal gorgon is a finding of a gorgon, (13) implies that in any world u, if *e* is successful in u, *e* is made successful by a finding of a gorgon in u. So using (13) right-to-left, we can conclude that Perseus is searching for a gorgon. Similar reasoning establishes the validity of

(4b) and (4c). And in the same way, (21) makes (2) valid.
This leaves us with the problem of (6), repeated here:

(31) a. Perseus seeks a gorgon.
  b. Perseus seeks a mortal gorgon or an immortal gorgon.

(31a) does not entail (31b), and (13) and (24) correctly allow for (31a) to be true while (31b) is false (but, also correctly, not the converse). Yet in $\mathcal{L}_x$, 'a gorgon' and 'a mortal gorgon or an immortal gorgon' are the very same quantifier. So in $\mathcal{L}_x$, it is unacceptable to stipulate meaning-postulates that distinguish (31a) from (31b). From this we should conclude that the semantics of (31a) and (31b), as well as the meaning-postulates to be obtained from (13) and (24), cannot be correctly formulated in $\mathcal{L}_x$ (or in intensional$_{pw}$ type-theory, since the quantifiers are intensionally$_{pw}$ the same as well).

The case of (31) is one of the main motivations for use of $\mathcal{L}_m$, since, interpreted in $\mathcal{L}_m$, there is no reason to think that 'a gorgon' and 'a mortal gorgon or an immortal gorgon' will be the same quantifier, that is, the same function from inputs of type im to outputs of type m. This is so even if the outputs obtained from each for the same input are necessarily equivalent. The question is whether, for example, the propositions *a gorgon sleeps* and *a mortal gorgon or an immortal gorgon sleeps* are literally identical. Certainly, they are the same proposition$_{pw}$, but that is just a reflection of the limitations of intensional$_{pw}$ type-theory that we already saw (note 14, page 50) in connection with the difference between trying to avoid a war with France versus trying to avoid a nuclear or non-nuclear war with France. On a structured conception of proposition (see, e.g., King 1996), the equivalent propositions are not identical, since properties like *mortal* and *immortal* or *nuclear* and *non-nuclear* figure in only one of the pair. If we think of semantic values of type m as *states of affairs* instead of propositions, constituents of the world rather than representations of such constituents, nothing changes: properties figure in one state that are missing in the other, so the states cannot be identified.

The solution to the problem of (31), therefore, is to make $\mathcal{L}_m$ the official language of semantic representations (though we can still use $\mathcal{L}_x$ where the difference is immaterial). The $\mathcal{L}_m$-meaning of **char** may map ⟦Q⟧ to one function of type $(em)m$ while it maps ⟦Q' or Q''⟧ to a different function of this type, even though, at any world w, the set of which ⟦Q⟧'s extension at w is the characteristic function is the union of the counterpart sets for ⟦Q'⟧ and ⟦Q''⟧ (the conditions on **char** will take care of the inference from (31b) to (31a)). Using $\mathcal{L}_m$ also has the desirable side-effect of handling more familiar intensionality issues, and, along with definition by cases, allows us to dispense with the schematic nature of (13), (21) and (24) entirely.

We are still not done with weakening inferences, which occupy a central position in our discussion because of their controversial nature. But it is worth assessing (13), (21) and (24) against other types of inference.

The following example extrapolates an attitude fallaciously:

(32) x seeks an F; x does not seek a G; ∴ x seeks an F which is not G.[33]

Intuitively, this is invalid. Suppose Perseus merely wishes to observe gorgons. So he seeks a gorgon, but does not seek a mortal gorgon (he doesn't care which type of gorgon he observes). (32) would allow us to infer that he seeks an immortal gorgon, yet he is really indifferent. (13) explains why the conclusion is false: it is not necessary for the success of his search that he find an *immortal* gorgon.

Suppose we change the second premise of (32):

(33) x seeks an F; □(no F is (a) G); ∴ x seeks an F which isn't (a) G.

The first premise makes it necessary for success that x find an F, so if it is *necessary* that no F is G, success occurs only if an F that is not G is found. Assuming the search *could* be made successful this way, (13) implies the validity of (33). But it might be objected to this result that the first premise may be true because x seeks an F which *is* a G. Recall our mathematician who does not keep up with the news and seeks a counterexample to Fermat's Last Theorem because he needs one for the result he is trying to obtain: how could finding, or getting, a number that is *not* a counterexample, make his search successful and meet his need?

---

[33] Johan van Benthem asked me how this type of case fares in my approach.

The problem here is that □ in (33) is being construed as metaphysical necessity, whereas our preferred reading of □ is as a universal quantifier over worlds which permit anything conceivable consistent with logical possibility. For the ill-informed mathematician of the previous paragraph, a counterexample to Fermat's Last Theorem is perfectly conceivable. Therefore the second premise is false in his case. If it *is* inconceivable for an agent that an *F* is *G*, then the conclusion that the agent seeks an *F* which isn't *G* is acceptable.

Finally, we consider a "mixed" inference, where some premises are (perforce) relational, and others notional:

(34) Perseus needs a mirrored shield. Perseus will get everything he needs. ∴ Perseus will get a mirrored shield.

Mixing a notional understanding of the first premise with the inevitable relational reading of the second (take it to mean that he *will* get everything he *now* needs), (34) seems valid, and not obviously more complex than its all-relational reading. We can explain this because of the form we attribute to the second premise:

(35) **(every)**λ$\mathcal{Q}$.
if((some)λe.need(e) and subject(e)(per) and char($\mathcal{Q}$)(e)) then
(some)λe.getting(e) and agent(e)(per) and $\mathcal{Q}$λx.theme(e)(x)

which in higher-orderese says that every property of properties characterizing a need of Perseus's is a property of the property of being a theme of a getting by Perseus. The argument therefore consists in two simple steps: first, instantiate $\mathcal{Q}$ with **a(mirrored(shield))**, then apply *modus ponens* using (34)'s first premise.

10 THE SERENDIPITY PROBLEM

Bracketing issues about the analysis of the modalities expressed in (13), (21) and (24), one appealing feature of these clauses is that they explain the relatively problematic concept of characterization in terms of relatively less problematic concepts: concepts for familiar thematic relations, and for events such as findings and gettings. Understanding of an area of discourse is improved by such an analysis. But there are cases which threaten to show that the theory of characterization needs more, perhaps less transparent, resources.

Suppose that Richard III seeks a horse, but a war horse, not a cart horse. In the circumstances at Bosworth, finding Charger would make his search a success. Suppose also that Charger is a conscript: in civilian life, Charger is Nag, a hard-working cart horse. It follows that Richard III's search could be made a success by finding a war horse (Charger) *and* could be made a success by finding a cart horse (Charger). And since 'Richard III seeks a war horse', by (13), implies that his search cannot be successful unless he finds a war horse, it follows that his search cannot be successful unless he finds a war horse or a cart horse. So by (24), we have established

(36) Richard III seeks a war horse or a cart horse

contradicting the conditions of the example. The problem can obviously be duplicated for 'Richard III wants a war horse' or 'Richard III owes me a war horse'.

Even though a course of events $\bar{e}$ in which Richard III finds a cart horse can make his search e a success (because the cart horse is a war horse) the fact that he finds a cart horse is *irrelevant* to $\bar{e}$'s making e a success. So one way round our difficulty would be to add constraints formulated in terms of relevance. It would be unfortunate if this introduced a new primitive into the account,[34] but we can think of it instead as shorthand for a *modal* filter that excludes the problem cases: the idea is to exploit the fact that a finding can make Richard III's search a success whether or not any of its themes is a cart horse, while it is not the case that a finding can make his search a success whether or not any of its themes is a war horse. Apart from a division of cases, the formulation is straightforward.

Say that two QNP's in $D^{\mathcal{M}}_{(ib)b}$ are *independent* iff, taking each as a set of sets, neither is a subset of the other. We distinguish the dependent case from the independent case. In the dependent case, the truth of a search ascription with the contained QNP implies the truth of the disjunction of the two quantifiers. For example, if Richard III seeks a

---

[34] This problem case is from (Forbes 2003), where, unfortunately, I introduced new primitives to handle it. In an earlier draft of this chapter, (36) had 'needs' in place of 'seeks', but I am now unsure that requirement verbs should be subject to the filter developed in this section.

war horse, then he seeks a war horse or a horse; if Perseus seeks every gorgon, then he seeks every gorgon or every mortal gorgon. These are acceptable inferences, since their oddity is surely pragmatic.

The modal filter comes into play for independent cases, such as (36). We say that (36) is true iff (a) ◇(some course of events $\vec{e}$ makes the search successful, $\vec{e}$ has a finding of a war horse as a part, and $\vec{e}$ does not have a finding of a cart horse as a part); and (b) ◇(some course of events $\vec{e}$ makes the search successful, $\vec{e}$ has a finding of a cart horse as a part, and $\vec{e}$ does not have a finding of a war horse as a part). (36) is false because (b) fails: finding a cart horse that is not a war horse does Richard III no good. Similarly, though the gorgons are a superset of the daughters of Phorcys and Ceto, Perseus can seek every gorgon without seeking every gorgon or every daughter of Phorcys and Ceto. This is because no $\vec{e}$ makes his search for every gorgon successful if $\vec{e}$ includes a finding of each daughter of Phorcys and Ceto, but does *not* include a finding of each gorgon.

So the two disjuncts communicate with each other (with the obvious generalization to more than two). A generalization for the case of independent Q and Q' can be obtained with a minor change to (24), as italicized:

(37) **(char(Q or Q'))(e)** iff (i) (either G: $G = {}^{\wedge}\lambda\vec{e}_0$.for Q x *but not for Q' x, there is some e' which is part of $\vec{e}_0$ such that Fe' and x is a theme of e'*, or $G = {}^{\wedge}\lambda\vec{e}_0$.for Q' x *but not for Q x, there is some e' which is part of $\vec{e}_0$ such that Fe' and x is a theme of e'*)[◇(for some $\vec{e}$ such that ${}^{\vee}G\vec{e}$, $R\vec{e}e$)]; and (ii) □(for any $\vec{e}$ such that $R\vec{e}e$, either for Q x, there is some e' which is part of $\vec{e}$ such that Fe' and x is a theme of e', or for Q' y, there is some e'' which is part of $\vec{e}$ such that Fe'' and y is a theme of e'').

Suppose it is essential to Charger to have been sired by Prancer. Then if ◇ expresses metaphysical possibility, we must either say that, in view of (37), no-one seeks Charger unless they seek Charger or a horse sired by Prancer, or else that the case does not fall under (37). Since someone *could* seek Charger or a horse sired by Prancer, either ◇ is not metaphysical possibility here, or 'Charger' (type-raised) and 'a horse sired by Prancer' are not independent. Here it seems best to appeal to the notion of conceivability that was introduced precisely to deal with cases which made trouble for our account of **char** because world-to-world variation is missing among metaphysically possible worlds. If we admit worlds not evidently in conflict with what we know *a priori*, there *are* not-sired-by-Prancer worlds where finding Charger makes Richard III's search a success. This allows the appropriate instance of (37) to come out true where it needs to.

11 NEGATIVE QUANTIFIERS

A determiner DET is *left-upwards entailing* ($\uparrow^L$) iff DET A (IS) C and A ⊆ B entail DET B (IS) C. The determiners 'at least n' are the paradigms of $\uparrow^L$ determiners ('at least three gorgons live in Crete, all gorgons are monsters, therefore at least three monsters live in Crete'). Similarly, DET is *right-upwards entailing* ($\uparrow^R$) iff DET A (IS) B and B ⊆ C entail DET A (IS) C. In addition to 'at least _', 'every' is a paradigm $\uparrow^R$ determiner. Since 'at least one' is upwards entailing on both sides, we write '⇈' as shorthand for its properties.

DET is *left-downwards entailing* ($\downarrow^L$) iff DET A (IS) C and B ⊆ A entail DET B (IS) C. 'Every' is the paradigm $\downarrow^L$ determiner, so 'every' is ⇃↾. An example of the converse, a ↿⇂ determiner, is 'only', if it is a determiner at all (see Larson and Segal 1995:301).

Finally, DET is said to be *right-downwards entailing* ($\downarrow^R$) iff DET A (IS) B and C ⊆ B entail DET A (IS) C. The determiners 'at most n', including 'no' ('at most zero'), are the paradigm R↓ determiners. Since they are also L↓, they are ⇊. A ⇊ determiner is called *negative* and a QNP whose determiner is ⇊ is called a *negative quantifier*.[35]

The reader already familiar with this classification of determiners has probably noticed that none of the examples of notional readings whose semantics we have given has involved a negative quantifier. There is a reason for this. Following the standard pattern, we would give the semantics (38b) for the notional reading of (38a):

(38) a. Perseus seeks no unicorn.
  b. **(some)λe.seeking(e) and agent(e)(perseus) and char(no(unicorn))(e)**

---

[35] Not every determiner falls into one of these four groups. For example, the determiners 'exactly n' are neither $\uparrow^L$ nor $\downarrow^L$ and neither $\uparrow^R$ nor $\downarrow^R$.

But (38b) represents (38a) as saying that Perseus is agent of a search; whereas it seems (38a) would be true if Perseus is in his armchair at home (this is certainly so for the relational reading). According to (38b), 'Perseus seeks no unicorn, in fact he does not seek anything at all' is a notional contradiction.

Perhaps (38b) misrepresents (38a) because ⟦no⟧ is a fusion of two semantic components, a negation operator NEG and an existential determiner ONE. In deriving a type-theoretic semantics for (38a), the story would go, NEG should be introduced in a higher position so that it has the 'seeks'-VP in its scope. This results in an interpretation for (38a) that makes it synonymous with 'Perseus does not seek a unicorn', interpreting ONE as 'at least one'. The resulting semantics would simply be the wide-scope negation of the semantics of 'Perseus seeks a unicorn', which ensures that (38a) is true if Perseus is merely sitting in his armchair.

If this is the *whole* story, the higher positioning of NEG must be obligatory. But there is a sense in which findings or gettings of *absences* can make searches successful, or meet needs, or satisfy desires. Decomposition plus higher-positioning of NEG seems wrong for the following cases:

(39) a. The admissions committee is looking for no grade less than B.
 b. The applicants need no grade less than B.
 c. The referee wants no biting.

Thinking of a committee member scanning a single transcript, it is quite hard to hear the reading of (39a) in which NEG has a higher position. The higher-position readings are easier to hear in (39b) and (39c), but lower-position NEG is still more natural. In (39c), for instance, we would normally take it that the referee has a positive preference that the contestants not bite each other, which is not asserted by "the referee doesn't want any biting", this latter being consistent with the referee's not caring either way.[36] Note that the preferred reading does not entail the wide-scope reading in this case, since the referee may have inconsistent attitudes.

---

[36] Strictly-speaking-consistent, that is. For whatever reason, "the referee doesn't want any biting" is often understood as (39c); see further (Horn 2001:308–30).

To the propositionalist who accepts the NEG+ONE account of 'no', the ambiguities in the cases in (39) are unsurprising. Propositionalism allows for two different higher positions at which NEG might be interpreted: with scope over the embedded verb but not the main verb ('wants not to have any biting') or with scope over both verbs ('does not want to have any biting'). But if propositionalism is incorrect for search verbs, as Chapter 4 argued, (39a) suggests that NEG can be interpreted *in situ*. Presumably this could also be true for the preferred readings of (39b) and (39c), so the ambiguities of these cases provide no differential support for propositionalism.

For our own approach, it is important that we do not imply that the *occurrence* of a finding is required for the search for no grade less than B to be a success, or the *occurrence* of a getting for the desire for no biting to be satisfied. Certainly, we would naturally say that the Committee's search for no grade less than B in a particular transcript is a success if, in the usual sort of circumstances, it finds no grade less than B. But there is no difference between *finding no* grade less than B and *not finding* a grade less than B. To find no grade less than B is not to *be* the agent of a finding of some sort; it is *not* to be the agent of a finding of some sort. Hence, there is no requirement that a finding must occur. Similarly, getting no biting is just *not getting any biting*, so does not necessarily involve the occurrence of a getting. That is, with extensional verbs v, readings of v+QNP with 'no'-QNP are all derived with NEG in higher position.

Our clauses (13) and (21) are compatible with this. The explanation that (13) (page 106) implies for **char(no(F))(e)** is that in any course of events $\bar{e}$ that makes a success of e, *for no F* is there a finding of that F in $\bar{e}$. Where e is the admissions committee's search for no grade less than B, this is exactly right. For the same reason, (21) has exactly the lack of commitment to findings that is required. Thus, our clauses apply straightforwardly to QNP's with ⇓ determiners falling under them. Perhaps that is some confirmation of them.

According to Richard (2001:115), QNP's with ⇓ determiners raise another problem, namely, one of *relevance*.[37] In the course of his search for a gorgon, Perseus may find something irrelevant to his

---

[37] In (Forbes 2003) I used a similar notion of relevance for what I have here called the serendipity problem and analysed instead as a modal filter.

goals, say, a unicorn. And if a gorgon is all he is searching for, (38a), 'Perseus seeks no unicorn', should be true. But on our account and the first iteration of Richard's, it would not be, since, in the case of our account, a finding of a gorgon that makes the search successful may also be a finding, simultaneously, of a unicorn. So it is false that no unicorn is a theme of the finding. Therefore, Richard suggests, to make 'Perseus seeks no unicorn' come out true in this case, we should require instead that no unicorn is a theme whose being a theme *explains why* the finding makes the search a success.

This will lead to some complications it might be better to avoid. Fortunately, we have discerned an ambiguity in (38a), between a reading with higher NEG that says Perseus does not seek a unicorn, and a reading with lower NEG to be construed along the same lines as the preferred readings of the cases in (39). If Perseus is looking for a gorgon, but has no objection to stumbling across a unicorn (especially if it is accompanied by a gorgon), then the appropriate reading of (38a) is with higher NEG: 'seeks no unicorn' means 'does not seek a unicorn'. And this reading is true in the imagined circumstances, without any appeal to explanatory relevance, since Perseus is not the agent of a search that is successful only if a unicorn is found.

A reading with lower NEG, by analogy with the cases in (39), should imply that finding a unicorn ends the search in failure. Finding a unicorn should defeat the search in the same way as finding a grade less than B on a candidate's transcript defeats the search for no grade less than B: the search of the transcript is abandoned, the applicant rejected. Since Perseus has no strong objection to stumbling across a unicorn, it is presumably false that he seeks no unicorn in this strong sense of being the agent of a search characterized by the property of being a property of no unicorn, a search that ends in failure if a unicorn is found. Hence no counterexample to (13) as it stands arises, and so the example does not establish the need for an appeal to explanatory relevance.

The claim of ambiguity in (38a) that we are relying on here might be challenged. Richard has an argument that, at least with some determiners, higher-NEG readings are problematic. Given what we have said about 'no', we should expect two readings for 'Perseus seeks *at most two* gorgons' (he believes that three is more than he can handle). These readings would be generated by the hypothesis that 'at most' is a composite of NEG and an operator MORE THAN. Interpreting NEG in higher position would then produce 'Perseus doesn't seek more than two gorgons', which, as with (38a) and no matter what it conveys, is clearly true if he is sitting in his armchair. But the 'Literary Example' (Richard 2001:113–14) argues that this is not (ever?) an available reading of 'Perseus seeks at most two gorgons'. The example is as follows:

(40) a. Odile seeks a man who has read Proust and a man who has read Gide, but is indifferent between finding one man who has read both versus two men who have each read a different one.
b. Odile seeks more than one man.
c. Odile seeks at most one man.
d. Odile does not seek more than one man.

Since Odile is indifferent between finding one man and finding two, both (40b) and (40c) are false.[38] But (40d) is the interpretation of (40c) with higher NEG. So (40d) and (40c) must have the same truth-value. Since (40b) and (40c) are false, this means (40b) and (40d) are false. But (40b) and (40d) cannot both be false.

Clearly, the example shows that 'at most' is not *always* interpreted by decomposing its meaning into NEG and MORE THAN and deriving the meaning of the encompassing VP by introducing NEG above the main verb. And perhaps that is all that Richard intended – to show conclusively that another reading exists. For the non-propositionalist, this will be a reading in which NEG is interpreted *in situ*, giving 'at most' the same meaning as 'no more than', while for the propositionalist, it could be a reading in which NEG is interpreted in the embedded clause above the covert verb, giving 'seeks to find at most'

---

[38] Richard says, surely correctly, that it is a condition of adequacy of any account of intensional transitives that it allow cases of this sort, where 'seeks at least $n + 1$' and 'seeks at most n' are both false while 'seeks some' is true. His account allows for this (p. 111) as does mine (in some worlds, the search is made successful by one or more findings of n in total, in others, by one or more findings of $n + 1$ in total, with no reducibility to n). But there will be trouble for Moltmann's (1997) 'minimal situation' theory, since a *minimal* situation in which Odile finds a man who has read Proust and a man who has read Gide is presumably always one where Odile finds just one man.

the same meaning as 'seeks not to find more than'.

However, the Literary Example does not show that (40c) is unambiguous and always interpreted with NEG lower than the main verb. It only shows that if we agree that (40b) and (40c) are both false, one possible reading that (40c) can have in isolation, namely, (40d), is not consistent with the facts. Indeed, (40d) is clearly true in the example, not just because it is the negation of the false (40b), but in its own right, in terms of our intuitive understanding of it. Consequently, it still seems that we do not have to employ the concept of explanatory relevance, since the Literary Example is consistent with the ambiguity we perceived in 'Perseus seeks no unicorn' that circumvents the problem of irrelevant themes.

Concentrating on lower NEG readings, we note that by the lights of (13), weakening inferences with ⇃⇂ determiners are valid: if the Admissions Committee is looking for no grade less than B, then it is looking for no grade less than C, since if there is a course of events that makes the search successful in which no grade less than B is a theme of a finding, then there is a course of events that makes the search successful in which no grade less than C is a theme of a finding; and if a course of events of the former kind is necessary for success, so is one of the latter kind.

Perhaps surprisingly, disjunctions of negative QNP's have conjunctive force, like other kinds of QNP disjunctions. This is not evident if we consider only examples like 'Perseus seeks no unicorn or no minotaur' – we tend to read this in a way that makes it a consequence of 'Perseus seeks no unicorn'. But for 'the Admissions Committee is looking for no grade less than B or no letter of recommendation that is less than adulatory', there is to my ear a reading that implies, roughly, that the Committee will be satisfied if it finds no grade less than B on the candidate's transcript, and will be equally satisfied if it finds no less-than-adulatory letter of recommendation in the candidate's file. This is implied by (24) and (37). So these meaning postulates are applicable to *all* the disjunctions we have considered, including disjunctions of negative quantifiers.

7

Verbs of Creation and Depiction

For verbs of creation ('assemble', 'bake', 'build', 'manufacture', and so on), it is not lexical meaning by itself which gives rise to marks of intensionality, but rather the combination of lexical meaning with the semantic effect of a particular grammatical construction, progressive aspect. One, or perhaps two, marks of intensionality are exhibited in the contrast between

(1) a. Nigella prepared a meal.
b. Nigella was preparing a meal.

Unlike (1a), (1b) does not imply that a meal was prepared, for Nigella may have abandoned her cooking before so much as the semblance of a meal began to take shape. So (1b) can be true even if no meal exists. It may also be argued that in the imagined circumstances, there was no particular meal such that Nigella was preparing *it*. So we have unspecificity in addition to existence-neutrality, as with, for example, requirement verbs, though in progressive aspect only.

The proposal that verbs of creation in progressive aspect be given the same semantic treatment as intensional transitives generally, is found in (Bennett 1977) and is worked out in a Montagovian way in (Zucchi 1999); also, Richard (2001:104) classifies creation verbs as intensional transitives 'in the progressive'. Since creation verbs are action verbs, Davidsonian event semantics is appropriate for them (*cf.* the examples in (1)). This suggests we should be able to apply our own account of ITV's to show that the special features of examples like (1b) are well-explained by the hypothesis that the **char** primitive occurs in their semantics.

1 PARSONS' THEORY

One outcome a semantics for the progressive must avoid is making progressive sentences entail their non-progressive counterparts; for example, (1b) should not entail (1a). Parsons (1990:170–1) proposes to secure this result by employing two semantics primitives, **cul** and **hold**. **Cul** would appear in the semantics of the perfective (1a) and **hold** in the semantics of the imperfective (1b). (1a)'s semantics will say explicitly that the event of preparing *culminated*, (1b) merely that it *held*. So there is no (1b)-to-(1a) implication.

The problem of blocking the entailment from progressive to non-progressive counterpart is not restricted to sentences with creation verbs, since, independently of whether culmination brings some product into existence, holding does not imply culminating. For instance, if Agatha was crossing St. Charles Avenue, it does not follow that she crossed it, since she may have boarded a convenient streetcar when she reached the neutral ground in the middle. We need to block the progressive-to-non-progressive inference here too; so we use **cul** and **hold** in general.[1]

In addition to **hold**, we employ a predicate of events, **in-progress**, which is more evocative of the progressive.[2] A Parsons-style contrast between progressive and non-progressive is then exhibited by

(2) a. Agatha was crossing a street.
 b. **(some)λe.crossing(e) and held((in-progress)(e)) and agent(e)(agatha) and (some(street))λx.theme(e)(x)**.
 c. Agatha crossed a street.
 d. **(some)λe.crossing(e) and culminated(e) and agent(e)(agatha) and (some(street))λx.theme(e)(x)**.

---

[1] The inference from progressive to non-progressive is known as the 'imperfective paradox'. See (Parsons 1990:167–70) for discussion and references.

[2] **In-progress** is from (Parsons 1990:171) where it is (almost) recommended. I retain **hold** as a carrier of tense information.

As required, (2d) is not a consequence of (2b), in the absence of some rather unlikely meaning-postulates.

But the (2b)-pattern is inappropriate for creation verbs:

(3) a. Nigella was cooking a meal.
 b. **(some)λe.cooking(e) and held((in-progress)(e)) and agent(e)(nigella) and (some(meal))λx.theme(e)(x).**

In (3b), **(some(meal))λx.theme(e)(x)** asserts the sometime existence of a meal, while, as we noted above, Nigella may have stopped cooking before bringing any meal into existence.

Parsons' response to this problem is to deny such a possibility. He writes (1990:174):

> In northern California one can visit Jack London State Park and see the house that Jack London was building when he died. At least this is what the tourist guides say. It isn't much of a house – only a foundation and parts of some walls. But native speakers of English call it a house...people describe unfinished houses as houses, and my analysis assumes that this is correct usage.

I do not think we can be satisfied with this response. How much has to have been built for an unfinished house to be a house is a vague matter: if someone describes a foundation and parts of some walls as a house, and if nothing of importance turns on whether we say 'house' or 'beginnings of a house', we will be happy to allow 'house'. But accommodation has its limits. The process of building a house starts when the ground is broken: at that point, 'Jack is building a house' is true (or if not at that point, at least when the first brick is laid). However, we would not, except in jest, point to empty ground, or a single brick, and say "there's the house Jack was building when he died". We can be generous, yet still have a problem with situations in which the progressive statement is true though not enough has been done to justify the application of the predicate in the verb's direct object ('house', 'meal', etc.).

One might simply insist that the truth of the progressive statement and applicability of the predicate *never* come apart in the way envisaged in the previous paragraph. But cases in which we provide a more detailed description of the goal of the creation process make so insisting seem rather dogmatic. Perhaps Jack was building a *three-storey* house: he knew the plans he had begun to follow were for such a house, he had ordered the appropriate materials, he possessed the required skills, and so on. But on the assumption that the parts of the walls he left do not rise above the knee, I doubt we would say that there is a three-storey house in Jack London State Park. There would have to be something three-storeyish about the standing house-parts to justify this claim (*mutatis mutandis*, if it was a three-course meal that Nigella was preparing). Apparently, an adequate approach to creation verbs in the progressive should not interpret direct objects as thematic.[3]

2 CHARACTERIZING PROCESSES OF CREATION

We will defend the proposal that obtaining the correct entailments is to be accomplished by use of **char**: when we use a creation verb in the progressive, we are characterizing a process or course of events in a certain way. So for (4a) we have (4b):

(4) a. Jack was building a house.
 b. **(some)λe.building(e) and held((in-progress)(e)) and agent(e)(jack) and char(a(house))(e).**

Goodman's idea that we use QNP's to make classifications seems as well-suited to (4a) as to examples with more standard intensional transitives. What (4a) says, according to (4b), is that Jack was agent of an event classifiable as an a-house-building, or in our official terminology, of an event, in this case a process of building, that is characterized by the property of being a property of a house.

Is the use of **char** merely permitted, or rather required, in the presence of **in-progress**? There are two considerations why a house might instead be the *theme* of *e* even though *e* is still in progress. One is the

---

[3] Zucchi (1999:187) argues that 'an unfinished *F* is an *F*' will reintroduce the incorrect inference from progressive to non-progressive. Call the thing Jack left when he died Domus Interruptus. Then Jack built Domus Interruptus, and according to Parsons, Domus Interruptus is a house. So Jack built a house after all. However, though the inference is generally incorrect – *cf.* the cases in (2) – I suppose Parsons could make an exception for creation verbs, granted that the progressive implies the existence of at least an *unfinished* F.

consideration of *modal determinacy:* it may be that, given the plans which are being followed, only one metaphysically possible house can be assembled from the available prefabricated parts, so that in all close worlds in which *e* culminates, the same house is brought into existence. There is also the consideration of *sufficient completeness*, according to which there will normally be a point before the culmination of *e* at which enough has been done to speak of *e*'s having a house as a theme.

Modal determinacy by itself is insufficient for **(some(house))λx. theme(e)(x)**, since the thematic attribution implies that some house exists, which is incorrect if the house parts have been delivered but no assembly has yet taken place. Sufficient completeness looks more likely, with or without modal determinacy, but there is still a residual conflict between saying that a house is being brought into existence and saying that a house exists, or that it is being built and also exists: if it exists, how can it still be in the process of being brought into existence or being built? 'Exists' in this context is functioning as an "achievement verb" for reporting the achievement of a creation process's culmination.[4] Perhaps it will be replied that the building event can continue even though the creation process is over. But such continued building is more like building *onto*, and there is no problem about the existence of *y* if *x* is being built onto *y*: it is the status of *x* that is in question. So thematic attributions that use the predicate in the direct object of a creation verb appear to be anomalous: the progressive demands that QNP's which are direct objects of creation verbs be treated as characterizations of the underlying event.

However, modal determinacy rules out anti-relational ('no particular') construals of progressive sentences like (4a). That is, there appears to be a sense in which *there is* a particular house that is being built, if the building process results in the same house in the various possible worlds in which it culminates. This use of 'there is'

---

[4] Achievement verbs are one of the four groups distinguished in (Vendler 1967), the others being state verbs, activity verbs, and accomplishment verbs. The difference between achievement and accomplishment verbs is that the latter are true of events in which an outcome-directed process unfolds, such as *climbing* a ladder, while the former are true of events with which an accomplishment culminates, such as *reaching* the top.

does not express actual existence; it is rather a possibilist quantifier (Forbes 1989:5–6). So if (4b) gives (4a) the sense 'but no particular house', (4a) is false in cases where modal determinacy holds, and that is the wrong result.[5] This could reasonably be taken as another piece of evidence that **char(Q)(e)** is non-committal as to whether or not particular items are in question.[6] Alternatively, it may be said that **char(Q)(e)** expresses 'no particular one', but with verbs of creation this excludes only actually existing items. This does not mean that merely possible objects can be themes of creation-processes, however, since 'theme' is existence-entailing in both its positions.

In the previous chapter, we gave an exact account of what is meant by **char(Q)(e)** where e is an event of search, or a state of needing, wanting, or owing. The account was formulated in terms of necessary conditions for certain outcomes. In the literature on the progressive there is an approach to their semantics which we can think of as an implicit analysis of **char(Q)(e)**, for e a creation event, that plays the same theoretical role as our postulates governing characterization of searches. For example, Asher (1992) bases his account of the progressive on the idea that what makes an event-kind K a crossing of a street, say, is that even if in some particular case the putative street-crosser fails to get across, still, agents of events of kind K *normally* get across.[7]

This idea enables Asher to draw interesting connections between the progressive, generics, and default reasoning, based on the principle of Normal Success: if a ϕ-ing by x is in progress, then normally there is a subsequent state in which x has ϕ-ed (see his (A0), 1992:470). 'Normally' is a modal operator ranging at w over worlds that are normal relative to w, and the existential neutrality of creation-verb phrases is explained by the fact that w may not be in its

---

[5] The objection assumes transworld identity is governed by certain *constitutional sufficiency* principles (Forbes 2002b). If these are incorrect (McKay 1986; Robertson 1998), then there is no such phenomenon as modal determinacy and the problem dissolves.

[6] The anti-relational conjunct that expresses 'but no particular house' would have to say that it is not possible that some house is actually a theme of the building-event.

[7] The first account of progressives of this general type was (Dowty 1977); see (Landman 1992) for an approach slightly different from Asher's and (Szabó 2004) for critical discussion of Dowty and Landman.

own norm-set. In other words, something abnormal occurs at w, preventing the house-building from concluding successfully.

The literature on the progressive distinguishes between 'telic' and 'atelic' verbs. Telic verbs have as their associated event-kinds, kinds of events which 'have natural endpoints or completions' (Asher 1992: 469). By contrast, atelic event-kinds, such as running on the spot, simply cease to continue, for whatever reason. Two questions we can ask about accounts of the progressive like Asher's are, first, whether the tie between use of the progressive and the normality of reaching the natural endpoint of events of the associated kind is sufficiently tight; and, second, whether the account generalizes from the telic verbs with which it is motivated to atelic verbs, since the latter can also be used in the progressive.[8]

Regarding the first question, it is unclear whether the tie is sufficiently tight. For example, someone may have been climbing K2 when he slipped and fell to his death. But it is not true that someone who is climbing K2 is doing something that normally results in having climbed K2, because almost all expeditions to K2 end in failure. Zucchi gives the similar case of being blown up crossing a minefield (Asher 1992:475). Asher responds (p. 493) that in cases like this the subject is only *trying* to climb K2 or *trying* to cross the minefield. But this seems to have an element of the stipulative about it. An alternative stipulation that appears to be supported just as well is that these cases involve only climbing *on* K2 or crossing *through* the minefield. However, there is no conclusive objection here, since it may be that these are borderline cases: the *general* kind of activity that the agent is involved in usually gets people to the tops of mountains or the other sides of fields, but this norm conflicts in an irresolvable way with more specific ones for the cases in question. So we will not put much weight on these examples.

A bigger difficulty arises when we try to extend the account to atelic verbs. Suppose Gene is singing in the rain. Asher (p. 481) says that this is true iff the 'completion' of the singing occurs. But if we assume that Gene is simply singing snatches of this song and that, completion just amounts to his stopping, say because he is tired. So

---

[8] For further discussion of the telic/atelic distinction in the context of event semantics, see (Higginbotham 2000:63–73).

we would have to say that Gene is *not* singing in the rain, if in fact his singing in the rain will go on forever. Obviously, this is the wrong verdict. Though a world in which Gene sings in the rain forever is rather strange, in particular if we add that it is normal in this world for singing in the rain, once it starts, to go on forever, there is no trace of conceptual incoherence in describing what Gene is doing as singing. The moral appears to be that whether or not a course of action is singing has to do with its occurrent features, and is not dependent on how things turn out in any non-actual worlds.

The same is true of all other atelic cases, so a uniform account of the progressive cannot build dependence on how things (normally) turn out into the semantics. What appears to be happening in the telic case is that sensitivity to how things turn out in certain worlds determines the appropriateness of a particular prepositional phrase used to attribute a goal. There is a cautionary Chinese proverb about a man who decides to travel to the Moon, and looks for a tall tree to climb; as the proverb says, the initial stages of the trip go well. Here we would say that the man is climbing *towards* the Moon, but not that he is climbing *to* the Moon. A person who falls overboard can start swimming *to* the shore if the shore is only a hundred yards away, but if it is a hundred miles away, the swimmer can at best swim *towards* the shore. The difference is between specifying a goal versus a direction, and how things turn out in certain worlds determines only the goal-attribution. That the aspiring astronaut is climbing, or the man overboard swimming, is not disputable.[9]

Our Parsons-style account of the progressive is a good fit with this description, since it separates out event-kind predication, the progressive element, and the goal-attribution. How things go in other worlds does not bear either on the correctness of (say) **swimming(e)** or **held((in-progress)(e))**. But with the use of a telic verb there comes, explicitly or implicitly, a goal attribution (Agatha was crossing the street *to the other side*), and it is this attribution that is sensitive to outcomes in other worlds. For example, **((goal)(e))(the shore)** is true

---

[9] These cases involve sentient agents, but we see the same phenomenon with inanimate agents, as in Asher's example (p. 478), 'the ball is rolling off the table'. If the ball has insufficient momentum to reach the table's edge, it would not be said to be rolling off the table, but it would still be rolling *along* the table *towards* the edge.

only if the agent is not unrealistically distant from the shore.

Applying the general approach under discussion to verbs of creation, we would say that Jack's actions constitute a process of building a house because such actions normally lead to a house being built. With creation verbs, which are certainly telic, the role of characterization is like that of goal-attributions with verbs of movement. Someone who has no idea how to build houses and has assembled all the wrong materials would not be said to be building a house. This means that it is at least necessary for **char(Q)(e)** that the sorts of actions the agent is performing typically lead to a state in which Q**(exists)** is true. However, by contrast with the account of characterization we developed for search verbs, the principles of default logic that govern when **char(Q)(e)** is appropriate with creation verbs are not special-purpose; they apply to all telic verbs.[10]

3 VERBS OF DEPICTION

Physical depiction verbs are a species of creation verb, in that the end result of a physical depiction is a concrete artefact, a carved piece of wood, say, or a distribution of paint across the surface of a piece of canvas. This means that depiction verbs are doubly intensional. First, in the manner of creation verbs in the progressive: someone can be carving a figure, but if interrupted early enough, no sculpture is made. And second, in the regular way noted on page 48: Guercino drew a dog, 'surely a specific dog', according to the Norton Simon curators, while the Pompidou Centre's curators take the opposite tack for Braque's *Little Harbour in Normandy*: 'it appears this work was painted from imagination, since the landscape depicted cannot be identified'.

---

[10] The discussion in this section rules out explaining progressive in terms of non-progressive. What about the converse direction, proposed in (Szabó 2004)? It certainly seems that (2c) entails (2a), but whether that should be a consequence of the semantics, as opposed to a special meaning-postulate, is dubious if instantaneous events are possible. It may seem to make *prime facie* sense to say 'when God was creating the world, Lucifer interrupted with some suggestions'. However, if we are referring to the instantaneous consequence of the *fiat lux*, Lucifer could not, strictly speaking, have *interrupted*, and use of the progressive seems wrong.

That there are two ways a depiction VP can be notional is a problem if **char(Q)(e)** is to be used to capture both manifestations of notionality. One solution is to permit each manifestation to have its own *locus* of characterization. Depiction verbs like 'paint' and 'carve' are anyway ambiguous between creative and non-creative senses, and this ambiguity can be captured by postulating an underlying light verb, 'make' or 'do', in the creative use: to paint the Forth Railway Bridge, creatively, is to make a painting that is of the Forth Railway Bridge, which is to be the agent of a making characterized by 'a painting of the Forth Railway Bridge'; whereas to paint the bridge, in the sense of keeping it looking good, is simply to be the agent of a painting that has the bridge as its theme. So in the creative sense, there is a making event that can be characterized, and within that characterization there is the PP complement of a relational noun, which may be interpreted either notionally or relationally. The debate about *The Aldrovandi Dog* is therefore a debate over which of (5b) or (5c) is the truth expressed by (5a):

(5) a. Guercino painted a dog.
 b. **(some)λe.making(e) and cul(e) and agent(e)(guercino) and (some(painting))λx.theme(e)(x) and (a(dog))λy.of(x)(y).**
 c. **(some)λe.making(e) and cul(e) and agent(e)(guercino) and (some(painting))λx.theme(e)(x) and char(a(dog))(x).**[11]

According to (5b), a dog is such that the painting Guercino made is of *it*, whereas (5c) says only that the painting he made is an a-dog painting. (5b) treats 'of a dog' as a genuine prepositional phrase, in which 'of' has a non-trivial if abstract meaning of type *i(ib)*; for an alternative, see (Carpenter 1997:134–5). In (5c) we have extended characterization from a relation between acts of depiction and

---

[11] An anonymous reader noted that 'sketch an *F*' and 'made a sketch of an *F*' will presumably get the same semantics, but argued that they are not synonymous: if Guercino is blindfolded, given a pen, and told to sketch a dog, he may *sketch* a dog, but not *make a sketch* of a dog, because the pen has been filled with water. I think I share this intuition, but I doubt that the example involves the light 'make' of (5). If we replace 'make' with 'do', which lacks a "heavy" reading in this context, I believe the difference disappears: Guercino sketches a dog, and also does a sketch of a dog. So the intuition of non-synonymy depends on giving 'make' a heavier sense.

properties of properties to allow it to hold between depictions themselves and properties of properties.

Notice that nothing is accomplished by the proposal that with depiction verbs, "notional" readings are really statements about images, for instance, that (5a) means in the "notional" sense that Guercino painted a dog-image. For 'dog-image' is just 'image of a dog', which is again ambiguous between relational and notional readings. So this proposal would just lead us to apply **char(a(dog))** to an image in the painting, rather than the painting (the reader convinced that this is how it should be done can easily adapt the forms proposed in this chapter).[12]

The notional reading of the non-progressive (5a) is captured in (5c) by a characterization of the painting. This leaves us free to use **char** again to express the progressive by characterizing the *making*. The progressive VP 'was painting a dog' allows relational and notional readings just like (5a). So the relational construal of 'was painting a dog' involves makings characterized by paintings of such-and-such things, as in (6b) below, while the notional construal involves makings characterized by paintings characterized by such-and-such properties of properties, as in (6d) below.

Since **char** demands a quantifier as argument, in characterizing the making we have to avoid predicating the quantifier of a property of type *ib*, since the result would be a type *b* argument for **char**, which is a type mismatch. So we use a relative clause construction: makings may be characterized by such quantifiers as 'a painting which, for some dog, is such that the said dog is its theme' or 'a painting which is characterized by the property of being a property of a dog'. The relative pronouns 'which' and 'that' are translated by **which** and **that**. These form what are essentially subsective adjectives, which in turn produce complex nominals. Thus 'a dog that is fierce' becomes 'a ((that is fierce)-dog)', in which 'that is fierce' extracts from ⟦dog⟧

---

[12] Another possibility, suggested by the anonymous reader of the previous note, is that (5a) means "notionally" that Guercino painted an imaginary dog. If this means that he copied a mental image of a dog, then it probably is relational, in the way that if I copy Guercino's painting, I draw a specific dog. But (i) not all painting from imagination is copying mental images, and (ii), to copy a mental image of a dog you must first imagine a dog, and this has a notional sense that still remains to be explained.

the (characteristic function of the) fierce dogs. In the semantics, **that** takes λx.fierce(x) as input and produces the output **that(λx.fierce(x))**, which then modifies **dog** to produce a well-typed input for **a**: **a((that (λx.fierce(x)))(dog))** (so **that** is of type $(ib)((ib)(ib))$). Following this treatment in the representations of the progressive below, 'painting of a dog' in its relational reading (6b) is '(that is of a dog)-painting', and in its notional reading (6c) is '(that the property of being a property of a dog characterizes)-painting'. For intelligibility, (6c) employs an intermediate representation, **a(painting of a dog)**:

(6) a. Guercino is painting a dog.
  b. **(some)λe.making(e) and holds((in-progress)(e)) and agent(e)(guercino) and char(a((that(λx.(a(dog))λy.of(x)(y)))(painting)))(e).**
  c. **(some)λe.making(e) and holds((in-progress)(e)) and agent(e)(guercino) and char(a(painting of a dog))(e).**
  d. **char(a(painting of a dog))(e) = char(a((that(λx.(char(a(dog))(x))))(painting)))(e).**

For uniformity with the semantic representations in (6), one might now revise (5b) and (5c), so that, for example, (5b) directly expresses 'some (that is of a dog)-painting', like (6b). But there are a number of degrees of freedom in applying the core idea, and I will not search out reasons to fix upon a single candidate among the equivalents that present themselves.

Depiction verbs do not create special logical difficulties. Though some doubt that seeking a mortal gorgon implies seeking a gorgon, the claim that drawing a sleeping gorgon implies drawing a gorgon will probably elicit less resistance. And there is no disjunction problem: if someone draws a dog or a cat, that can only be because they drew a dog, or drew a cat, or drew something whose kind is one or other, but which cannot be determined from the image.[13]

---

[13] Characterization by quantifiers also seems also seems to account for examples of pseudo-agentives, drawn to my attention by Friederike Moltmann, such as 'the picture portrays a dog'. Here there is a state of portraying, characterized by **a(dog)**.

4 DEPICTION VERBS AND THE DEFINITENESS EFFECT

One puzzling behaviour of depiction verbs is that it is only with a restricted range of QNP's that they form VP's that sustain notional readings. By contrast, there is no such restriction for search verbs or desire verbs. Comparing the two groups in:

(7) a. Gertrude seeks exactly two Pharaohs' tombs.
    b. Gertrude seeks another Pharaoh's tomb.
    c. Gertrude seeks every Pharaoh's tom.

and

(8) a. Gertrude drew exactly two Pharaohs' tombs.
    b. Gertrude drew another Pharaoh's tomb.
    c. Gertrude drew every Pharaoh's tomb.

we see that all the examples in (7) are easily read notionally, but (8c) contrasts with (8a) and (8b): a notional reading of (8c) is hard to hear. (8c) might mean that for each Pharaoh's tomb, Gertrude made a drawing of it; or it might mean that she made a drawing in which all Pharaohs' tombs appear. But it is hard to understand "Gertrude drew every Pharaoh's tomb, but no particular tombs".[14] We have the same problem with "Gertrude drew most Pharaohs' tombs" and "Gertrude drew the Pharaoh's tomb/the Pharaohs' tombs". The elusiveness of notional readings for depiction VP's with these determiners in the direct object NP is robust across languages.[15]

It will be argued here that it is not just a matter of the relational readings being *preferred*: there *are* no notional readings of depiction-verb phrases when the complement is an 'every'-NP. Apparent counterexamples dissolve on closer inspection. There are two angels in Verrocchio's *Baptism of Christ*, but it is likely that his pupil Leonardo painted one of them. Yet even if we agree that neither of them painted any particular angels, the claim 'Verrocchio painted every angel', made in the context of a dispute about attribution,

---

[14] Zimmerman makes a similar observation about 'compare' (1993:159).

[15] This claim is based on a survey I carried out at Logica 2003 in the Czech Republic. Languages represented included Czech, French, Italian, German, Portuguese, Spanish, Dutch, and Danish.

would not demand a notional reading. In such a context, we are relationally quantifying over the angel-images in the scene (a similar quantification seems to occur in 'Verrocchio painted every angel praying'). In the same vein, Perseus, mistakenly thinking that gorgons are real, may make an artist's impression of Euryale, Medusa and Stheno, based on stories he has heard about them that he wrongly thinks are factual. So Perseus drew every gorgon/drew the three gorgons; and this must be notional, it may be said, since gorgons don't exist. But although it is true that he drew no real gorgons, it is not true that he drew no particular gorgons. He was not just making them up: he drew particular fictional ones (recall the discussion in Section 3.3). In 'Perseus drew every gorgon' the quantifier is therefore relational, over fictional characters.

For a different kind of case, suppose Audubon is preparing a field guide to birds. Then we may say that he drew every bird, even if there were no particular birds he drew. But 'he drew every bird' implicitly involves quantification over *kinds* of bird: we are saying that for each kind of bird, he drew a bird (no particular bird) of that kind. Here we have a relational 'each kind of bird' and a notional indefinite 'a bird'. Similarly, for some drawings there may be a number n such that there *ought* to be n F's in the drawing, and if n F's are drawn, we can say the artist drew every F. For instance, in a drawing of a spider from above, there ought to be eight legs, and if there are, the artist has drawn every leg. But this is like the bird case: for each kind of leg (front left, front right, first middle left, etc.), the artist drew a leg (no particular one) of that kind.[16] Absent better examples, therefore, I maintain that notional interpretations of depiction VP's with 'every'-QNP's or the others mentioned above are simply unavailable.

What might explain this? It appears to be the determiner that is crucial, and there is a striking match between the determiners that

---

[16] Timothy Williamson suggested the case of a flower with rotational symmetry which normally has exactly eight petals. Here there is no ordinary notion of petal-type, but we can still say that to draw every petal is for there to be some admissible petal-arrangement in which every petal-position has a petal (but no particular petal) drawn in it. A double-quantifier account may also be correct for an example suggested to me (p.c.) by Thomas Hofweber, 'In his novel, Tolstoy portrayed every unhappy marriage'. Alternatively, an account of generics may illuminate the non-relational reading of this sentence.

force relational readings on depiction VP's and those that do not occur naturally in existential contexts such as 'there is/are' and 'there must be':

(9) a. There are exactly two Pharaohs buried here.
  b. There is no Pharaoh buried here.
  c. There are more obscure than famous Pharaohs buried here.
  d. ?There is every Pharaoh buried here.[17]
  e. ?There are most Pharaohs buried here.
  f. ?There is some but not every Pharaoh buried here.

This suggests that to explain the special feature of (8c) we should look to an account of the 'definiteness effect' exhibited in (9).

A persistent idea, going back to (Milwark 1977), is that the determiners which are natural in existential contexts are not really quantificational. For instance, Reuland and ter Meulen (1987:14) contrast NP's which are used to "modify" the conversational domain – these are non-quantificational – with those whose meanings may be defined as generalized quantifiers (properties of properties) over the current conversational domain. The indefinite NP 'a Pharaoh' is a non-quantificational domain-modifier – 'a Pharaoh is buried here' *adds* to the conversational domain – while the universal 'every Pharaoh' is simply quantificational. The claim is then that only non-quantificational NP's are natural in existential contexts.

But this discourse-theoretic criterion is *prima facie* extensionally incorrect. $\downarrow^R$ determiners such as 'no', 'at most three' and 'very few' pattern with existential determiners as regards acceptability in existential contexts – see (9b) – but are not used to modify the conversational domain. For example, in terms of file-change semantics (Heim 1983), an assertion of 'a Pharaoh is buried here' will start a new "card", whereas 'no Pharaoh is buried here' will not.[18]

---

[17] Special cases: there is a "list" usage that allows 'every' and (perhaps) 'most' (Milwark 1977:n.1) and there is an idiomatic use of 'every', roughly synonymous with 'good', as in 'there is every reason to believe/doubt/expect'.

[18] However, (Kamp and Reyle 1993:333, 458–61) treats $\downarrow^R$ determiners as domain modifiers: such determiners introduce a discourse referent that is neutral between being an individual and being a set, and a cardinality condition is placed on this dis-

To avoid this objection, a defender of the discourse-theoretic criterion will have to insist on decomposition of $\downarrow^R$ determiners (see, e.g., McNally 1997:102–3, 106–7). If 'there is no Pharaoh buried here' is underlyingly 'not: there is a Pharaoh buried here' then a domain-modifying determiner occurs within the existential context. Our discussion of decomposition of 'no' in Section 6.11 is consistent with this account, but the general strategy faces certain difficulties. One technical problem is how exceptive constructions are to be allowed for. 'There is no Pharaoh but/except Ramses II buried here' needs 'no' to license 'except' if the latter is to be part of the determiner (Moltmann 1997:21). We also have 'But/except for Ramses II, there is no Pharaoh buried here'; however, it appears that plausible semantic accounts of exceptives require a more intimate association between 'but' or 'except' and the determiner than would be provided by taking this latter form as the fundamental one (von Fintel 1991:96–100 argues that the fundamental form is the one in which the exceptive is right-adjacent to the NP).

Perhaps a deeper difficulty for the decompositional defense of the discourse-theoretic criterion is that it loses plausibility when it is extended – as it must be – to other $\downarrow^R$ determiners. For example, we would have to maintain that 'there are very few Pharaohs buried here' is underlyingly 'it is not the case that there are more than very few Pharaohs buried here'. This goes from less to more complex.

A better way of defining which determiners are acceptable in existential contexts, due to Keenan (1987, 2003), is as follows.[19] Monadic determiners can be regarded as relations between sets, defined in the obvious ways: EVERY(A)(B) iff $A \subseteq B$, NO(A)(B) iff $A \cap B = \emptyset$, and so on. 'EVERY(A)(B)' is of the form Rxy, and we read 'EVERY(A)(B) iff $A \subseteq B$' as saying that $\langle A,B \rangle$ belongs to the (graph of the) EVERY relation iff $A \subseteq B$. We call A the *restriction* set and B the *coda* set. Where Ð is any determiner, the main concepts we employ are:

---

course referent. But this is an unintuitive extension of the notion of discourse referent, and I note that such referents fail to support anaphora: 'There are no/few/at most two Pharaohs buried here, because they couldn't afford a Pyramid' is unsuccessful, though a pronoun of laziness standing for 'Pharaohs' is acceptable: '...because they preferred to be inside a Pyramid'.

[19] I largely employ the terminology and definitions of (Keenan 2003).

(10) a. Đ is *conservative in first argument* (cons₁) iff whenever A ∩ B = A ∩ C, ĐAB = ĐAC.
   b. Đ is *conservative in second argument* (cons₂) iff whenever A ∩ C = B ∩ C, ĐAC = ĐBC.
   c. Đ is *cardinal* iff whenever |A ∩ B| = |E ∩ F|, ĐAB = ĐEF.
   d. Đ is *co-intersective* iff whenever A ∩ B̄ = E ∩ F̄, ĐAB = ĐEF.
   e. Đ is *proportional* iff for finite A, B, E and F, iff whenever |A ∩ B|::|A ∩ B̄| = |E ∩ F|::|E ∩ F̄|, ĐAB = ĐEF.

These criteria give *invariance conditions*. For example, conservativity in first argument says that the truth-value of ĐAB remains the same under all changes to the coda set that preserve its intersection with the restriction set.[20] Thus the restriction set contains all domain elements relevant to evaluation of the sentence. So we say that the restriction set is the *local universe* for cons₁ determiners (Keenan 2003:200). Similarly, conservativity in second argument says that the truth-value of ĐAB remains the same under all changes to the restriction set that preserve its intersection with the coda set. So the coda set is the local universe for a cons₂ determiner.

The determiners which occur naturally in existential contexts are the cons₂ determiners (and boolean compounds thereof).[21] This is easy to check for positive cases. And it is also easy to see that 'all' and 'most' fail to be cons₂; for example, it may be that the students who did well and the philosophy majors who did well are the same people, but granted that there are many more students than philosophy majors, perhaps all philosophy majors did well but not all students did ('all' is co-intersective and 'most' is proportional; both are cons₁).

Granted the extensional correctness of Keenan's criterion, it is pointless to augment it with discourse-theoretic conditions. What

---

[20] Conservativity in first argument is usually just called *conservativity* in the GQ literature. The standard criterion is a linguistic one, that Đ A ARE B iff Đ A ARE A THAT ARE BS. (10a) is easily seen to be equivalent to ĐAB = ĐA(A ∩ B). If A were not the local universe for Đ, putting the narrower A ∩ B for B should sometimes make a difference.

[21] In (9a)–(9c) the cons₂ determiners are all cardinal as well, but Keenan argues (2003:202–4) that there are cons₂ non-cardinal determiners in natural language, such as 'at least two...besides John'. He gives 'mostly' and 'only' as examples of cons₂ non-cons₁ determiners. Though these are controversial examples of determiners, classifying them as such means that we need the more general notion of conservativity₂.

requires explanation here is why it should be exactly the non-cons$_2$ determiners that make for direct-object NP's that block notional readings of depiction-verb phrases.

5 THE PURE INVENTORY ACCOUNT

The empirical generalization that is of interest to us is that, for any depiction verb-phrase [v[ᴅɴ]], a notional reading is permitted iff the determiner ᴅ is one for which, in sentences of the form ᴅAB, the coda set B is the local universe. Since intensional transitives generally allow notional readings, the failure of the determiners for which the coda set B is not the local universe to permit a notional reading is what needs to be explained. Scoping a QNP complement above its transitive verb is the default in many types of syntax, and intensional transitives are the special case, allowing the *in situ* interpretation that permits semantics such as (6c). But *within* this special case, the behaviour of non-cons$_2$ determiners with depiction verbs is an extra quirk, not mere conformity to the default requiring no further comment.

The explanation of the restriction to cons$_2$ determiners has to do with the way in which notional descriptions of depictions are evaluated, and is best presented in terms of a contrast with cases where there is no restriction on the determiners that permit notional readings. Why, for instance, does "Gertrude seeks every Pharaoh's tomb", have a notional reading? Well, "Gertrude seeks at least one Pharaoh's tomb" certainly has such a reading, and one sort of situation that makes this reading true is that in which Gertrude is the agent of a search that is governed by the intention to find at least one Pharaoh's tomb, the intention she could announce with "I'm going to find at least one Pharaoh's tomb". But Gertrude might instead be the agent of a search that is governed by the intention to find every Pharaoh's tomb, the intention she could announce with "I'm going to find every Pharaoh's tomb". And if possession of the existential intention is a truthmaker for a notional reading of "Gertrude seeks at least one Pharaoh's tomb", there can hardly be any obstacle to possession of the universal intention being a truthmaker for a notional reading of "Gertrude seeks every Pharaoh's tomb". A similar case can be made for a notional reading of "Gertrude seeks most Pharaoh's tombs". It is the generality of the intention, marked by the QNP in its expression, that the notional reading captures.[22]

By contrast, in depiction-verb phrases, the use of non-cons$_2$ determiners makes it hard to see what kind of truthmaker a notional reading could have. For (11a), we require both (11b) and (11c):

(11) a. Guercino drew a dog.
b. There is a drawing, or part of a drawing, of which Guercino is sole author.
c. (Most of) a dog is in that drawing, or part thereof.

(Henceforth we suppress 'most' and 'part'.) (11c) has a reading in which 'a dog' functions as a quantifier over the domain of the context, and a situation in which both this reading of (11c), and (11b), are true, is a truth-maker for the relational reading of (11a).

But (11c) also has what we will call a *pure inventory* reading, in which there is no implication that the drawing is of some specific dog. (In the case of *The Aldrovandi Dog*, a pure inventory would list, among other things, a dog, a castle, a tower, more than three trees, and so on.) The idea is that a pure inventory can be made on the basis of inspection of the picture by someone who has the relevant recognitional capacities for the types of thing depicted, but who need not have any particular capacity to recognize specific objects (exactly Goodman's notion of classification). On the pure-inventory reading of (11c), (11c) and (11b) jointly characterize truthmakers for the notional reading of (11a).[23]

A truthmaker for (12a) on the one-drawing disambiguation would be a state of affairs in which (12b) (= (11b)) and (12c) are both true:

(12) a. Guercino drew every dog.
b. There is a drawing of which Guercino is sole author.
c. Every dog is in that drawing.

---

[22] The reader is spared the longer version of this paragraph which uses modal variation in outcome conditions in place of governing intentions.

[23] Pure inventory readings are neutral on whether or not a particular thing is depicted, so they are weaker than notional readings if the latter include 'but no particular one' as part of their content.

A relational reading of (12c) produces a truthmaker for the relational reading of (12a). But by contrast with (11a), there is no notional reading of (12a), and that seems to trace to there being no pure inventory reading of (12c). In turn, that (12c) has no pure-inventory reading can be explained in terms of the non-cons$_2$ property of 'every'. Both (11c) and (12c) have the ÐAB form, in which the coda set B is *things in the drawing*. 'Things in the drawing' is itself ambiguous between a relational and a pure-inventory sense, and in (11c)'s pure inventory sense, we invoke pure-inventory senses twice: 'a dog is among the things in the drawing'.[24]

But in (12c), Ð cannot use the coda set B as a local universe: since 'every' is co-intersective, the things determining the truth-value of 'every'-sentences are rather the elements of A ∩ B̄, where B̄ is things that are not in the drawing. The constitutive relevance of things not in the drawing compels 'every dog' to function as a quantifier over the full domain of discourse of the context (animals owned by Aldrovandi, say). Similarly, with proportionality determiners like 'most', |A ∩ B| has to be compared with |A ∩ B̄|. So for 'most dogs are in the drawing' the facts about things not in the drawing are again truth-value determining, compelling 'most dogs' to function as a quantifier over the domain of discourse of the context.

We get the same effect with cons$_2$ determiners and VP negation: 'at least one dog is in the drawing' has a pure-inventory reading, but for 'at least one dog is not in the drawing', the inner 'not' (rather than a non-cons$_2$ determiner) makes facts about things not in the drawing truth-value determining, which in turn compels 'at least one dog' to be a quantifier over the domain of discourse of the context.

This account distinguishes between the *absence* of a notional reading and the *impossibility of the truth* of a notional reading. There is a good sense in which it is impossible that Guercino drew ℵ$_ω$ dogs, in no matter how many drawings. But 'Guercino drew ℵ$_ω$ dogs' has a

---

[24] It is a good question how 'dog' retains its literal meaning in the pure-inventory reading of 'a dog is in the drawing'. Perhaps, as is argued in (Walton 1973), it is because of an implicit 'it is make-believedly the case' operator, which interacts scopally with 'a dog'; or perhaps it is because of a pragmatically licensed shift or widening of the extension of 'dog' to include dog-images (Partee 2003). But a simpler answer is that 'a dog is in the drawing' in the pure-inventory sense is derivative upon 'the drawing is an (a dog)-drawing', in which '(a dog)-drawing' is explained in terms of **char**.

notional reading, and '$\aleph_\omega$ dogs are in the drawing' has a pure-inventory reading. Yet no notional and pure-inventory readings exist for (12a) and (12c), thanks to the non-cons$_2$ determiners.

The absence of these readings raises one final puzzle, namely, how the overall strategy for interpreting the area of discourse in question is to guarantee the absence of the reading. In any approach which involves recovering from writing or speech some underlying representation which is then semantically interpreted, one way we can prevent a particular reading from arising is to block the recovery process from producing an underlying representation whose interpretation would be the unwanted reading. An alleged notional reading of (12a) would have, in our current vocabulary, the semantics

(13) **(some)**λe.making(e) and cul(e) and agent(e)(guercino) and
 (a(drawing))λx.theme(e)(x) and char(every(dog))(x)

and the problem is that there is no anti-relational meaning for this to express. However, it is within the resources of type-theory to block (13) from being derived. I will not pursue details here, but one method would be to use the *feature-constrained* types of (Moortgat 2002), arranging things so that non-cons$_2$ determiners have a feature that is passed by **char** up through the relevant lambda term in which the **char**-subterm is embedded, a feature that cannot be checked by a QNP whose nominal is headed by a relational noun derived from a depiction verb.

A Montagovian alternative is to allow (13) to stand but to impose a meaning-postulate which makes it equivalent to the single-sketch relational reading. The meaning-postulate would be applicable whenever a depiction-noun occupies the position of **drawing** in (13). But this strategy is acceptable only if we agree that the idea of characterization by a property of properties is neutral between relational and anti-relational ('but no particular one(s)') readings, otherwise the original difficulties with the Montagovian approach discussed in Section 5.1 will arise over again.

8

Substitutivity

Referential opacity is the term commonly used for the phenomenon of substitution-failure, for example, the failure of 'seek/fear/caricature Hyde' to entail 'seek/fear/caricature Jekyll'. Richard (2001:109) remarks that a treatment of intensional transitives that does not examine referential opacity could seem like a critical discussion of *Paradise Lost* that ignores the Prince of Darkness. So for completeness, I end with a brief presentation of the 'hidden indexical' theory of opacity I favour,[1] along with a discussion of how it is to be integrated into the semantics for ITV's that has been developed here.[2]

1 SUBSTITUTION AND SIDE-EFFECTS

A properly formulated rule of substitution (Identity Elimination, '=E' for short) requires that when an occurrence of a term t in the minor premise is replaced by a term t' whose coreferentiality with t is guaranteed by the major premise, *no other changes* are effected; especially, the substitution must have no *side-effects*. But this is vague: substituting t' may produce a conclusion *shorter* than the minor premise, and no-one would object to that. What we want to

---

[1] The sobriquet 'hidden indexical theory' is due to Schiffer; see (Schiffer 1992; 1995; 1996). Prominent examples of the genre include (Crimmins 1992, Richard 1990).

[2] My basic approach has not changed from that of (Forbes 2000a); however, I think the current chapter improves on that paper in a number of respects.

avoid are side-effects that change truth-condition, for it is change of truth-condition that opens the door to change of truth-value.

Two illuminating examples of truth-condition-changing side-effects are the following, respectively from (Quine 1961:22) and (Fine 1989:222–3; see also Linsky 1967:104):

(1) a. Giorgione is Barbarelli.
    b. Giorgione was so-called because of his size.
    c. Therefore, Barbarelli was so-called because of his size.

(2) a. The man behind Fred is the man in front of Bill.
    b. The man behind Fred saw him leave.
    c. Therefore, the man in front of Bill saw him leave.

In (1) the conclusion has a truth-condition different from premise (1b)'s because the substitution has the side-effect of changing the reference of 'so', which in (1b) refers to the name-type of which the preceding 'Giorgione' is a token.[3] In (2), the substitution produces a truth-condition different from (2b)'s since it has the side-effect of altering the reference of the anaphoric 'him'. As these examples suggest, it is no trivial matter to formulate a universally adequate rule of =E, since the ways in which disruptive side-effects might be triggered in natural language appear to be quite open-ended.

The moral Quine drew from substitution-failure is that the notion of objectual satisfaction cannot be applied to the open sentences obtained by replacing the substitution-resistant term with a variable, and that consequently, existential or universal generalization ("quantifying in") makes no sense. This moral seems to be supported by the two examples above, for it looks as if neither of the following is interpretable if regarded as inferred from (1b) or (2b) respectively:

(3) a. Someone is so-called because of his size.
    b. Someone saw him leave.

---

[3] For the notion of name-type I employ, see (Kaplan 1990). In his analysis of Quine's views, Fine (1989:216) says that the occurrence of 'Giorgione' in (1b) is 'not purely referential...because [it] is not used solely to pick out [the] object'. This does not seem right: 'so' is used to refer to 'Giorgione', but that does not affect the semantics or "use" of 'Giorgione' in any way.

We can imagine parents, for ideological reasons, christening their unfortunate child 'someone'. But this is not the existential quantifier that is supposed to figure in (3a), which cannot serve as an antecedent to 'so-called'. (It is a difficulty for a substitutional semantics for quantifiers that it predicts that (3a) is not just meaningful, but *true*, in virtue of the true substitution-instance (1b).) In (3b), 'him' remains an anaphoric pronoun. It is therefore in search of an anchor, since we have rendered it anchorless by replacing the complex description that embedded its anchor 'him' with the simple 'someone'. As a result, the only anaphoric pronouns that can be used as direct object of 'saw' are third-person reflexives. So (3b) as it stands is at best an open sentence.

With these two examples to hand, along with familiar quotational ones, we might be tempted to generalize to the conclusion that whenever substitution fails, the mechanism that accounts for the failure also blocks quantifying in. But on the face of it, intensional verbs refute such a generalization. In the example below,

(4) a. Superman is Clark
 b. Lex fears Superman
 c. Lex fears Clark
 d. There is someone Lex fears

we appear to have substitution-failure in the move from (4b) to (4c), yet (4d) is perfectly intelligible, whether or not it is validly inferred.[4]

Among the possible responses to these judgements about (4) are

---

[4] Substitution-failure in (4) might be challenged even by those who admit it for *that*-clauses. For in *that*-clause examples, e.g., 'fears that Superman will interfere'/ 'fears that Clark will interfere', it is not given as part of the set-up that the *proposition* that Superman will interfere is identical to the *proposition* that Clark will interfere. So it is natural to look to non-identity of those propositions as the source of the substitution-failure. But in objectual attitude examples, no analogous move is possible; e.g., in our case, it *is* given as part of the set-up that Superman is Clark. However, the strongest argument for substitution-failure, that substitution disrupts psychological explanation, applies equally to propositional and objectual ascriptions. We can explain Lex's furtive behaviour by ascribing to him (i) fear of Superman and (ii) the belief that Superman is nearby. A single substitution disrupts this, whichever ascription we make it in; recall Ch. 3.1, *ad fin*. Arguments like this for substitution-failure have been challenged in a series of papers by David Braun (2000, 2001a, 2001b), but his objections bear equally on propositional and objectual ascriptions.

first, that (4d) is straightforwardly deducible from (4b) precisely because there is *no* substitution-failure in such attitude ascriptions;[5] second, that there *is* substitution-failure, but the mechanism responsible for it, though still present in the likes of (4d), does not render the quantifying-in unintelligible;[6] and third, that there is substitution-failure, the mechanism responsible for it *does* block quantifying in, but the existential generalization effected in (4d) is only performed *after* the mechanism has been removed. The third option is the one we will explore here.

2 'SO-CALLED'

Despite the name, we need not insist that hidden indexical theories posit hidden *indexicals* – any covert device that contributes to truth-conditions in a way that substitution disrupts will work. The theory developed below takes its inspiration from the overt 'so' in (1b), which might be regarded as a pronoun, or as a demonstrative. The latter categorization conveniently ushers Kaplan-style semantics for demonstratives onstage (Kaplan 1989), but my formulations will be consistent with either, though I will use Kaplan's apparatus.

It may be worthwhile to begin with the overt case, the 'so' in (1b). The special feature of this use of 'so' is that its reference is often visibly displayed in the *linguistic* context, as in (1b). If we keep to this simple case, avoiding examples in which the reference of 'so' is to something extra-sentential, we can display the interpretation by

---

[5] The *locus classicus* of this view is (Salmon 1986); more recent defenses include (Braun 1998) and (Soames 2002). Soames's 'many propositions asserted' theory makes substitution-resistance a pragmatic phenomenon by singling out just one as the semantics, while (Bealer 1993) offers a 'many propositions' account on which all the propositions are meanings of the sentence (p. 42). Without gainsaying the appeal of many-propositions theories, I think it is undercut if there is a workable one-proposition account that explains substitution-failure without using entities as obscure as Bealer takes the full Fregean hierarchy of modes of presentation to be (p. 19).

[6] Perhaps the 'paratactic' analysis of (Davidson 1969) falls into this category. 'There is someone such that Lex fears him to be nearby' could be 'there is someone of whom Lex fears the following: he is nearby' (Hornsby 1977). However, the paratactic analysis has trouble with objectual ascriptions. 'Lex fears the following person: Superman' permits substitution, so the paratactician who believes in opacity is forced to be a propositionalist.

linking each occurrence of 'so' to an occurrence of some other expression. For (1b), taking 'so-called' to be 'called so', this produces

(5) Giorgione was called so because of his size.[7]

Here the interpretation is one in which 'so' is linked to the token of 'Giorgione'. (5) exhibits a kind of deferred ostension, in which the type is referred to *through* a demonstration of the token, as if 'called so' meant 'called by the name-type of which *that* one is a token'.[8]

A more elaborate example:

(6) If Caravaggio$^{(1)}$ was called so$^{(1)}$ for his place of birth and Guercino$^{(1)}$ was called so$^{(2)}$ for his squint, then Guercino$^{(2)}$ was called so$^{(3)}$ for his squint and Caravaggio$^{(2)}$ was called so$^{(4)}$ for his place of birth.

We have superscripted distinct tokens of expressions of the same type (e.g., 'so$^{(4)}$' for the fourth occurrence of 'so'), which permits us to stipulate a *context* for (6) as a function. The most likely is the context μ defined by:

(7) $\mu(1) = \langle 1, \text{'Caravaggio'} \rangle; \mu(2) = \langle 1, \text{'Guercino'} \rangle; \mu(3) = \langle 2, \text{'Guercino'} \rangle; \mu(4) = \langle 2, \text{'Caravaggio'} \rangle.$

In μ, the first 'so' demonstrates the first 'Caravaggio', the third 'so' the second 'Guercino', and so on. We can display μ in a more visually intelligible way by dropping (6)'s superscripts and putting in links:

---

[7] The link notation admits of an obvious interpretation in terms of displaying the reference of a demonstrative. But it can equally well be understood as tracing a quasi-*anaphoric* connection, in which 'so' refers not to the reference of what it is linked to, but to the expression itself or its type (in Forbes 1990, 1996, I called 'so' a "logophor", by analogy with 'anaphor'). Links are used in the semantics of anaphor by Evans; see his (1977:Sec.III).

[8] Generally, though, description theories of deferred ostension do not fare well; see (Borg 2002:495–504). The demonstrative gloss of 'so' goes back to (Thomason 1979: 209). But Montalbetti (2003:133) argues that 'so' cannot always be treated as a demonstrative, because of examples like 'Giorgione was so-called because of his size, as was Pepino'. The sloppy reading of this is easy to get, the strict reading harder. But if we replace 'so-called' with 'called by *that* name', the strict reading (Pepino was called 'Giorgione') is to my ear the only one available.

(8)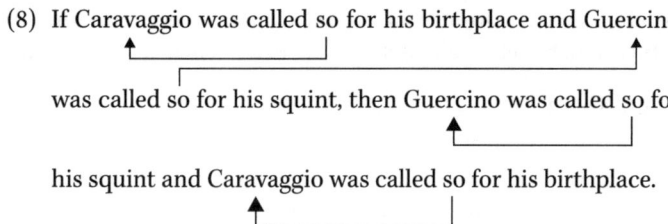
If Caravaggio was called so for his birthplace and Guercino was called so for his squint, then Guercino was called so for his squint and Caravaggio was called so for his birthplace.

But there is no syntactic or semantic reason to rule out a context in which, say, all four "so"'s refer to, or *via*, the first 'Caravaggio'.

It may be tempting to call (6) a logical truth, because superscripts that merely number tokens of a type do not affect logical form, and so we seem to have an instance of $(\phi \wedge \psi) \to (\psi \wedge \phi)$. But with the referents of its occurrences of 'so' unspecified, (6) is no more a logical truth than $\phi(that) \to \phi(that)$ is in Kaplan's system (the two occurrences of 'that' need not be coreferential – see the discussion in Kaplan 1989:587). There are in fact two notions of logical truth applicable to sentences like (6). First, there is logical truth *in a context*: once a context has been fixed, as in (8), it may be that the truth-value of the sentence-in-context is insensitive to changes in the interpretation of its non-logical vocabulary. (6) in the context μ defined by (7) is logically true in this restricted way. There is also logical truth *simpliciter*, the property of being true no matter the interpretation of non-logical vocabulary and no matter the context (so long as it assigns each 'so' a referent). (6) lacks this property, since, for instance, it is false in a context μ that includes $\mu(2) = \langle 1, \text{'Caravaggio'}\rangle$, on the intended interpretation, since Guercino was not called 'Caravaggio' for any reason. A 'so'-free sentence is logically true *simpliciter* iff it is a logical truth of conventional first-order logic.

For a slightly more formal treatment, we introduce a three-place predicate y to represent 'x is called t for/because of y' (crude but convenient). We stipulate that there are two sorts of individual constants, those that name individuals which are not elements of the lexicon, and quotation names of constants of that sort. And we require that (i) $[\![\underline{c}]\!] = c$ if $\underline{c}$ is a quotation name of c, and (ii) $\langle x,y,z\rangle \in [\![y]\!]$ only if y is a quotation-name $\underline{c}$ and $[\![c]\!] = x$. This allows Barbarelli to be called 'Giorgione' or not, though we cannot say that Barbarelli is called 'Giorgione' for no reason.

We want (3a) to be uninterpretable rather than merely false, so we might decree that it is not even well-formed. Assuming (3a) has a regimentation like '(some x: person(x))[$y(x$, so, his size)]', it would either be '$y(x$, so, his size)' that is classified as ill-formed, or the syntax would prevent the prefixing to it of '(some x: person(x))'. But neither of these is desirable, as is shown by the validity of

(9) Giorgione is so-called because of his size.

Therefore, someone is so-called because of his size.

Trouble arises only if 'so' tries to link to something other than 'Giorgione'. So the problem must be purely semantic. In a first-order framework, we can allow some 'so$^{(i)}$'s to be undefined, so that the derivation of a semantic value for (3a) "crashes" when it calls ⟦so$^{(i)}$⟧. In a type-theoretic approach, (3a) would involve a type mismatch.[9]

3 'AS SUCH'

In the hidden indexical semantics for attitude ascriptions we will develop here, substitution-failure is explained by the covert presence of an 'as such' which links to the word or phrase being substituted. For example, on the reading on which (10a) resists substitution, it can be paraphrased as (10b):

---

[9] To explain why (3a) cannot be inferred by Existential Introduction (∃I) from (1b), we sketch a simple inference system for y and 'so'. Proofs are in sequent-to-sequent format, links are allowed to cross the turnstile (cf. (9)), each line is a context, 'So'-I is $\Sigma \vdash y(t, \underline{c}, \zeta) \Rightarrow \Sigma \vdash y(t, \text{so}, \zeta)$, and 'So'-E is $\Sigma \vdash y(t, \text{so}, \zeta) \Rightarrow \Sigma \vdash y(t, \underline{c}, \zeta)$. In the I-rule a 'so' is introduced and linked to an occurrence of c anywhere to the left on the same line, and in the E-rule such a link is erased and 'so' replaced with $\underline{c}$. Call an expression to which a link points *targeted*. Then =E requires that no term in the minor premise that is being substituted be targeted, and ∃I and ∀I say that the constant being replaced cannot be targeted. There is also a general prohibition against "removing" formulae with targeted terms. For example, ∨E and ∃E disallow discharge of assumptions with targeted terms, and →E and ∧E cannot be applied if the antecedent or eliminated conjunct has a link from the consequent or retained conjunct. No 'so' in a premise can link to another premise. In applications of →I, links to terms in the discharged assumption shrink to follow their targets across ⊢, while in ¬E, neither major nor minor premise may contain a 'so'. (9) is derived by applying 'so'-E, ∃I, and 'so'-I, in that order.

(10) a. Lex fears Superman
     b. Lex fears Superman as such.

For Lex to fear Superman as such, Lex has to stand in the fearing relation to Superman in a special way: roughly, Lex is disposed to respond fearfully when Superman is presented to him, in thought or perception, in a specific way, namely, as Superman. The effect of 'as such' is to invoke the mode of presentation in question and use it to alter the extension of 'fears', granted the latter is a binary relation.[10]

But what exactly *is* the mode of presentation? As a proof of possibility, suppose that thinkers sort information (and misinformation) about what they take to be different objects into *dossiers* (Grice 1969), in a way that does not guarantee a one-one map between dossiers and the objects those thinkers create stores of information about. Dossiers may be active or inactive (be online or offline) and an effect of processing a name is that a particular dossier is brought online, a dossier which may be just one of many on the same subject. A mode of presentation of x may be understood as the capacity to activate *this* dossier, whose subject is x (perhaps as opposed to *that* one, whose subject is, again, x). Of course, *any* expression may have the capacity to activate a dossier holding corresponding information (*cf.* the discussion of the Moses illusion on page 170). But this is activation *by content*. The cognitive significance of a name should rather be thought of as the capacity to activate *by label*. We need not agonize here over the question of how Fregean this notion of mode of presentation is. It is certainly "private": there is no possibility that two people share the same mode of presentation of anything, since

---

[10] Terry Parsons informs me that medieval philosophers investigated 'reduplicatives', which employ 'as' and repeat the subject term: 'a human, as a human, is rational, as a biped, not'; see, for example, (Burley 2000:267–83). I am pleased with the pedigree. In (Forbes 1990, 1996, 2000a) I developed an account of substitution-failure which postulated a covert version of the 'so' of 'so-called'; I employed 'as such' in (Forbes 2000b). The same account could be formulated with a reduplicative *qua*. Nothing of substance seems to turn on the choice of covert term we make here. My use of 'as such' as an opacity-inducer is not unusual. For example, in (Fodor 2004a:31) we find: "To have the concept DOG is to be able to think about dogs as such...The 'as such' marks the intentionality of concept possession. Since extensionally equivalent concepts can be distinct, your being able to think about Granny's favourite animals doesn't *ipso facto* manifest your possession of DOG".

their dossiers are theirs alone. But there are notions of 'kind' on which two people can have modes of presentation of the same kind.

A mode of presentation might be invoked metalinguistically, as the 'Superman' mode of presentation. But the idea to be pursued here is that the 'as' of 'as such' is an opacity-inducing operator for which Davidson's semantic innocence thesis is incorrect;[11] so a *name* following 'as' will invoke a mode of presentation rather than occur quoted in a description of it. For example, in 'Lex fears Clark, not as such but as Superman', the 'Superman' invokes a mode of presentation of a certain extraterrestrial without necessarily referring to the extraterrestrial himself.

A simple way of implementing this is to introduce a function π which associates with each name n a way of thinking of $[\![n]\!]$. $[\![As]\!]$ then makes an operator out of $\pi(n)$ which can modify extensions. At the atomic level, the type-theoretic semantics would be:

(11) a. Lois seeks Superman;
      b. ((as(such))(seeks(superman)))(lois).

Regarding (11b) as a sentence of $\mathcal{L}_x$, $[\![\textbf{superman}]\!]$ is an element of D_i, and $\pi(\text{'}\textbf{superman}\text{'})$ an element of a special domain D_θ of modes of presentation. If (11b) is a sentence of $\mathcal{L}_m$, we can do without the special domain D_θ, since quantifier-meanings (type $(im)m$) can serve instead.[12] For the $\mathcal{L}_x$ case, $[\![\textbf{such}]\!]$ is a token of the same type as that

---

[11] Davidson's famous comment on Frege is 'If we could recover our pre-Fregean semantic innocence...it would seem to us plainly incredible that...words [in the content sentences of attitude attributions] mean anything different, or refer to anything else, than is their wont when they come in other environments' (Davidson 1969:172). That the thing to say about 'as' is that it creates contexts for which semantic innocence is wrong was suggested to me by Mark Richard (p.c.).

[12] This is what Thomason's account of substitution-failure depends on. He assigns names type $(im)m$, and different functions may be assigned to names which are intuitively coreferential, reflecting the idea that coreferential names combined with the same property-expression may yet produce different propositions. For example, if the proposition **callas(sings)** and the proposition **kalogeropoulou(sings)** are distinct, then **callas** and **kalogeropoulou** are different functions of type $(im)m$, even though Maria Callas *is* Mary Kalogeropoulou. And if **callas** and **kalogeropoulou** are distinct, then worshipping Callas need not be the same thing as worshipping Kalogeropoulou. Our approach retains a type i semantics for names, but entities of type $(im)m$ are finegrained enough to be modes of presentation.

'**such**'-occurrence is linked to. ⟦**As**⟧ is an operation which applies π to its input ⟦**such**⟧ and maps the resulting mode of presentation to functions of type $(ib)(ib)$: if f is this map, ⟦**as**⟧ = $f\pi$. Intuitively, then, ⟦**as(such)**⟧ accepts a function of type ib, say ⟦**seeks(superman)**⟧, and outputs a related function of type ib – in this example, one which maps an individual to $\top$ iff that individual seeks Superman *as such*. The effect of ⟦**as(such)**⟧ on ⟦**seeks(superman)**⟧ is therefore to delete agents from its extension, or functionally, to change the output, for some inputs, from $\top$ to $\bot$.[13] We can stipulate that **as** is the *only* primitive expression which uses π. Cognitively, this means that the mode of presentation is ignored when processing ⟦**seeks(superman)**⟧, with its hyperintensional verb. So to this extent, we respect Davidson's semantic innocence thesis: ⟦**superman**⟧ simply provides Superman to ⟦**seeks**⟧.[14]

On this account, if we substitute 'Clark' for 'Superman' in (11a), the input to ⟦**as(such)**⟧ will be the same as before, namely, ⟦**seeks(clark)**⟧ (which is no different from ⟦**seeks(superman)**⟧). But if $\pi(\text{'superman'}) \neq \pi(\text{'clark'})$, the substitution may have the side-effect of changing the meaning of **as(such)**, since ⟦**as**⟧ is now looking at a different mode of presentation of the Man of Steel. If Lois seeks Superman but does not seek Clark, ⟦**seeks(superman)**⟧ will map Lois to $\top$, and the ⟦**as(such)**⟧ obtained from (11b) does not alter this. But the ⟦**as(such)**⟧ obtained after substituting **clark** in (11b) will be a different function of type $(ib)(ib)$ – one whose output for the input ⟦**seeks(superman)**⟧ maps Lois to $\bot$. So substitution fails in the extensional $\mathcal{L}_x$.

In assigning a single mode of presentation to each name, the

---

[13] Here I am assuming that to seek x as so-and-so is sufficient for seeking x, *simpliciter*. For other attitudes, it is perhaps less clear cut. If Lois admires Superman but not Clark, why should we say she stands in the admiration relation to a certain extraterrestrial, rather than that she does not? Scepticism on this point naturally leads to the view that, at the atomic level, there are no binary attitude relations, only ternary ones of type $\langle i, i, m \rangle$, where m is a mode of presentation of an individual. But for such a sceptic, the semantics of **as(such)** given here can easily be recast so that its effect is to select a particular triple $\langle a, b, m_b \rangle$ over another $\langle a, b, m'_b \rangle$. (Thanks to Kelly Gaus for the observation and discussion that led to this note.)

[14] It would be possible to fold the application of π into the semantics of 'such', but the case of 'as Clark' or 'as Superman' suggests that application of π is part of the meaning of 'as'. Formally, of course, the articulation of ⟦**as**⟧ as $f\pi$ is unnecessary: there is just a single function from names to $(ib)(ib)$-functions. But we want to make explicit the point at which modes of presentation are employed.

above semantics restricts itself to languages which are in the Fregean sense "ideal": each expression has exactly one sense, shared by all with mastery of the language, and exactly one reference. However, the model of modes of presentation as powers to activate particular dossiers by label makes modes of presentation unshareable. For shareability, $\pi(n)$ should be a *kind* of mode of presentation. The kind for 'Superman' would be the property of having the power to activate a thinker's 'Superman'-dossier by label: $\lambda y.\lambda x.x$ activates y's 'Superman'-dossier by label. This allows the output of π to be constant across a range of thinkers. So for (12a) we have (12b):

(12) a. Everyone admires Superman;
  b. **(everyone)**λx.**((as(such))(admires(superman)))**(x).

In evaluating (12b) in $\mathcal{L}_x$, ⟦**as**⟧ uses π to obtain an element of D_θ that is now conceived of as an abstraction from the various individual modes of presentation of Superman. Like ⟦**admires(superman)**⟧, ⟦**as(such)**⟧(⟦**admires(superman)**⟧) is an *ib*-function, but one that maps to $\bot$ those agents ⟦**admires(superman)**⟧ maps to $\top$ but whose particular mode of presentation of Superman that is relevant to the admiration is not of the right kind, say because the agent admires Superman as Clark only. There will also be cases where the final outcome is $\bot$ because the agent has never encountered the name 'Superman'. $\pi($**'superman'**$)$ is still defined, because kinds of modes of presentation are not person-relative. While such agents admire Superman if they admire Clark as such, it is straightforwardly false, and comes out that way on our approach, that they admire Superman as such.

Agents can have different dossiers labelled with the same name. So in certain contexts, it might be unclear whether 'Harold admires Aristotle' attributes admiration of the philosopher or the shipping magnate. One view about this case is that since the ascriber presumably has a determinate intention which it is, a specific proposition is literally expressed, and the audience is just out of luck so far as grasping it is concerned. This is neutral on whether or not 'admires Aristotle' is 'admires Aristotle as such', but if it is the latter, the view in question should hold that the speaker's intention is enough to guarantee that $\pi($**'aristotle'**$)$ is a kind of mode of presentation of whichever of the two Aristotles is the right one. On the other hand, if the quandary of the audience is given more weight in deciding whether or not a specific proposition is literally expressed, then we may want to require that in contexts lacking other cues, the ascriber must say something like 'Harold admires Aristotle the shipping magnate' or 'Harold admires Aristotle the philosopher'. This still leaves it open whether or not there is also a covert 'as such', but if there is, we have, in the name-description terms, an explicit announcement of which of the Aristotles π('**aristotle**') presents.

A knowing ascriber's referential intention is *prima facie* of less help in the special case where an unknowing agent has two dossiers labelled with the same name, and the dossiers are about the same individual. This is the structure of Kripke's 'Paderewski' case (Kripke 1979), in which an agent, Peter, believes, or seems to believe, that Paderewski has some musical talent, and also that Paderewski has no musical talent. This is because, on one occasion of encountering Paderewski, he does not realize it is the same person as on another occasion – he thinks, incorrectly, that there are two Paderewskis. For an ascriber who knows Peter's situation, making an objectual ascription which exploits this knowledge requires use of name-description terms, as in 'Peter admires Paderewski the pianist and doesn't admire Paderewski the politician'; for without the qualifiers (or something covert to the same end) the ascriber contradicts himself.[15] Covert 'as such' cannot effectively *replace* 'the pianist' and 'the politician', but seems to have a familiar role in blocking attempted substitutions based on the identity 'Paderewski the pianist *is* Paderewski the politician'. Such substitutions are illegitimate in cases where the difference between Peter's two ways of thinking matters. But it is not clear that a satisfactory account can be built on the idea

---

[15] Kripke himself uses such qualified terms to clarify his meaning (Kripke 1979:279, n.37). I still stand by the broad thrust of the views I expressed about the Paderewski case in (Forbes 1990, IV). However, I there rejected Kripke's insistence that we answer the question 'Does Peter, or does he not, believe that Paderewski has musical talent?' on the grounds that, after all, we are not obliged to answer the question 'Was Aristotle, or was he not, fond of dogs?' in a context where it is entirely unclear which Aristotle is being referred to. I would now say, in a corresponding objectual case, that Peter seeks Paderewski (because he seeks Paderewski the pianist, because he seeks Paderewski the pianist *as such*); and that, while he does not seek Paderewski the politician as such, this does not entail that he does not seek Paderewski, because it does not entail that he does not seek Paderewski the politician.

that the presence of 'the pianist' and 'the politician' itself suffices for substitution-failure. A covert 'as such' linked to 'Paderewski the pianist' explains it, the role of 'the pianist' being to indicate which of Peter's modes of presentation it is that π should output (so there is strong pragmatic pressure to interpret ascriptions using 'the pianist' and 'the politician' opaquely). The associated kind of mode of presentation is the property of having the power to activate a thinker's 'Paderewski'-dossier by the indicated combination of label *and* content.

Though we will not pursue the details here, our apparatus can also be extended to demonstrative ascriptions, though substitution-failure is less common in these cases because modes of presentation are less likely to be invoked (Forbes 1987:14–15). But an ascriber who knows that he is demonstrating the same person, by direct and deferred means respectively, may still say 'Lex fears *that* guy but not *that* guy', pointing first to the Man of Steel attired as Superman, performing some act of superheroism, then, second, to a picture of the Man of Steel attired as Clark, say on *The Daily Planet* website. One possibility is that each 'that guy' is covertly 'that guy as such', where the 'as such' invokes a kind of demonstrative mode of presentation, or way for things to look (granted some vagueness). For example, the kind of way for things to look invoked by the second 'as such' would be paradigmatically satisfied by ways the Man of Steel looks when he is acting as Clark in a normal situation (no fancy dress parties).

If **as(such)** blocks substitution by a mechanism not very different from 'so-called', why does quantifier introduction seem unproblematic with attitude ascriptions? As (9) shows, we *can* existentially generalize 'Giorgione is so-called because of his size', first by eliminating 'so-called', then by applying $\exists I$, then by introducing 'so-called' with a link across the turnstile or 'therefore' to the 'Giorgione' of the premise (*cf.* n.9, p. 157).[16] Our semantics for 'as such' makes it factive on **seeks**, since it never converts a mapping to $\bot$ into a mapping to

---

[16] Do these steps presuppose an existential commitment in the premise that is not there? Semantic innocence requires that the reference of a name not change when used in opaque contexts, but this cuts both ways. An atheist who says 'Darius worships Ahura Mazda' either speaks archly, or uses 'Ahura Mazda' in the same way as in 'Ahura Mazda is the chief god of the Zoroastrians', from which we may infer 'the Zoroastrians have a god'. But the god is a mythical object. See further (Salmon 2002).

T. So we can move from **((as(such))(seeks(superman)))(lois)** to **(seeks (superman))(lois)**. The latter is the substitution-permitting reading of 'Lois seeks Superman', and so entails **(someone)λx.((seeks(x))(lois))**. The difference with (9) is that 'as such' is covert, thus the presence of the elimination step is hidden, and no subsequent reintroduction is made; this exaggerates the contrast with (9).

We are saying that the semantics of ascriptions of objectual attitudes about the Man of Steel to Lois by those aware of her ignorance standardly involves covert **as(such)**. That the phenomenon is semantic, as opposed to pragmatic, is easily accommodated by a drawing of the semantics/pragmatics distinction in the style of (Recanati 2003), where the semantic (truth-evaluable) content of an utterance is derived partly from the lexical meanings of its overt constituents, and partly by 'primary pragmatic processes'. Such processes could certainly include 'enrichment' of the basic sentence-meaning by insertion of **as(such)**. But a more traditional account of the semantics/pragmatics distinction could also account for the presence of **as(such)**. The traditional account sees the truth-evaluable content of an utterance as arising out of the lexical meanings of its overt constituents combined with values from context for the context-dependent parameters that the lexical meanings include (see, e.g., Stanley 2002). On this view, we end up with the likes of (12b) because speakers intentionally select **as(such)** as part of the proposition to which they are about to give voice elliptically.

4 OPACITY AND UNSPECIFICITY TOGETHER

At the subatomic level, where does **as(such)** operate? The substitution-*permitting* reading of the relational 'Lois seeks Superman' is

(13) **(some)λe.seeking(e) and agent(e)(lois) and theme(e)(superman).**

And although it is not the only possible choice, the most natural way of formulating the substitution-*resistant* reading is to let ⟦**as(such)**⟧ be a function which determines whether or not Superman is a theme constituent of the seeking according to the way he is represented in the seeking; that is, by how the agent of the seeking thinks of him. So we allow that Superman may be a theme of a seeking, but not a theme *as Superman:*

(14) **(some)λe.seeking(e) and agent(e)(lois) and ((as(such))(theme(e)))(superman)**.

Here ⟦**theme(e)**⟧ in $\mathcal{L}_x$ is an *ib*-function, mapping to ⊤ exactly the themes of some particular event *e*. But if this function is first operated on by ⟦**as(such)**⟧, the result is an *ib*-function which sends Superman to ⊥ if, in *e*, Lois is, as we say, only looking for Clark. The $\mathcal{L}_m$-interpretation of **((as(such))(theme(e)))(superman)** according to the Russellian is that it is the proposition that Superman is theme of *e* under the 'Superman' guise. For the Fregean, an equally good candidate is the *state of affairs* that Superman is theme of *e* under the 'Superman' mode of presentation.[17]

For a notional case, suppose that Tex is the owner of a fine collection of stuffed chucks: moorchuck, waterchuck, fieldchuck, and so on. But his collection lacks a woodchuck. However, Tex has no interest in collecting hogs, and for whatever reason, believes that some but not all woodchucks are groundhogs. Tex wants to add the *pure* woodchuck to his collection. Notionally, we have

(15) a. Tex seeks a woodchuck that isn't a groundhog.
b. **(some)λe.seeking(e) and agent(e)(lois) and char(a woodchuck that isn't a groundhog)(e)**.
c. **a woodchuck that isn't a groundhog = a((that(λx.not(groundhog(x))))(woodchuck))**.[18]

Clearly, nothing prevents substitution in (15b). So, since being a woodchuck is the same as being a groundhog, it follows that Tex seeks a woodchuck that isn't a woodchuck.

This is as it should be, but there is also a true ascription of a notional attitude to Tex that does not convict him of absurdity, one on which neither 'woodchuck' nor 'groundhog' can be replaced by

---

[17] As these paraphrases indicate, there is no difficulty in providing a sub-atomic semantics for the ternary atomic semantics mentioned in note 13.

[18] Recall the discussion of 'which' and 'that' on p. 140. I have simplified by ignoring the second indefinite 'a'.

the other. We can paraphrase this true ascription as "Tex seeks a woodchuck that isn't (also) a groundhog, as such", in which 'such' links to "woodchuck that isn't a groundhog". The semantics is then

(16) **(some)λe.seeking(e) and agent(e)(tex) and
((as(such))(char(a woodchuck that isn't a groundhog)))(e).**

When 'such' targets a nominal, π maps the nominal to a conception of a property. For a complex nominal such as "woodchuck that isn't a groundhog", π might encode a subsidiary composition of conceptions. Or it may be that for a complex nominal m formed from simples $e_1...e_n$, the value of π is a conception constituted by an implicit grasp of how $[\![e_1]\!]...[\![e_n]\!]$ compose together to form $[\![m]\!]$. This is an issue which, fortunately, we need not go into:[19] either way, Tex's conception of the property *woodchuck that isn't a groundhog* will be distinct from his conception of the property *woodchuck that isn't a woodchuck*, because his conception of the property *woodchuck* is distinct from his conception of the property *groundhog*. Each conception involves the idea of being the same sort of animal as *these*, but there is nothing in either conception to indicate that the animals in the two groups of exemplars are themselves of the same kind. Or so it will be if the conceptions are distinct: if instead Tex has only now been taught the word 'groundhog' as an alternative to 'woodchuck', then the attitude ascribed in (15a) is no more intelligible than is seeking a woodchuck that isn't a woodchuck.

5 SIMPLE SENTENCES

An obvious question to ask is what selection constraints there are on the use of **as(such)**. There appear to be very few. This is brought out by examples of 'simple sentences' advanced by Jennifer Saul (1997a, 1997b). Saul points out that in addition to sentences with verbs that are normally classified as intensional, we have an intuition of substitution-resistance for sentences such as

---

[19] See the exchange between Fodor and Peacocke (Peacocke 2004:90–92; Fodor 2004b:106–7).

(17) a. Clark entered the phone booth and Superman came out.
b. Superman has more success with women than Clark.

Saul says that in the absence of psychological vocabulary, we cannot offer any of the usual explanations why substitution should fail in the examples in (17). So the intuition of substitution-failure must be in error, and in need of debunking explanation. The implication, of course, is that the intuition of substitution-failure in *standard* cases, like (11a) and (15a), being no stronger as an intuition, is just as good a candidate for debunking explanation: a semantic justification of the kind that has been constructed here is unmotivated.

One philosopher's *modus tollens* being another's *modus ponens*, we will instead extend our hidden indexical semantics to examples like those in (17). One reason to do this is because we can. But another is that speakers who produce statements like those in (17) regard themselves as saying something true, and would reject the results of substitution. For example, in a review of recent books about Shostakovich, the historian Orlando Figes wrote

(18) Shostakovich always signalled his connections to the classical traditions of St. Petersburg, even if he was forced to live in Leningrad. (*The New York Review of Books*, 10th June 2004, p. 14.)

Perhaps signalling connections is intensional, but being forced to live somewhere is not. And Figes would undoubtedly reject interchange of 'St. Petersburg' and 'Leningrad' as wrong in both clauses. The question is whether 'wrong' here means literally false; better, the question is why it *shouldn't* mean this.[20]

Another factual case concerns the double life of one Stephanie Vowell, who dances at a "gentleman's club" in Las Vegas under the stage-name 'Trixie'. In an interview in *The New York Times* titled 'The Philosopher Stripper' (I am not making this up – see 2nd June 2004), we read:

Trixie is not just a stage name, it's a persona that safeguards Ms. Vowell's psyche and gets her better tips. Trixie is a dumb blonde with no college

---

[20] The intensionality in (18) is unnecessary; Figes could have made a similar point with 'Shostakovich always retained connections with...'.

education. [Ms. Vowell went to college – GF]... "Trixie is an entertainer, a caretaker," Ms. Vowell said. "You don't ever want to meet Stephanie... Stephanie is boring...so plain that *I* wouldn't want a lap dance with her," Trixie said... "Look, you can't kiss your kids with the same mouth that comes in here and takes a dollar... That's why you put on your make-up, you put on your war paint, you put on your attitude."

Note how in this passage the author switches easily between psychological ('want to meet', 'is boring') and non-psychological contexts ('with no college education') which resist substitution equally. This suggests that whatever we say about apparent substitution-failure, it should not sharply distinguish the two sorts of context.

One thought about the examples in (17) is that they involve some kind of hidden reference to *ways of dressing*. For example, (17a) might be paraphrased 'Clark, so-attired, entered the phone booth, and Superman, so-attired, came out'. Here there is reference to the way Clark dresses in acting as Clark, and to the way he dresses in acting as Superman. But this is insufficiently general, since Clark, acting as Clark, may dress as Superman to go to a fancy dress party. Use of 'as such' allows a greater level of generality. So (17b), for example, could be paraphrased as 'Superman, as such, has more success with women than Clark, as such'. For the Man of Steel, like the Philosopher Stripper, leads a double life: sometimes he is acting as the protagonist of one life, sometimes as the other (the changeover points often occur in phone booths). Acting as Superman results in things going better for him with women than does acting as Clark.

Implementing this formally for (17b) is complicated by the latter's use of the generic present and the comparative, but for (17a) we have:

(19) **(some)λe.entering(e) and ((as(such))(agent(e)))(clark) and (the pb)λx.theme(e)(x) and [(some)λe.exiting(e) and ((as(such))(agent(e)))(superman) and (the pb)λx.theme(e)(x)]**.

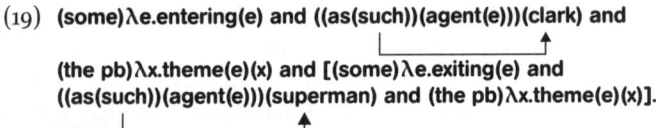

agent(e) is of type *ib* and **as(such)** is of type (*ib*)(*ib*). There are events *e*, for example, certain phone-booth-exitings, such that ⟦**agent**⟧(*e*) is a function that maps Clark to ⊤; but if Clark is acting as Clark in those exitings (he just needed to make a phone call), ⟦**(as(such))**⟧ (⟦**agent**⟧(*e*)) maps Clark to ⊥ if **such** points to 'Superman'. Note that

((as(such))(agent(e)))(clark) does not mean that Clark is acting as Clark *while* he is agent of *e*, but rather that Clark is acting as Clark *in being* agent of *e*.[21] In other words, in participating in *e* in the way of an agent, the Man of Steel is presenting himself as Clark.

So selection constraints on **as(such)** seem to be essentially two. First, there must be, broadly speaking, distinct aspects in the history of an object, such as distinct functions or distinct roles, for **as(such)**-modification to have an effect (though in the absence of multiple aspects, modification is merely redundant, as opposed to being ill-formed or otherwise uninterpretable). Second, modification must apply to something that can be intelligibly relativized to the range of aspects in play. For example, since acting as Trixie is not the same as acting as Stephanie, Trixie can be agent of a kissing acting as Trixie in that kissing, without Stephanie being agent of it acting in it as Stephanie. On the other hand, 'Leningrad, as such, is identical to St. Petersburg, as such', is initially puzzling, though this might be stated in opposition to 'Leningrad, as such, is distinct from St. Petersburg, as such', the latter saying that the Czarist aspects of the city's heritage are different from the Soviet aspects.[22]

The proposal, then, is that on some occasions of use of (17a) and its ilk, the literal meaning of the speech act is given by (19) and its ilk. These uses of (17a) would only be made by someone who knows that Clark is Superman, but for such speakers, **as(such)** is an optional element which they can silently employ in sincere avowals of (17a). Or so we should say if we would like typical uses of the various examples above to come out true, *ceteris paribus*, when knowledgeable speakers intend something true.

But David Braun and Jennifer Saul have argued that the statements knowledgeable speakers make with the examples in (17) are

---

[21] An explanation in terms of 'while' would be vulnerable to substitutions instantiating 'A while B, B is temporally co-incident with C, ∴ A while C'. Here I am responding to Barry Schein's example 'Superman outscored Clark' (Schein 2005), a one-clause variant of a case due to Joseph Moore (Moore 1999).

[22] The case of names associated with a specific period of an object's history is discussed at length in (Zimmerman 2005). Zimmerman proposes a Montagovian semantics keyed to special features of this case. But while I have no quarrel with his description of our actual use of names like 'Leningrad' and 'Karl-Marx-Stadt', I would not go so far as to build its features into the semantics. The hidden indexical semantics operates at a level of abstraction above these details.

false, and judging them to be true is an error (Braun and Saul 2002). Anyone who advances an error thesis owes an explanation of why competent subjects make the error, and Braun and Saul propose to assimilate these cases to others in the psychological literature where facts the subject knows are not brought to bear because they are in some way obscured by features of the task in question. For example, most subjects, if asked how many animals of each kind Moses took on the ark, answer 'two', and only subsequently realize their mistake. This 'Moses illusion' seems to be a consequence of two factors. The question embodies a pragmatic presupposition that it was Moses who took animals on the ark, but because they first process the interrogative "how many", subjects focus on recalling a number, and pass over the presupposition unthinkingly.[23] But this is not the whole story, since few will answer 'two' to the question 'How many animals of each kind did Caligula take on the ark?' The fact that there are major and salient respects of similarity between Moses and Noah is also playing a role.

Braun and Saul propose that judging the examples in (17) to be true is making a broadly similar sort of error. There is something the subject believes ('it was Noah who took animals on the ark', 'Superman is Clark'), but features of the task, for example the task of evaluating the sentences in (17), screen off this belief. It might be, they speculate, that subjects keep their information about the Man of Steel in two files, a 'Superman' file and a 'Clark' file (Braun and Saul 2002:20). The 'Superman' file contains 'has much success with women', and the 'Clark' file contains 'has little success with women'. This seems to support (17b), and would be paradigmatic support if the two files matched up to two individuals, as is normally the case. So not stopping to consider the identity, to remind themselves that this case is not the normal one, subjects avow the truth of (17b).

One problem with this is that it ignores the *producers* of examples like those in (17). Unlike the formulators of trick questions, who know they are implicating falsehoods, speakers who produce, say, (17b), take themselves to be communicating the plain truth (I intend

---

[23] Generalizing from my own case, I predict that subjects would be less likely to answer 'two' if the question were rephrased as 'Moses took some animals on the ark; how many of each kind?'

this formulation to be neutral between literally stating the plain truth versus merely implicating it or engaging in pretense). It is hard to see how any explanation of why *they* are in error can be right if it depends on something like 'not stopping to consider the identity' on their part. For the way they formulate their remarks is explained by their awareness of the identity, and they know that effects such as the rhetorical punch of (18) depend on their respective audiences being aware of it. (We can imagine Professor Figes rolling his eyes and groaning inwardly as an error theorist earnestly points out to him that since Leningrad *is* St. Petersburg, he might as well say Shostakovich was forced to live in St. Petersburg; or Ms. Vowell's possibly less restrained reaction if an error theorist explained to her that since Stephanie *is* Trixie, a kiss from Stephanie's mouth is *ipso facto* a kiss from Trixie's.)

There is a concomitant asymmetry among consumers of these statements in response to "correction". Asked to reconsider, subjects who answered 'two' to the Moses-question will immediately see their mistake if they have the knowledge of the Bible that is the norm in societies where Christianity is the dominant religion. But readers of (18) would do no such thing. Those who feel the rhetorical punch of Figes' remark do so precisely because they know that Leningrad is St. Petersburg. It is perverse to attribute to them an error which, coincidentally, issues in the judgement they would have made if they had got Figes' intended interpretation right. Their judgement is better explained by supposing that they grasp the true, substitution-resistant proposition that the producer was trying to communicate, a proposition about Leningrad and St. Petersburg, each as such.[24]

If an error theory is implausible, why else might we deny that, say,

---

[24] Suppose we are told that (17b) ('Superman has more success with women than Clark') is asserted by Lois, *before* she discovers that Superman is Clark. Braun and Saul say that being told this would not lead us to revise our evaluation of (17b) as true (2002:11), which is supposed to show that we were not originally interpreting (17b) as involving hidden indexicals (since our evaluation stays the same on finding out that it does not). But if we do not revise our evaluation, that undermines Braun and Saul's view that the erroneous evaluation as true results from ignoring the identity; for we can no longer be ignoring it when we are told that (17b) is asserted in ignorance of it. And to the extent that we would be slow to revise our evaluation – a rather small extent, I believe – that only testifies to interference from what we know *we* would mean by (17b).

(17a) literally expresses (19)? One possibility is that (17a) merely implicates (19). Braun and Saul deny this too, but they do admit that in "special" contexts, (19) could be an implicature of (17a). Their example of a special context is that of Clark's parents, who know of his double life, and are discussing his activities (2002:13). But there seems to be little that is *special* about this context. *Each* example we have been discussing is effective only in contexts with a speaker and audience who are aware of the identity, aware or expecting that the other is aware of it, and so on.

Nevertheless, I see no reason to stop at the claim that (17a) conveys (19) only by a pragmatic mechanism. If this claim means we have to distinguish the way simple sentences work from the way attitude ascriptions work, it is phenomenologically dubious, as we noted above *re* the interview with Stephanie Vowell. Moreover, we may take it to be uncontested that (19) is the semantics of

(20) Clark, as such ('so-personified', 'as Clark', '*qua* Clark', etc.), entered the phone booth, and Superman, as such ('so-personified', 'as Superman', '*qua* Superman', etc.), came out.

The only difference between (20) and (17a) is that the opacity-inducer is explicit in (20). So (17a) can be regarded as an elided version of (20). If an elision procedure is at work in attitude ascriptions, it is no extravagance to postulate it for (17a) as well.

An alternative is to understand (20) to be a conversational implicature of (17a), something that has to be worked out. But recovering (20) from (17a) seems much closer to using a little real-world knowledge to recover the intended meaning from a scope ambiguity ('a flag flew from every building'), or the suppressed words from an ambiguous elision ('Perseus is more afraid of Medusa than Athena') than it is to recovering, say, 'this candidate is unqualified for the job' from 'this candidate has very neat handwriting'.[25] Additionally, the

---

[25] This example of conversational implicature is one of Grice's most famous (Grice 1989:33). (Barber 2000:304) proposes that for the likes of (17b), working out the implicature involves reasoning about what epistemic conditions would prompt someone who does not know the identity to assert the sentence. But this is entirely too roundabout: in following the interview with Ms. Vowell, I doubt we have any thoughts about hypothetical subjects who believe that Stephanie and Trixie are different people. More likely, we just see that to make sense of the interview, something akin to 'as such'

alleged implicature is resistant to cancellation. Surely no-one aware of the facts sincerely asserts 'Superman has more success with women than Clark', *unless* they intend to contrast the effects on women of his acting as Superman with the effects of his acting as Clark? Making the statement, then adding that no such contrast is intended, would bewilder a knowing audience.

A final objection I shall consider, due to Saul (1999), is that allowing hidden indexicals into the literal content of simple sentences gives speakers far too much room for manoeuvre. For example, it would commit us to judging that Clinton spoke the truth with

(21) I did not have an improper relationship with Miss Lewinsky

if Clinton distinguishes the intern *persona* and the mistress *persona* and associates 'Miss Lewinsky' with the former and 'Monica' with the latter. In the same way, Saul claims, it would be possible to avoid perjury charges with statements like 'No, I never showed the documents to Mr. Smith', or 'Ms. Jones never signed a contract with us', if we associate the names with an appropriate *persona*. This, she says, 'is clearly not the way our language works' (1999:111).

It is not so clear to me. First, the use of the word 'no' will be a problem for the defendant. If he is asked 'did you show the documents to Mr. Smith?' and replies 'No, I never showed them to Mr. Smith', the 'no' is already perjury, since it denies the propositional content of the question, in which 'Mr. Smith' is presumably used without any implicit 'as such'. And even in a case like (21), where 'no' does not occur, the defendant is in trouble. We would not say that (21) is literally false in the imagined case, where it means

(22) I did not have an improper relationship with Miss Lewinsky as such.

must be understood. But this undercuts Barber's main objection to a semantic account of substitution-failure in simple sentences, that the phenomenon would occur even among speakers of a language that lacked devices like '*qua*' or 'as such'. I have some difficulty seeing how. Barber introduces 'Supermanizing' and 'Clark Kentizing' to capture the implications (p. 304), but he explains these expressions in terms of 'appearing as Superman' and 'appearing as Clark'. He also suggests (*loc. cit.*) that the meaning of 'Supermanize' could be given as a list – wearing a red cape, etc. – but this gets modal cases wrong: consider 'Even wearing a *green* cape (and so on, changing most items in the list), Superman would have more success with women.'

But whether or not this avoids the charge of perjury depends on the exact definition of perjury. If perjury is 'false *or misleading* testimony while under oath to tell the truth' then (21) is perjury,[26] for Clinton knows that no-one else will understand it as (22), but rather as the contradictory of the prosecution's charge. The oath a witness takes is to tell, among other things, the *whole* truth, which cannot be done by (22) alone. So I doubt that allowing (22) to be the literal content of (21) in this type of case has counterintuitive consequences for our ordinary views about when someone speaks in a blameworthy way.

---

[26] This definition (my italics) is taken from http://www.adlergiersch.com/legal.cfm, though usually such definitions employ an adverb like 'knowingly'.

Bibliography

Almog, Joseph. 1998. The Subject Verb Object Class I. In *Philosophical Perspectives 12: Language, Mind and Ontology*, edited by J. Tomberlin. Basil Blackwell.

Anderson, Anthony. 1980. Some New Axioms for the Logic of Sense and Denotation: Alternative (0). *Noûs* 14:217–34.

Asher, Nicholas. 1992. A Default, Truth-Conditional Semantics for the Progressive. *Linguistics and Philosophy* 15:463–508.

Asher, Nicholas, and M. Morreau. 1995. What Some Generics Mean. In *The Generic Book*, edited by G. Carlson and F. Pelletier. Chicago University Press.

Authier, Marc, and Lisa Reed. 1999. *Structure and Interpretation in Natural Language*. Lincom Europa.

Barber, Alex. 2000. A Pragmatic Treatment of Simple Sentences. *Analysis* 60:300–8.

Barwise, Jon, and Robin Cooper. 1982. Generalized Quantifiers and Natural Language. *Linguistics and Philosophy* 4:159–219. Also in (Portner and Partee 2002).

Bealer, George. 1989. Fine-Grained Type-Free Intensionality. In *Properties, Types and Meaning*, I, edited by G. Chierchia, B. Partee and R. Turner. Kluwer Academic Publishers.

Bealer, George. 1993. A Solution to 'Frege's Puzzle. In *Philosophical Perspectives 7: Language and Logic*, edited by J. Tomberlin. Ridgeview.

Bealer, George. 1994. Property Theory: The Type-Free Approach v. the Church Approach. *The Journal of Philosophical Logic* 23: 139–171.

Bennett, Michael. 1977. A Guide to the Logic of Tense and Aspect in English. *Logique et Analyse* 20:491–517.

Bonomi, Andrea. 1999. The Progressive and the Structure of Events. *The Journal of Semantics* 14:173–205.

Borg, Emma. 2002. Pointing at Jack, Talking about Jill: Understanding Deferred Uses of Demonstratives and Pronouns. *Mind & Language* 17:489–512.

Braun, David. 1998. Understanding Belief Reports. *The Philosophical Review* 107:555–95.

Braun, David. 2000. Russellianism and Psychological Generalizations. *Noûs* 34:203–36.

Braun, David. 2001a. Russellianism and Explanation. In *Philosophical Perspectives 15: Metaphysics*, edited by J. Tomberlin. Basil Blackwell.

Braun, David. 2001b. Russellianism and Prediction. *Philosophical Studies* 105:59–105.

Braun, David, and Jennifer Saul. 2002. Simple Sentences, Substitution, and Mistaken Evaluations. *Philosophical Studies* 111:1–41.

Burley, Walter. 2000. *On the Purity of the Art of Logic*. Translated by P. V. Spade. Yale University Press.

Carpenter, Bob. 1997. *Type-Logical Semantics*. The MIT Press.

Castañeda, Hector-Neri. 1967. Comments. In *The Logic of Decision and Action*, edited by N. Rescher. University of Pittsburgh Press.

Castañeda, Hector-Neri. 1968. On the Logic of Attributions of Self-Knowledge to Others. *The Journal of Philosophy* 65:439–56.

Chalmers, David. 2002. Does Conceivability Entail Possibility? In *Conceivability and Possibility*, edited by T. Gendler and J. Hawthorne. Oxford University Press.

Chierchia, Gennaro. 1989. Anaphora and Attitudes *De Se*. In *Semantics and Contextual Expressions*, edited by R. Bartsch, J. v. Benthem and P. v. E. Boas. Foris.

Chierchia, Gennaro, and Sally McConnell-Ginet. 2000. *Meaning and Grammar*. 2nd. ed. The MIT Press.

Cohen, Ariel. 1999. *Think Generic!* Palo Alto: CSLI Publications.

Cooper, Robin, and Terence Parsons. 1976. Montague Grammar, Generative Semantics, and Interpretive Semantics. In *Montague Grammar*, edited by B. Partee. Academic Press.

Crimmins, Mark. 1992. *Talk About Belief*. The MIT Press.

Davidson, Donald. 1967. The Logical Form of Action Sentences. In *The Logic of Decision and Action*, edited by N. Rescher. Pittsburgh: University of Pittsburgh Press.

Davidson, Donald. 1969. On Saying That. In *Words and Objections: Essays on the Work of W. V. Quine*, edited by D. Davidson and G. Harman. Reidel.

Davidson, Donald. 1985. Adverbs of Action. In *Essays on Davidson: Actions and Events*, edited by B. Vermazen and M. Hintikka. Oxford University Press.

Davies, Martin. 1987. Tacit Knowledge and Semantic Theory: Can a Five per cent Difference Matter? *Mind* 98:441–62.

DeCarrico, Jeanette. 1983. On Quantifier Raising. *Linguistic Inquiry* 14:343–6.

Den Dikken, Marcel, Richard Larson, and Peter Ludlow. 1996. Intensional "Transitive" Verbs and Concealed Complement Clauses. *Rivista di Linguistica* 8:331–48. Also (slightly abridged) in *Readings in the Philosophy of Language* edited by Peter Ludlow, The MIT Press, 1997, 1041–53.

Dennett, Daniel. 1982. Beyond Belief. In *Thought and Object*, edited by A. Woodfield. Oxford University Press.

Dignum, F., J-J. Ch. Meyer, and R. J. Wieringa. 1996. Free Choice and Contextually Permitted Actions. *Studia Logica* 57:193–220.

Dowty, David. 1977. Towards a Semantic Analysis of Verb Aspect and the English "Imperfective" Progressive. *Linguistics and Philosophy* 1:45–78.

Dowty, David. 1979. *Word Meaning and Montague Grammar*. Reidel.

Dowty, David. 1989. On the Semantic Content of the Notion of 'Thematic Role'. In *Properties, Types and Meanings II: Semantic Issues*, edited by G. Chierchia, B. Partee and R. Turner. Kluwer Academic Publishers.

Dowty, David, Robert Wall, and Stanley Peters. 1981. *Introduction to Montague Semantics*. Kluwer Academic Publishers.

Enç, Mürvet. 1991. The Semantics of Specificity. *Linguistic Inquiry* 22: 1–25.

Evans, Gareth. 1977. Pronouns, Quantifiers and Relative Clauses (I). *The Canadian Journal of Philosophy* 7:467–536.

Evans, Gareth. 1981. Following a Rule: Objectivity and Meaning. In *Wittgenstein: To Follow a Rule*, edited by S. Holtzman and C. Leich. Routledge.

Evnine, Simon. 1999. Believing Conjunctions. *Synthese* 118:201–27.

Fiengo, Robert, and Robert May. 1996. Interpreted Logical Forms: A Critique. *Rivista di Linguistica* 8:349–73.

Fine, Kit. 1989. The Problem of *De Re* Modality. In *Themes from Kaplan*, edited by J. Almog, J. Perry and H. Wettstein. Oxford University Press.

Fodor, Janet Dean. 1979. *The Linguistic Description of Opaque Contexts*. Garland.

Fodor, Jerry. 2004a. Having Concepts: A Brief Refutation of the Twentieth Century. *Mind and Language* 19:29–47.

Fodor, Jerry. 2004b. Reply to Commentators. *Mind and Language* 19:99–112.

Fodor, Jerry, and Ernest Lepore. 1996. The Pet Fish and the Red Herring: Why Concepts Aren't Prototypes. *Cognition* 58:243–76. All references are to the revised version in (Fodor and Lepore 2002b).

Fodor, Jerry, and Ernest Lepore. 2001. Why Compositionality Won't Go Away: Reflections on Horwich's "Deflationary" Theory. *Ratio* 14:350–68. All references are to the revised version in (Fodor and Lepore 2002b).

Fodor, Jerry, and Ernest Lepore. 2002a. The Emptiness of the Lexicon: Reflections on Pustejovsky. *Linguistic Inquiry* 1998:269–88. All references are to the revised version in (Fodor and Lepore 2002b).

Fodor, Jerry, and Ernest Lepore. 2002b. *The Compositionality Papers*. Oxford University Press.

Forbes, Graeme. 1987. Indexicals and Intensionality: A Fregean Perspective. *The Philosophical Review* 96:3–31.

Forbes, Graeme. 1989. *Languages of Possibility*. Basil Blackwell.

Forbes, Graeme. 1990. The Indispensability of *Sinn*. *The Philosophical Review* 99:535–63.

Forbes, Graeme. 1996. Substitutivity and the Coherence of Quantifying In. *The Philosophical Review* 105:337–72.

Forbes, Graeme. 2000a. Objectual Attitudes. *Linguistics and Philosophy* 23:141–83.
Forbes, Graeme. 2000b. Substitutivity and Side-Effects. unpublished ms. *www.tulane.edu/~forbes*.
Forbes, Graeme. 2002a. Intensionality I. *Proceedings of the Aristotelian Society*, Supplementary Volume 76:75–99.
Forbes, Graeme. 2002b. Origins and Identities. In *Individuals, Essence and Identity: Themes of Analytic Metaphysics*, edited by A. Bottani, D. Giaretta and M. Carrara. Reidel.
Forbes, Graeme. 2003. Meaning-Postulates, Inference, and the Relational/Notional Ambiguity. *Facta Philosophica* 5:49–74.
Fox, Chris, and Shalom Lappin. 2001. A Framework for the Hyperintensional Semantics of Natural Language with Two Implementations. In *Logical Aspects of Computational Linguistics*, edited by P. de Groote, G. Morrill and C. Rotoré. Springer.
Frege, Gottlob. 1967. The Thought: A Logical Enquiry. In *Philosophical Logic*, edited by P. Strawson. Oxford University Press.
Gamut, L. T. F. 1991. *Logic, Language and Meaning Volume II: Intensional Logic and Logical Grammar*. Chicago: University of Chicago Press.
Garber, Marjorie, and Nancy Vickers, eds. 2003. *The Medusa Reader*. Routledge.
Geach, Peter. 1967. Intentional Identity. *The Journal of Philosophy* 64:627–32. Reprinted in *Logic Matters* by Peter Geach, Basil Blackwell 1972, pp. 146–53.
Goodman, Nelson. 1949. On Likeness of Meaning. *Analysis* 1:1–7.
Goodman, Nelson. 1976. *Languages of Art*. Hackett Publishing Company.
Grice, H. P. 1969. Vacuous Names. In *Words and Objections: Essays on the Work of W. V. Quine*, edited by D. Davidson and J. Hintikka. D. Reidel.
Grice, Paul. 1989. *Studies in the Way of Words*. Harvard University Press.
Harley, Heidi. 2004. Wanting, Having, and Getting: A Note on Fodor and Lepore 1998. *Linguistic Inquiry* 35:255–67.
Heim, Irene. 1983. File Change Semantics and the Familiarity Theory of Definiteness. In *Meaning, Use and Interpretation of Language*,

edited by R. Bäuerle, C. Schwarze and A. v. Stechow. Walter de Gruyter.

Herburger, Elena. 2000. *What Counts: Focus and Quantification*. The MIT Press.

Higginbotham, James. 1986. Davidson's Program in Semantics. In *Truth and Interpretation: Perspectives on the Philosophy of Donald Davidson*, edited by E. LePore. Basil Blackwell.

Higginbotham, James. 1989. Elucidations of Meaning. *Linguistics and Philosophy* 12:465–517.

Higginbotham, James. 2000. On Events in Linguistic Semantics. In *Speaking of Events*, edited by J. Higginbotham, F. Pianesi and A. C. Varzi. Oxford University Press.

Horn, Laurence. 2001. *A Natural History of Negation*. CSLI Publications.

Hornsby, Jennifer. 1977: Saying Of. *Analysis* 37:177–85.

Hornstein, Norbert. 1995. *Logical Form: From GB to Minimalism*. The MIT Press.

Horwich, Paul. 1998. *Meaning*. Oxford University Press.

Horwich, Paul. 2006. *Reflections on Meaning*. Oxford University Press.

Huddleston, Rodney, and Geoffrey K. Pullum. 2002. *The Cambridge Grammar of the English Language*. Cambridge University Press.

Jennings, R. E. 1994. *The Genealogy of Disjunction*. Oxford University Press.

Kamp, Hans. 1979. Semantics versus Pragmatics. In *Formal Semantics and Pragmatics for Natural Language*, edited by F. Guenthner and S. Schmidt. Reidel.

Kamp, Hans, and Uwe Reyle. 1993. *From Discourse to Logic*. Kluwer Academic Publishers.

Kaplan, David. 1986. Opacity. In *The Philosophy of W. V. Quine*, edited by L. E. Hahn and P. A. Schilpp. Open Court.

Kaplan, David. 1989. Demonstratives. In *Themes from Kaplan*, edited by J. Almog, J. Perry and H. Wettstein. Oxford University Press.

Kaplan, David. 1990. Words. *Proceedings of the Aristotelian Society*, Supplementary Volume 64:93–117.

Katz, Graham. 2000. Anti Neo-Davidsonianism. In *Events as Grammatical Objects*, edited by C. Tenny and J. Pustejovsky. CSLI Publications.

Keenan, Edward. 1987. A Semantic Definition of "Indefinite NP". In *The Representation of (In)definiteness*, edited by E. Reuland and A. t. Meulen. The MIT Press.

Keenan, Edward. 2003. The Definiteness Effect: Semantic or Pragmatic? *Natural Language Semantics* 11:187–216.

King, Jeffrey. 1996. Structured Propositions and Sentence Structure. *The Journal of Philosophical Logic* 25:495–521.

Kratzer, Angelika. 1998. Scope or Pseudo-Scope: Are There Wide-Scope Indefinites? In *Events and Grammar*, edited by S. Rothstein. Kluwer.

Kripke, Saul. 1972. Naming and Necessity. In *Semantics of Natural Language*, edited by D. Davidson and G. Harman. Reidel.

Kripke, Saul. 1979. A Puzzle About Belief. In *Meaning and Use*, edited by A. Margalit. Reidel.

Kripke, Saul. 1980. *Naming and Necessity*. Basil Blackwell.

Lahav, Ron. 1989. Against Compositionality: The Case of Adjectives. *Philosophical Studies* 57:261–79.

Landman, Fred. 1992. The Progressive. *Natural Language Semantics* 1:1–32.

Larson, Richard. 1985. The Syntax of Disjunction Scope. *Natural Language and Linguistic Theory* 3:217–64.

Larson, Richard. 2002. The Grammar of Intensionality. In *Logical Form and Natural Language*, edited by G. Preyer and G. Peter. Oxford University Press.

Larson, Richard, and Gabriel Segal. 1995. *Knowledge of Meaning*. The MIT Press.

Larson, Richard, Marcel den Dikken, and Peter Ludlow. 1997. Intensional Transitive Verbs and Abstract Clausal Complementation. *Linguistic Inquiry* (forthcoming).

Larson, Richard, and Sungeun Cho. 2003. Temporal Adjectives and the Structure of Possessive DP's. *Natural Language Semantics* 11:217–47.

Lewis, David. 1972. General Semantics. In *Semantics of Natural Language*, edited by D. Davidson and G. Harman. Reidel.

Lewis, David. 1973. *Counterfactuals*. Basil Blackwell.

Linsky, Leonard. 1967. *Referring*. Humanities Press.

Loewer, Barry. 1976. Counterfactuals with Disjunctive Antecedents. *The Journal of Philosophy* 73:531–7.

Ludlow, Peter. 1994. Conditionals, Events, and Unbound Pronouns. *Lingua e Stile* 29:165-83.

McKay, T. J. 1986. Against Constitutional Sufficiency Principles. In *Midwest Studies in Philosophy XI: Studies in Essentialism*, edited by P. A. French, T. E. Uehling and H. K. Wettstein. University of Minnesota Press.

McNally, Louise. 1997. *A Semantics for the English Existential Construction*. Garland Publishing.

McShane, Marjorie. 2005. *A Theory of Ellipsis*. Oxford University Press.

Makinson, David. 1984. Stenius' Approach to Disjunctive Permission. *Theoria* 50:138-47.

May, Robert. 1985. *Logical Form: Its Structure and Derivation*. The MIT Press.

Milwark, G. L. 1977. Toward an Explanation of Certain Peculiarities of the Existential Construction in English. *Linguistic Analysis* 3:1-29.

Moltmann, Friederike. 1997. Intensional Verbs and Quantifiers. *Natural Language Semantics* 5:1-52.

Montague, Richard. 1960. On the Nature of Certain Philosophical Entities. *The Monist* 53:159-94.

Montague, Richard. 1974. The Proper Treatment of Quantification in Ordinary English. In *Formal Philosophy: Selected Papers of Richard Montague*, edited by R. Thomason. Yale University Press.

Montalbetti, Mario. 2003. Reference Transfers and the *Giorgione* Problem. In *Anaphora: A Reference Guide*, edited by A. Barss. Basil Blackwell.

Moore, Joseph. 1999. Saving Substitutivity in Simple Sentences. *Analysis* 57:91-105.

Moortgat, Michael. 2002. Categorial Grammar and Formal Semantics. Forthcoming in *The Encyclopedia of Cognitive Science*, John Wiley 2005.

Muskens, R. 2005. Sense and the Computation of Reference. *Linguistics and Philosophy* 28:473-504.

Nolan, Daniel. 1997. Impossible Worlds: A Modest Approach. *Notre Dame Journal of Formal Logic* 38:535-72.

Noordhof, Paul. 2002. Imagining Objects and Imagining Experiences. *Mind and Language* 17:426-55.

Osherson, D. N., and E. E. Smith. 1981. On the Adequacy of Prototype Theory as a Theory of Concepts. *Cognition* 9:35–58.

Parsons, Terence. 1990. *Events in the Semantics of English*. The MIT Press.

Parsons, Terence. 1995. Thematic Relations and Arguments. *Linguistic Inquiry* 55 (4):663–79.

Parsons, Terence. 1997. Meaning Sensitivity and Grammatical Structure. In *Structures and Norms in Science*, edited by M. L. Dalla Chiara, K. Doets, D. Mundici and J. v. Benthem. Kluwer Academic Publishers.

Partee, Barbara. 1973. Some Transformational Extensions of Montague Grammar. *The Journal of Philosophical Logic* 2:509–34.

Partee, Barbara. 1974. Opacity and Scope. In *Semantics and Philosophy*, edited by M. Munitz and P. Unger. NYU Press.

Partee, Barbara. 1984. Compositionality. In *Varieties of Formal Semantics*, edited by F. Landman and F. Veltman. Foris.

Partee, Barbara. 1986. Noun-Phrase Interpretation and Type-Shifting Principles. In *Studies on Discourse Representation Theory and the Theory of Generalized Quantifiers*, edited by J. Groenendijk, D. d. Jongh and M. Stokhof. Foris.

Partee, Barbara. 1997. Genitives – A Case Study. In *Handbook of Logic and Language*, edited by J. van Benthem and A. ter Meulen. The MIT Press.

Partee, Barbara. 2003. Privative Adjectives: Subsective Plus Coercion. *Presuppositions and Discourse: Essays offered to Hans Kamp*, edited by R. Bäuerle, U. Reyle and T. E. Zimmermann. Elsevier.

Peacocke, Christopher. 1979. *Holistic Explanation*. Oxford University Press.

Peacocke, Christopher. 1981. Demonstrative Thought and Psychological Explanation. *Synthese* 49:187–217.

Peacocke, Christopher. 1987. Depiction. *The Philosophical Review* 96:383–410.

Peacocke, Christopher. 1999. *Being Known*. Oxford University Press.

Peacocke, Christopher. 2004. Interrelations: Concepts, Knowledge, Reference and Structure. *Mind and Language* 19:85–98.

Pelletier, Jeffrey. 1994. The Principle of Semantic Compositionality. *Topoi* 13:11–14.

Pietroski, Paul. 2002. Function and Concatenation. In *Logical Form and Natural Language*, edited by G. Preyer and G. Peter. Oxford University Press.

Pietroski, Paul, and Norbert Hornstein. 2002. Does Every Sentence Like This Exhibit A Scope Ambiguity? In *Belief and Meaning*, edited by W. Hinzen and H. Rott. Hansel-Hohenhausen.

Portner, Paul, and Barbara Partee, eds. 2002. *Formal Semantics: The Essential Readings*. Basil Blackwell.

Quine, W. V. 1956. Quantifiers and Propositional Attitudes. *The Philosophical Review* 53:177–87. Page references are to the reprinted version in Quine 1966:185–96.

Quine, W. V. 1960. *Word and Object*. The MIT Press.

Quine, W. V. 1961. Reference and Modality. In *Reference and Modality*, edited by L. Linsky. Oxford University Press.

Quine, W. V. 1966. *The Ways of Paradox*. Harvard University Press.

Quine, W. V. 1979. Intensions Revisited. In *Contemporary Perspectives in the Philosophy of Language*, edited by P. A. French, T. E. Uehling and H. K. Wettstein. University of Minnesota Press.

Recanati, François. 2000. Relational Belief Reports. *Philosophical Studies* 100:255–72.

Recanati, François. 2003. *Literal Meaning*. Cambridge University Press.

Reimer, Marga. 2002. Do Adjectives Conform to Compositionality? In *Language and Mind: Philosophical Perspectives* Volume 16, edited by J. Tomberlin. Basil Blackwell.

Reuland, Eric, and Alice ter Meulen. 1987. Introduction. In *The Representation of (In)definiteness*, edited by E. Reuland and A. t. Meulen. The MIT Press.

Richard, Mark. 1990. *Propositional Attitudes*. Cambridge University Press.

Richard, Mark. 1995. Defective Contexts, Accommodation, and Normalization. *The Canadian Journal of Philosophy* 25:551–70.

Richard, Mark. 2001. Seeking a Centaur, Adoring Adonis: Intensional Transitives and Empty Terms. In *Figurative Language: Midwest Studies in Philosophy* Volume 25, edited by P. French and H. Wettstein. Basil Blackwell.

Robbins, Philip. 2002. How to Blunt the Sword of Compositionality. *Noûs* 36:313–34.

Robertson, Teresa. 1998. Possibilities and the Arguments for Origin Essentialism. *Mind* 107:729–49.

Robertson, Teresa. 2003. (In the Fiction/Myth) The Number Seventeen Crosses the Rubicon. *Southwest Philosophy Review* 19:125–34.

Rooth, Mats, and Barbara Partee. 1982. Conjunction, Type-Ambiguity, and Wide-Scope 'Or'. In *Proceedings of the First West Coast Conference on Formal Linguistics*, edited by D. Flickenger, M. Macken and N. Wiegand: Stanford University.

Salmon, Nathan. 1986: *Frege's Puzzle*. The MIT Press.

Salmon, Nathan. 1989. The Logic of What Might Have Been. *The Philosophical Review* 98:3–34.

Salmon, Nathan. 2002. Mythical Objects. In *Meaning and Truth*, edited by J. Campbell, M. O'Rourke and D. Shier. Seven Bridges Press.

Saul, Jennifer. 1997a. Substitution and Simple Sentences. *Analysis* 57:102–8.

Saul, Jennifer. 1997b. Reply to Forbes. *Analysis* 57:114–8.

Saul, Jennifer. 1999. Substitution, Simple Sentences, and Sex-scandals. *Analysis* 59:106–12.

Schein, Barry. 1993. *Plurals and Events*. Cambridge, Mass: The MIT Press.

Schein, Barry. 2002. Events and the Semantic Content of Thematic Relations. In *Logical Form and Natural Language*, edited by G. Preyer and G. Peter. Oxford University Press.

Schein, Barry. 2005. *Conjunction Reduction Redux*. Unpublished ms.

Schiffer, Stephen. 1992. Belief Ascription. *The Journal of Philosophy* 89:499–521.

Schiffer, Stephen. 1995. Descriptions, Indexicals, and Belief Reports: Some Dilemmas (But Not the Ones You Expect). *Mind* 104:107–31.

Schiffer, Stephen. 1996. The Hidden Indexical Theory's Logical-form Problem: a Rejoinder. *Analysis* 56:92–7.

Smith, E. E. 1988. Combining Prototypes: A Selective Modification Model. *Cognitive Science* 12:485–527.

Soames, Scott. 1987. Direct Reference, Propositional Attitudes, and Semantic Content. *Philosophical Topics* 15:47–87.

Soames, Scott. 2002. *Beyond Rigidity*. Oxford University Press.

Stalnaker, Robert. 1968. A Theory of Conditionals. In *Studies in Logical Theory*, edited by N. Rescher. Oxford University Press.

Stalnaker, Robert. 1984. *Inquiry*. The MIT Press.

Stanley, Jason. 2002. Making it Articulated. *Mind and Language* 17: 149–68.

Szabó, Zoltán Gendler. 2000. Compositionality as Supervenience. *Linguistics and Philosophy* 23:475–505.

Szabó, Zoltán Gendler. 2004. On the Progressive and the Perfective. *Noûs* 38:29–59.

Szabó, Zoltán Gendler, ed. 2005. *Semantics versus Pragmatics*. Oxford University Press.

Tanner, Ernest. 1995. *Athletics Deficits: The Adverse Effects on the University's Endowment*. Memo to the Tulane 2000 Steering Committee, April 26th, 1995.

Thomason, Richmond. 1979. Home is Where the Heart Is. In *Contemporary Perspectives in the Philosophy of Language*, edited by P. A. French, T. E. Uehling and H. K. Wettstein. University of Minnesota Press.

Thomason, Richmond. 1980. A Model Theory for Propositional Attitudes. *Linguistics and Philosophy* 4:47–70.

van Benthem, Johan. 1986. *Essays in Logical Semantics*. D. Reidel.

van Benthem, Johan. 1988. The Lambek Calculus. In *Categorial Grammars and Natural Language Structures*, edited by R. Oehrle, E. Bach and D. Wheeler. D. Reidel.

van Benthem, Johan. 1995. *Language in Action*. The MIT Press.

Vendler, Zeno. 1967. Verbs and Times. In *Linguistics in Philosophy*, edited by Z. Vendler. Cornell University Press.

von Fintel, Kai. 1991. Exceptive Constructions. *Semantics and Linguistic Theory I*, edited by S. Moore and A. Z. Wyner, CLC Publications (http://ling.cornell.edu/clcpubs/index.html).

Walton, Kendall. 1973. Pictures and Make-Believe. *The Philosophical Review* 82:283–319.

Wilk, Stephen R. 2000. *Medusa: Solving the Mystery of the Gorgon*. Oxford University Press.

Yablo, Steven. 1993. Is Conceivability a Guide to Possibility? *Philosophy and Phenomenological Research* 53:1–42.

Yablo, Steven. 2002. Coulda, Woulda, Shoulda. In *Conceivability and Possibility*, edited by T. Gendler and J. Hawthorne. Oxford University Press.

Zimmerman, Thomas Ede. 1993. On the Proper Treatment of Opacity in Certain Verbs. *Natural Language Semantics* 1:149–79.

Zimmerman, Thomas Ede. 2000. Free Choice Disjunction and Epistemic Possibility. *Linguistics and Philosophy* 8:255–90.

Zimmerman, Thomas Ede. 2001. Unspecificity and Intensionality. In *Audiatur Vox Sapentiae*, edited by C. Féry and W. Sternefeld. Akademie Verlag.

Zimmerman, Thomas Ede. 2004. Monotonicity in Opaque Verbs. *Semantics Archive*, http://semanticsarchive.net/

Zimmerman, Thomas Ede. 2005. What's in Two Names? *The Journal of Semantics* 22:53–96.

Zucchi, Sandro. 1999. Incomplete Events, Intensionality and Imperfective Aspect. *Natural Language Semantics* 7:179–215.

Index

A
achievement verb 134
adjective
    difference between intersective and subsective 27
    extensional 21
    intersective 20, 27, 94
    non-extensional 21
    privative 21, 94
    subsective 21, 34, 82, 94, 140
adjective detachment 21
adjunct 73, 76, 85, 86
admissibility condition 34
agent-relative possibility 104
Ahura Mazda 164
Almog, J. 65
ambiguity
    of 'for' 75
    of 'with' 88
Anderson, A. 34
anti-relational reading 50
argument of a verb 73, 74, 85
argument to a function 15, 16, 17
Asher, N. 65, 135–137
atelic verb 136
atomic versus sub-atomic semantics 74, 77, 164
attachment ambiguity 42, 56, 58, 59, 61
Authier, M. 16

B
Barber, A. 172, 173
bare plural 8, 42, 66
Barwise, J. 6
Bealer, G. 15, 35, 154
Bennett, M. 130
binary-branching tree 17, 18
boolean co-ordination 28
Borg, E. 155
Braun, D. 153, 154, 169–172

C
Callas, M. 67, 160
Carpenter, B. 16, 26, 28, 29, 82, 139
Castañeda, H-N. 53, 74
categorial syntax 16
cautionary Chinese proverb 137
Chalmers, D. 104
characteristic function of a set 22
characterization 83, 94, 121, 134, 135, 138, 139, 150
Chierchia, G. 53
Cho, S. 16
Churchill, W. 66, 69
closure of belief 91, 92
closure under entailment 93
coda set 145
Cohen, A. 65
collective/distributive distinction 64
compositionality

as one-one operation 34
function-argument model of 15
compounding 21
conditional logics for type-shifting 79
conjunctive force 97–99, 107–117, 129
conjunctive QNP 113
conservativity in first argument 146
conservativity in second argument 146
constitutional sufficiency principles 135
conversational implicature 108, 172
Cooper, R. 6, 16
co-ordinated phrase 20
co-ordinator 20
creative vs. non-creative senses of physical depiction verbs 139
Crimmins, M. 151

D

Davidson, D. 69, 73–75, 130, 154, 159–160
Davies, M. K. 5
DE context 112
De Morgan distribution 108
de re/de dicto distinction 41
DeCarrico, J. 58
decomposition
 of 'at most' 128
 of 'lack' and 'omit' 45
 of 'no' 125, 145
default existential closure 85
default reasoning 135
definiteness effect 144
den Dikken, M. 55, 56, 58, 59, 65, 66
Dennett, D. 42
descriptive pronoun 103
detachment
 adjective 21
 nominal 21
 of adjuncts 75
determiner
 cardinal 146
 co-intersective 146
 conservative in first argument 146
 conservative in second argument 146
 intersective 80, 83
 left-downwards entailing 124
 left-upwards entailing 124
 non-quantificational 144
 proportional 146
 quantificational 22
 right-downwards entailing 124
 right-upwards entailing 124
Dignum, F. 109
direct translation 32
differential explanation 31
dossiers 158
downward entailing context 112
Dowty, D. 74, 135
Dream-Elimination 75

E

ellipsis 57
Enç, M. 41
error thesis 170
Evans, G. 5, 103, 155
Evnine, S. 91
exceptive construction 145
existence-independence 46–47
existential context 144, 145, 146
extension
 of a predicate 5, 6
 of a sentence 6
extensional adjective 21
extensional construal 39, 45, 60, 61
extensional expression 11

F

famous deeds description-theory 13
Figes, O. 167, 171
file-change semantics 144
Fine, K. 152
flexible intension 9
Fodor, J. 3, 5, 79, 158, 166
Fodor, J. D. 45
Forbes, G. 14, 96, 122, 127, 135, 151, 155, 158, 162, 163
Fox, C. 35
free-choice 'any' 96, 111
Frege, G. 53, 159
function
    black box 1
    characteristic 22
    deterministic 1
    one-one 34

G

Gamut, L. T. F. 110
Garber, M. 39
Gaus, K. 160
Geach, P. 46
generalized co-ordination 117
generic 65, 66, 135
generic present 168
Goodman, N. 69, 77–81, 83, 101, 133, 148
gorgon myth 39
governing intention approach 72, 82, 94, 105, 116, 148
Grice, P. 158, 172

H

Harley, H. 55
he* 53
Heim, I. 110, 144
Herburger, E. 75
hidden indexical 151, 154, 157, 167, 171, 173
Higginbotham, J. 5, 45, 75, 136
higher-order intensional logic 15, 110
Hob-Nob sentence 46
Hofweber, T. 143
Horn, L. 126
Hornsby, J. 154
Hornstein, N. 41
Horwich, P. 3, 5
Huddleston, R. 74
hyperintension as structured entity 14
hyperintensional expression 13
hyperintensional logic 15

I

imperfective paradox 131
implicature cancellation 109, 173
independent quantifiers 122
indifference explanation 95–96
intended interpretation 30, 33, 35
intension
    constant 10
    flexible 9
intension as generalization of extension 9
intensional expression 11
intensional sense of 'find' 102
intensionalism, global 11
intensionality of 'it is necessary that' 11
intensional$_{pw}$ 38, 44, 50, 96, 97, 110, 119
intentional logic 15
intersective adjective 20, 27, 94
intersective determiner 80, 83
invariance condition 146
iterated co-ordinators 115

J

Jack London State Park 132

Jacovides, M. 65
Jennings, R. 111

K

K2 136
Kamp, H. 67, 109, 144
Kaplan, D. 43, 53, 66, 102, 152, 154, 156
Katz, G. 77
Keenan, E. 80, 145, 146
King, J. 119
Kratzer, A. 75
Kripke, S. 10, 13, 162

L

labelled constituent 19
Lahav, R. 5
lambda-abstraction 24
lambda-conjunction 85
lambda-conversion 28
Landman, F. 135
Lappin, S. 35
Larson, R. 6, 16, 38, 54–58, 60–62, 65, 75, 95, 110, 124
Lepore, E. 3, 5, 79
Lewis, D. 14, 31–32, 95, 108
Linsky, L. 152
Literary Example 128
local universe of a determiner 146
Loewer, B. 109
logical truth
    in a context 156
    simpliciter 156
Ludlow, P. 54–58, 75

M

Makinson, D. 109, 110
mark of intensionality 46, 102
McKay, T. 135
McNally, L. 145
meaning-postulate 32, 34, 70, 71, 80, 83, 107, 119, 132, 138, 150

Milwark, G. 144
mixed inference 121
modal determinacy 134
modal subordination 103
modal variation 102–105, 124
Moltmann, F. 45, 72, 100, 128, 141, 145
Montague, R. 67, 69–70, 71, 72, 77, 84
Montalbetti, M. 155
Moore, J. 169
Moortgat, M. 86, 150
Morreau, M. 65
Moses illusion 158, 170
Muskens, R. 33

N

need
    instrumental *vs.* non-instrumental 106
NEG+ONE account of 'no' 126
negation problem 62
negative polarity 45, 112
negative quantifier 124
Nolan, D. 106
nominal 20, 33, 58, 78, 80, 166
nominal detachment 21
nominal modifier 27, 81
nominals from relative clauses 140
non-committal reading 48–51, 71, 81, 83, 103, 135
non-extensional adjective 21
non-relational reading 50
Noordhof, P. 62
normal form for compound QNP's 116
noun phrase 19
nuclear war with France 50, 119
number-words as subsective adjectives 82

O

objectual attitude verb 39
Osherson, D. 3

P

Paderewski 162
Paradise Lost 151
paratactic analysis 154
Parsons, T. 16, 45, 54, 62–63, 65, 73–74, 77, 85, 86, 131–133, 137, 158
Partee, B. 5, 16, 20, 21, 27, 54, 58, 61, 98, 110, 149
partitive, covert 111
Peacocke, C. 31, 53, 72, 82, 91, 166
Pelletier, J. 5
pet-fish problem 3, 5
Pietroski, P. 41, 74
piranha enthusiast 5
positioning
    postfix 20
    prefix 20
possibilist quantifier 135
possible-worlds profile 9, 30, 31
Prince of Darkness 151
principle of Normal Success 135
privative adjective 21, 94
property
    first-order 25
    of properties 24
    second-order 25
proposition 10
proposition, Russellian 14
propositional anaphora 56, 59
propositional answer-set 109
propositional attitude verb 39, 64
propositional attitudes, logic of 91
proposition$_{pw}$ 39, 119
pseudo-cleft construction 61
Pullum, G. 74
pure inventory reading 148

Q

quantificational determiner 22
quantified noun phrase 22
quantifying in 69
Quine, W.V.O. 41–43, 52–54, 152

R

Raffman, D. 96
Rankin, I. 95
real versus mythical 46
realistic world 100, 106
Recanati, F. 5, 45, 109, 164
reduplicative 158
Reed, L. 16
Reimer, M. 5
relational/notional ambiguity 41, 44, 84
relational/notional ambiguity as scope ambiguity 44
relief from slooplessness 43
restriction set 145
Reuland, E. 144
reverse compositionality 79
Reyle, U. 144
Richard, M. 72, 94, 126–128, 130, 151, 159
rigid designator 10, 12
rigidly designating description 12
Robbins, P. 4
Robertson, T. 46, 135
Root, M. 98, 110

S

Salmon, N. 31, 46, 104, 154, 164
Saul, J. 166, 167, 169–172, 173
Schein, B. 74, 75, 76, 100, 169
Schiffer, S. 151
scope
    narrow 8, 44, 77
    of an attitude verb 50
    of an intensional expression 44

of an operator 34
wide 8, 125
wide versus narrow 41
scope ambiguity 8, 41, 43, 84, 172
scope island 41
Segal, G. 6, 124
selection constraint 166, 169
semantic innocence 159, 160, 164
semantic type 17
semantic value 29
set abstraction 24
simple theory of types 15, 16
slooplessness, mere relief from, 43
sloppy versus strict readings 155
small clause 62
Smith, E. 3
Soames, S. 14, 154
socialist realism 62
specific/unspecific distinction 41
specificity problem 62
Splash! 55
Stalnaker, R. 50, 108
Stanley, J. 164
Star-Trek transporter 105, 106
Stojanovic, I. 54
subsective adjective 21, 34, 82, 94, 140
subsective operator 73
substitutional semantics for quantifiers 153
sufficient completeness 134
systematic ambiguity of 'and' 28
Szabó, Z. 2, 109, 135, 138

T

telic verb 136
ter Meulen, A. 144
thematic labelling 86
thematic role 74–75
Thomason, R. 15, 32–34, 84, 107, 155, 159
truth-functional appropriateness in hyperintensional logic 33
t-weighted feature 3
type mismatch 140, 157
type of truth-values versus the type of meanings 32
type raising 27, 98, 117
type shifting 27

U

unbreakable predicate 78, 80
unique-agent stipulation 76

V

vacuous quantification 91
van Benthem, J. 28, 31, 79, 86, 120
Vendler, Z. 134
verb phrase 19
von Fintel, K. 145

W

Walton, K. 149
weakening inference 94, 96, 99, 102, 118, 120, 129
well-typed formula 17
whale-watching 55
wide scope/narrow scope distinction 41
Wilk, S. 39
Williamson, T. 143

Y

Yablo, S. 104

Z

Zernova, Y. 62
Zimmerman, T. E. 43, 45, 111, 142, 169
Zucchi, S. 130, 133, 136